Mastering SQL Server

From Basics to Expert Proficiency

Contents

Introduction

In the ever-evolving landscape of technology, relational databases continue to be a cornerstone for data storage and retrieval. Among the myriad of database management systems, Microsoft SQL Server stands out as a robust, scalable, and versatile platform. This book, "Mastering SQL Server: From Basics to Expert Proficiency," aims to equip readers with the knowledge and skills required to effectively harness the power of SQL Server, irrespective of their experience level.

SQL Server, a product of Microsoft, has been a prominent player in the world of database management since its inception. This book begins by exploring the fundamental concepts, followed by hands-on guidelines on installation and configuration, and progresses to more advanced topics such as query optimization, transactions, concurrency, and security. Each chapter is meticulously crafted to provide comprehensive coverage of the topics at hand, ensuring that readers build a solid foundation before moving on to more complex concepts.

The initial chapters focus on introducing SQL Server, its features, and the various editions available. Understanding the components and architecture of SQL Server is crucial for anyone looking to manage or develop on this platform. We delve into the database design principles and normalization techniques, providing readers with the necessary tools to create efficient and scalable database structures.

Subsequent chapters guide readers through the SQL Server Management Studio (SSMS), a powerful integrated environment for managing SQL infrastructure. Step-by-step instructions on writing basic and advanced SQL queries are provided, ensuring that readers gain proficiency in data manipulation and retrieval.

A significant aspect of database performance lies in the effective use of indexes. This book covers the various types of indexes, their creation, and maintenance, along with best practices for optimizing database performance. Additionally, the topics of stored procedures and functions are addressed, highlighting their role in procedural database operations and how they can be utilized to streamline complex tasks.

Transactions and concurrency control form the backbone of reliable database operations. The book provides an in-depth analysis of transaction management, including the ACID properties, isolation levels, and techniques for handling concurrency issues. Understanding these concepts is vital for maintaining data integrity and consistency in multi-user environments.

Security is a paramount concern in today's data-driven world. The final chapters of the book are dedicated to SQL Server security features, covering authentication methods, permissions, encryption, and best practices for safeguarding data. The book also touches upon auditing and monitoring techniques that help in maintaining a secure database environment.

"Mastering SQL Server: From Basics to Expert Proficiency" is designed to be a valuable resource for database administrators, developers, and anyone interested in mastering SQL Server. Through detailed explanations, practical examples, and industry best practices, this book aims to provide a comprehensive understanding of SQL Server, enabling readers to become proficient in managing and developing robust database solutions.

Chapter 1

Introduction to SQL Server

This chapter provides an overview of SQL Server, covering its history, features, and editions. It explains the components and architecture of SQL Server, compares it with other relational database management systems, and outlines its relevance to the relational model. The chapter also offers a guide on getting started with SQL Server and discusses common use cases for the platform.

1.1 What is SQL Server?

Microsoft SQL Server is a relational database management system (RDBMS) developed by Microsoft. Designed to manage and store information efficiently, SQL Server provides a robust suite of tools for data storage, retrieval, and management. It offers comprehensive solutions that support transaction processing, business intelligence, and analytics applications. SQL Server adheres to the ANSI SQL standard, making it a versatile platform for ensuring data consistency and integrity while enabling complex queries and operations.

SQL Server is built on a client-server architecture, where the database engine manages databases and handles requests sent by client applications. It is key to various data-driven applications, ranging from small personal projects to large enterprise solutions. One of its most powerful attributes is its capability to handle a wide range of business-critical applications with high transactional workloads, while ensuring data security and high availability.

SQL Server encompasses several key components that work together to provide its functionalities:

- 1. Database Engine: The core service for storing, processing, and securing data, the database engine provides controlled access and rapid transaction processing. It supports both the relational data and the structured data types, XML and JSON.

- 2. SQL Server Analysis Services (SSAS): SSAS provides online analytical processing (OLAP) and data mining functionality, which enable users to analyze and make informed decisions based on vast amounts of data. It supports the creation of multidimensional structures called cubes, which facilitate complex queries and analysis.

- 3. SQL Server Integration Services (SSIS): SSIS handles data extraction, transformation, and loading (ETL) processes, allowing users to integrate and consolidate data from various sources. It supports workflows, data cleansing, and migration operations, automating complex data tasks.

- 4. SQL Server Reporting Services (SSRS): SSRS is used for creating, managing, and delivering a range of interactive and printed reports. It supports different data sources and provides a web interface for publishing reports. SSRS enables users to create detailed operational reports, dashboards, and mobile reports.

- 5. SQL Server Management Studio (SSMS): SSMS is an integrated environment for managing databases. It provides tools for configuring, managing, and administering SQL Server instances and databases. SSMS includes functionalities like query execution, script writing, and performance tuning, making database management efficient and convenient.

- 6. Master Data Services (MDS): MDS is a master data management tool that helps organizations manage their key business data. It ensures data consistency and accuracy by providing a centralized repository for critical data entities, facilitating data stewardship and data governance.

FirstName	LastName	HireDate
John	Doe	1999-04-01
Jane	Smith	2000-06-15
Alice	Johnson	2001-09-10
Robert	Brown	2002-11-20
Emma	Davis	2003-02-05

The term SQL Server can be considered both in the context of the software product developed by Microsoft and the server environment in which it operates. The server can be either a physical machine or a virtual machine instantiated on a cloud environment.

The following example illustrates a simple SQL query executed in SQL Server Management Studio (SSMS). This query retrieves the top 5 rows from the Employees table ordered by the HireDate:

```
SELECT TOP 5
    FirstName,
    LastName,
    HireDate
FROM
    Employees
ORDER BY
    HireDate ASC;
```

Upon execution, the result might output the following rows:

This query demonstrates SQL Server's capability to process SQL commands and return ordered data results efficiently.

SQL Server also integrates with various Microsoft products, such as Azure, Visual Studio, and SharePoint. Its seamless integration with these tools enhances its versatility and functionality. Additionally, SQL Server supports high availability and disaster recovery (HA/DR) configurations through features like Always On Availability Groups and failover clustering, ensuring that databases remain available and recoverable in case of hardware or software failures.

SQL Server's compatibility with cloud services is another key feature, providing options for on-premises, hybrid, or fully cloud-hosted environments. For example, Azure SQL Database, a cloud-based service based on SQL Server, offers scalability, automatic patching, backups, and performance tuning, reducing the administrative overhead associated with traditional database management.

SQL Server's extensive suite of tools and integrations thus makes it a critical component for various applications, ensuring efficient data storage, retrieval, and management while maintaining a high level of performance, security, and reliability.

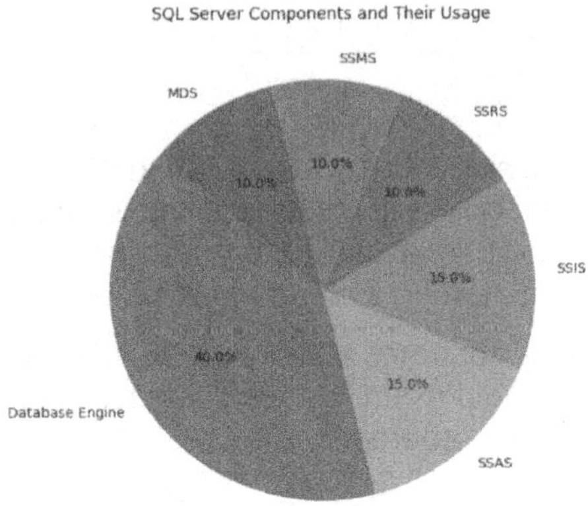

1.2 History and Evolution of SQL Server

SQL Server, a prominent relational database management system (RDBMS) developed by Microsoft, has undergone significant evolution since its inception. This section delves into the key milestones and advancements in the history of SQL Server.

Origins and Initial Release

SQL Server's roots can be traced back to a collaboration between Microsoft, Sybase, and Ashton-Tate that began in the late 1980s. The goal was to create a database management system to compete with market leaders like Oracle and IBM's DB2. The first version, SQL Server 1.0, was released in 1989 for IBM OS/2. This initial version provided foundational relational database capabilities, though its adoption was limited by the competition from more established databases.

Transition to Microsoft Windows

With the release of SQL Server 4.2 in 1993, Microsoft firmly positioned SQL Server to run on the Windows NT environment, marking a strategic shift from OS/2. The move aligned with Microsoft's broader enterprise strategy and allowed SQL Server to leverage the growing popularity of Windows NT. Improved stability and security were key enhancements introduced in this release.

Establishing Autonomy and SQL Server 6.0

The partnership between Microsoft and Sybase ended in 1994, with each company retaining the right to develop future versions of SQL Server independently. Microsoft's release of SQL Server 6.0 in 1995 represented its first standalone version. This release featured significant improvements, including an expanded feature set, enhanced robustness, and better performance, reflecting Microsoft's commitment to advancing the platform.

Introduction of Enterprise Editions

With SQL Server 6.5, released in 1996, Microsoft introduced the concept of Enterprise Edition to cater to large-scale enterprise environments. Features such as integrated support for internet applications, improved backup and restore capabilities, and advanced configuration options strengthened its position in the competitive RDBMS landscape.

SQL Server 7.0: A Major Overhaul

The launch of SQL Server 7.0 in 1998 marked a pivotal transformation, with a complete rewrite of the database engine. Key innovations in SQL Server 7.0 included:

- Introduction of a multi-instance architecture, allowing multiple database server instances on a single machine.
- Data Transformation Services (DTS) for data integration and transformation tasks.
- Improved query optimization and performance enhancements.

These features collectively enhanced scalability, reliability, and ease of administration, setting a new benchmark for subsequent versions.

SQL Server 2000 and XML Integration

SQL Server 2000 built upon the foundation of its predecessors and introduced native XML support, signaling Microsoft's embrace of emerging web standards. Key enhancements included:

- Indexed views for improved query performance.
- User-defined functions for modular programming.

- Improved security with integrated authentication modes.
- SQL Server Management Studio (SSMS), an integrated environment for managing SQL infrastructure.

SQL Server 2005: Enhanced Business Intelligence

Released in 2005, SQL Server 2005 was a landmark version with an emphasis on business intelligence (BI) capabilities. Major innovations included:

- SQL Server Integration Services (SSIS) replacing DTS, providing robust ETL (Extract, Transform, Load) functionality.
- SQL Server Reporting Services (SSRS) for comprehensive reporting solutions.
- SQL Server Analysis Services (SSAS) for online analytical processing (OLAP) and data mining.
- Enhanced security features such as data encryption and more granular permission settings.

These enhancements significantly broadened SQL Server's applicability in decision-making and business analytics environments.

SQL Server 2008 and 2008 R2: Greater Efficiency and Manageability

SQL Server 2008 introduced key features focused on data management efficiency and self-tuning capabilities:

- Policy-Based Management for consistent configuration enforcement across servers.
- Resource Governor to allocate system resources optimally.
- Enhanced data types like DateTime2 and FILESTREAM for managing unstructured data.
- Compressible backup and data compression features.

SQL Server 2008 R2, released in 2010, further built on these enhancements by introducing Master Data Services (MDS) and PowerPivot for Excel, enriching its data management and analysis capabilities.

SQL Server 2012: AlwaysOn and Columnstore Indexes

SQL Server 2012 introduced significant enhancements aimed at high availability, performance, and cloud readiness:

- AlwaysOn Availability Groups for high availability and disaster recovery.
- Columnstore indexes for faster data warehousing queries.
- Enhanced SSRS with Power View for interactive data visualization.
- SQL Server Data Tools (SSDT) for a unified development environment.

These innovations positioned SQL Server as a robust solution for modern enterprise environments.

SQL Server 2014: In-Memory Optimization

A major feature of SQL Server 2014 was the introduction of in-memory OLTP, code-named Hekaton, designed to improve transaction processing performance significantly.

- In-memory OLTP for high-speed data operations.
- Enhanced integration with Azure for hybrid cloud deployment.
- Buffer Pool Extension for SSD storage to expand the buffer pool size.

SQL Server 2016: Comprehensive Platform Enhancements

SQL Server 2016 was another milestone that introduced end-to-end performance improvements and security features:

- Always Encrypted to protect sensitive data.
- Temporal tables for time-based data retrieval.
- JSON support for parsing and storing JSON data.
- Stretch Database for dynamically stretching warm and cold transactional data to Azure.
- Enhanced analytics capabilities with R integration.

SQL Server 2017 and Beyond: Cross-Platform and Advanced Analytics

SQL Server 2017, breaking new ground, became the first version to run on Linux. Alongside cross-platform support, it introduced:

- Python integration for advanced analytics.
- Adaptive query processing for intelligent performance tuning.
- Graph database capabilities for complex relationship modeling.

The evolution of SQL Server reflects Microsoft's adaptive strategy to embrace emerging technologies and requirements, ensuring the platform remains a forefront choice for diverse database management needs. SQL Server 2019 further expanded these capabilities with features like Big Data Clusters and integrated machine learning models, showcasing its commitment to innovation.

```
SQL Server version history highlights:
- 1989: SQL Server 1.0.
- 1993: SQL Server 4.2 for Windows NT.
- 1995: SQL Server 6.0 (Microsoft's first independent version).
- 1996: SQL Server 6.5.
- 1998: SQL Server 7.0 (complete rewrite of the database engine).
- 2000: SQL Server 2000 (XML support).
- 2005: SQL Server 2005 (business intelligence focus).
- 2008: SQL Server 2008 and 2008 R2.
- 2012: SQL Server 2012 (AlwaysOn, Columnstore Indexes).
- 2014: SQL Server 2014 (In-Memory OLTP).
- 2016: SQL Server 2016 (Always Encrypted, Temporal Tables).
- 2017: SQL Server 2017 (cross-platform support, Python integration).
- 2019: SQL Server 2019 (Big Data Clusters, machine learning integration).
```

1.3 Features and Editions of SQL Server

SQL Server is a comprehensive, scalable, and efficient relational database management system (RDBMS) developed by Microsoft. It includes various features and is available in multiple editions tailored to different user needs, ranging from individual developers to large enterprises. This section explores the primary features of SQL Server and provides an overview of the available editions.

SQL Server offers a wide array of features that enhance its functionality, security, performance, and ease of management. These features can be broadly categorized into the following areas:

- Data Storage and Management

- Security
- Performance Tuning and Optimization
- Business Intelligence
- High Availability and Disaster Recovery
- Development and Integration Tools

Data Storage and Management

SQL Server supports a flexible storage system, including traditional row-based storage and columnstore indexes, which optimize storage and retrieval for large volumes of data. It provides robust data management features, such as:

- Scalability: SQL Server can handle vast amounts of data, making it suitable for both small applications and large enterprise solutions.
- FileTable: A feature that allows users to store files and documents in special tables in SQL Server and access them via Windows applications as though they were stored in the file system.
- In-Memory OLTP (Online Transaction Processing): This feature enhances performance by allowing tables to be stored in-memory, thereby reducing the latency of disk I/O operations.

Security

SQL Server provides strong security mechanisms to protect sensitive data:

- Encryption: Includes Transparent Data Encryption (TDE) for encrypting data at rest, and Always Encrypted for protecting sensitive data within applications.
- Authentication and Authorization: Supports Windows Authentication and SQL Server Authentication, along with fine-grained access controls via roles and permissions.
- Auditing: Enables tracking and logging of activities on the server to help meet compliance requirements.

Performance Tuning and Optimization

Optimizing performance in SQL Server involves various tools and features:

- Query Store: Automatically captures query performance data to help diagnose and fix performance issues.
- Dynamic Management Views (DMVs): Provide insight into the health, performance, and utility of the database instances.
- Indexes: Various indexing strategies, including clustered, non-clustered, and full-text indexes, help speed up data retrieval processes.

Business Intelligence

SQL Server includes capabilities that facilitate Business Intelligence (BI) applications:

- SQL Server Integration Services (SSIS): Supports data integration and workflow applications.
- SQL Server Analysis Services (SSAS): Provides online analytical processing (OLAP) and data mining functionalities.
- SQL Server Reporting Services (SSRS): Offers tools for designing, distributing, and managing reports.

High Availability and Disaster Recovery

SQL Server ensures data availability and integrity through various features:

- Always On Availability Groups: Provides high availability and disaster recovery through multiple replicas.
- Failover Clustering: Ensures server resilience through clustering of multiple servers for automatic failover.
- Backup and Restore: Supports comprehensive backup strategies, including full, differential, and transaction log backups.

Development and Integration Tools

SQL Server integrates seamlessly with development environments and supports a wide range of development tools:

- SQL Server Data Tools (SSDT): Integrates with Visual Studio to provide a development environment for SQL Server.
- T-SQL (Transact-SQL): An extension of SQL that adds programming constructs to SQL for complex queries, stored procedures, triggers, and more.
- APIs and Connectivity: Supports various APIs and connectivity options, including ADO.NET, JDBC, ODBC, and REST APIs.

SQL Server is available in several editions, each tailored for different performance and feature requirements. The primary editions are:

- Enterprise Edition: The most comprehensive edition, offering all available SQL Server features. It is designed for large-scale applications requiring high performance, scalability, and advanced security.
- Standard Edition: Provides essential features needed for mid-tier applications, suitable for many organizations that do not require the full capabilities of the Enterprise Edition.
- Web Edition: A cost-effective option tailored for web hosting. It includes features necessary to support web applications but omits some high-end features found in the other editions.
- Developer Edition: Includes all features of the Enterprise Edition but is licensed for development and testing purposes only, not for production environments.
- Express Edition: A free, entry-level edition ideal for learning and building small-scale applications. It includes core database functionalities but is limited in terms of performance and scalability.
- Azure SQL Database: A fully managed cloud-based edition of SQL Server available on the Microsoft Azure platform. It offers features tailored for cloud environments, including dynamic scalability, built-in high availability, and automated backups.

The choice of edition largely depends on the specific needs and context of the organization or individual using SQL Server. Each edition provides a different balance of capabilities, performance, and cost, making SQL Server a versatile solution for various database management requirements.

1.4 Components of SQL Server

SQL Server is an extensive and sophisticated relational database management system (RDBMS) that incorporates various components to manage data efficiently, ensure security, and provide high availability. Understanding the different components of SQL Server is crucial to harnessing its full potential. Each component interconnects within the architecture, playing a distinct role in database management, execution, and optimization.

1. Database Engine

The Database Engine is the core service for storing, processing, and securing data. It includes the relational engine, which executes queries and processes commands, and the storage engine, which manages database files, pages, indexes, and data retrieval. Central functionalities include:

- **Transaction Management**: Ensures ACID (Atomicity, Consistency, Isolation, Durability) compliance for transaction processing.
- **Query Processing**: Parses and executes T-SQL (Transact-SQL) statements, optimizing query plans to enhance performance.
- **Storage Management**: Handles physical storage on disk, maintains indexes, and performs data page management.
- **Concurrency Control**: Manages locks, isolation levels, and deadlock resolution to ensure data integrity in multi-user environments.

The Database Engine can be started and stopped using SQL Server Configuration Manager. Below is a sample command line for starting the SQL Server instance:

```
net start MSSQLSERVER
```

2. SQL Server Agent

SQL Server Agent is a background service responsible for automating various administrative tasks such as job scheduling, alerting, and executing scripts. Core functionalities include:

- **Job Scheduling**: Allows for the creation and management of jobs that can run at specified times or in response to specific events.

- **Alerting**: Monitors events and performance conditions, sending notifications or executing actions when certain thresholds are met.
- **Operators and Proxies**: Facilitates the management of automated tasks by defining operators (recipients for alerts) and proxies (security credentials).

An example of creating a SQL Server Agent job using T-SQL is illustrated below:

```
USE msdb;
GO
EXEC dbo.sp_add_job
    @job_name = N'Weekly Database Maintenance';
GO
EXEC dbo.sp_add_jobstep
    @job_name = N'Weekly Database Maintenance',
    @step_name = N'Index Rebuild',
    @subsystem = N'TSQL',
    @command = N'ALTER INDEX ALL ON [YourDatabase] REBUILD;',
    @retry_attempts = 3,
    @retry_interval = 5;
GO
EXEC dbo.sp_add_schedule
    @schedule_name = N'Weekly Schedule',
    @freq_type = 8,
    @freq_interval = 1,
    @active_start_time = 010000;
GO
EXEC sp_attach_schedule
    @job_name = N'Weekly Database Maintenance',
    @schedule_name = N'Weekly Schedule';
GO
EXEC dbo.sp_add_jobserver
    @job_name = N'Weekly Database Maintenance';
GO
```

3. SQL Server Integration Services (SSIS)

SSIS is a platform for data integration and workflow applications. It offers tools for ETL (Extract, Transform, Load) processes, enabling data movement and transformation using various data sources (e.g., SQL Server, Oracle, Excel). Key features include:

- **Data Flow Transformations**: Includes tasks such as data cleansing, data conversion, and aggregation.
- **Control Flow Elements**: Incorporates task automation, including file operations, data warehouse population, and data loading.

- **Event Handling**: Manages error handling, logging, and service recovery mechanisms.

Executing an SSIS package using DTExec utility is shown below:

```
dtexec /f "C:\Packages\MyPackage.dtsx"
```

4. SQL Server Reporting Services (SSRS)

SSRS provides functionalities for generating, managing, and delivering interactive and printed reports. It supports a variety of data sources and enables users to create reports using templates or custom designs. Main aspects include:

- **Report Builder**: A tool for creating reports with a user-friendly, drag-and-drop interface.
- **Report Server**: Responsible for storing, processing, and delivering reports.
- **Subscription Services**: Automates report distribution based on subscriptions and scheduled delivery.

Creating a simple report using SSRS involves the following steps:

```
1. Launch SQL Server Data Tools (SSDT).
2. Create a new Report Server Project.
3. Design the report layout using Report Designer.
4. Define the data source and datasets.
5. Deploy the report to the Report Server.
6. Access the report via the Report Manager web interface.
```

5. SQL Server Analysis Services (SSAS)

SSAS is used for online analytical processing (OLAP) and data mining capabilities. It allows for the creation of multidimensional models that provide fast query performance and data analysis. Important features include:

- **Cube Creation**: Enables the creation of OLAP cubes to provide summarized data for analytical processing.
- **Data Mining**: Offers algorithms and tools for data exploration, pattern discovery, and forecasting.
- **MDX and DAX Languages**: Supports MDX (Multidimensional Expressions) and DAX (Data Analysis Expressions) for complex querying and data manipulation.

6. SQL Server Management Studio (SSMS)

SSMS is an integrated environment for managing SQL Server infrastructure. It combines a broad range of graphical tools with rich script editors to provide access to SQL Server. Functionalities include:

- **Object Explorer**: Allows users to view and manage objects in a hierarchical format.
- **Query Editor**: Provides a feature-rich environment for writing and executing T-SQL scripts.
- **Database Diagrams**: Facilitates the design and visualization of database schemas.

The myriad of tools provided by SSMS enhances productivity and ensures effective database management.

Below is a practical example of querying a database using SSMS query editor:

```
SELECT FirstName, LastName, Email
FROM Employees
WHERE Department = 'Sales';
```

1.5 SQL Server Database Architecture

SQL Server database architecture is a complex yet systematic blueprint designed to manage, store, and retrieve data efficiently and reliably. Understanding this architecture is crucial for database administrators (DBAs) and developers to optimize performance, ensure data integrity, and solve complex problems. In this section, we delve into the foundational components and structures that constitute SQL Server's database architecture.

At the highest level, SQL Server can be viewed as comprising three major subsystems: the Relational Engine, the Storage Engine, and the SQL OS.

Relational Engine: The Relational Engine, also known as the Query Processor, is responsible for executing SQL queries. It includes several critical components:

- **Parser:** The parser checks the syntax of a SQL query to ensure it adheres to SQL Server's language rules.

- **Algebrizer:** This component resolves the names of database objects referenced by the query.
- **Query Optimizer:** The optimizer generates the most efficient execution plan by evaluating various strategies for query execution. It considers factors such as available indexes, statistics, join methods, and hardware resources.
- **Query Executor:** The executor carries out the execution plan provided by the optimizer.

Storage Engine: The Storage Engine handles the manner in which data is stored, retrieved, and managed within SQL Server databases. It consists of:

- **Access Methods:** These methods are responsible for the physical storage and retrieval of data. They manage operations such as table scans and index seeks.
- **Buffer Manager:** This subsystem manages the data pages (8 KB units of storage) within SQL Server's buffer cache (memory pool). It minimizes physical I/O operations by caching frequently accessed data.
- **Transaction Manager:** This ensures compliance with ACID properties (Atomicity, Consistency, Isolation, Durability) through mechanisms like locking, logging, and transaction recovery.
- **Lock Manager:** It regulates concurrent access to data by multiple transactions to preserve consistency and resolve conflicts.
- **Log Manager:** This component writes transaction logs to ensure that all transactions are durable and that a database can be restored to a consistent state in case of a failure.

SQL OS: The SQL OS is an abstraction layer that interacts directly with the underlying system's hardware and operating system. Key responsibilities include:

- **Schedulers:** These determine how SQL Server's worker threads (which perform database operations) are allocated CPU time.
- **Memory Managers:** These components handle SQL Server's memory allocation, avoiding the overhead of frequent memory allocation/deallocation at the OS level.

- **I/O Managers:** Responsible for efficient disk I/O operations, ensuring quick data storage and retrieval.

Database Files: A SQL Server database comprises several file types stored on the disk:

- **Primary Data Files (.mdf):** These are the main files containing startup information and pointers to other database files.
- **Secondary Data Files (.ndf):** Optional files that hold data and can be spread across multiple disks for better performance.
- **Transaction Log Files (.ldf):** These files record all transactions and modifications to the database. They are critical for recovery processes.

Pages and Extents: SQL Server organizes data storage in pages and extents.

- **Pages:** The basic unit of data storage; each page is 8 KB in size. Pages store various types of information, including data rows, indexes, and overhead information.
- **Extents:** Collections of eight contiguous pages (64 KB). Extents can be uniform (all pages from the same object) or mixed (pages from different objects).

Indexes: Indexes in SQL Server enhance the speed of data retrieval operations. They can be:

- **Clustered Indexes:** These define the physical order of data in a table. Each table can have only one clustered index.
- **Non-Clustered Indexes:** These provide a logical order of data and can exist in multiples for each table. They reference the data by pointing to the physical data in a clustered index or a conventional table structure.

Buffer Pool: This is the primary memory component from which data cache and procedure cache operate. It ensures that frequently accessed data resides in memory for quick retrieval, avoiding repetitive disk I/O.

The architecture of SQL Server allows for robust and scalable data management, capable of handling vast amounts of data efficiently while maintaining high availability and performance. Understanding each of these components and their interactions is vital for optimizing database operations and ensuring the integrity and durability of data within an enterprise environment.

1.6 Comparison of SQL Server with Other RDBMS

When comparing SQL Server with other relational database management systems (RDBMS), several factors must be considered to understand the strengths and weaknesses of each system. These factors include performance, scalability, security, support, and cost, among others.

Performance: SQL Server is known for its high performance, especially in environments that handle large volumes of transactions. It uses advanced query optimization techniques and indexing strategies to enhance performance. For example, SQL Server supports in-memory databases with In-Memory OLTP, which significantly boosts transaction processing speed.

Other RDBMS like Oracle also offer high performance and have similar advanced features, such as Oracle's Exadata and in-memory options. However, each system's performance can vary based on the specific workloads and hardware configurations.

In terms of comparative performance, executing a simple query like a select statement might look as follows:

```
SELECT * FROM Employees WHERE Department = 'Sales';
```

Scalability: SQL Server provides excellent scalability options. It supports horizontal and vertical scaling, making it suitable for both small applications and large enterprise systems. The introduction of features like Always On availability groups allows for high availability and disaster recovery across multiple servers.

MySQL, another popular RDBMS, also offers good scalability, especially with its support for clustering and replication. MySQL's InnoDB storage engine is particularly effective in providing high concurrent write and transaction handling.

For a comparison, configuring a read replica for scaling reads in MySQL might use commands such as:

```
CHANGE MASTER TO MASTER_HOST='master_host', MASTER_USER='
    user_name', MASTER_PASSWORD='password';
START SLAVE;
```

Security: SQL Server offers robust security features. It includes advanced data encryption capabilities, such as Transparent Data Encryption (TDE) and Always Encrypted, which ensure data protection both at rest and in transit. Additionally, SQL Server integrates with Active Directory for simplified user management and authentication.

PostgreSQL, as another RDBMS contender, provides an equally strong security framework with similar encryption features and support for various authentication methods, including Kerberos and GSSAPI. PostgreSQL's row-level security policies also allow for more granular access controls compared to SQL Server.

An example of creating encrypted columns in SQL Server is:

```
CREATE COLUMN MASTER KEY CMK_Sales
WITH
(
    KEY_STORE_PROVIDER_NAME = N'Windows Certificate Store',
    KEY_PATH = N'CurrentUser/My/...)
;

CREATE COLUMN ENCRYPTION KEY CEK_Sales
WITH VALUES
(
    COLUMN_MASTER_KEY = CMK_Sales,
    ALGORITHM = 'RSA_OAEP',
    ENCRYPTED_VALUE = ...
);
```

Support: Microsoft provides comprehensive support for SQL Server through its extensive documentation, community forums, and professional services. Additionally, SQL Server benefits from regular updates and improvements, ensuring it remains current with the latest technology and security standards.

In contrast, while MySQL and PostgreSQL have strong open-source communities and substantial support options, their support models may vary. MySQL, now owned by Oracle, offers commercial support, whereas PostgreSQL relies more on its extensive, active community for problem-solving and updates.

Cost: Cost is a significant factor in choosing an RDBMS. SQL Server operates under a commercial license model which means the enterprise edition, while feature-rich, can be more expensive. However, SQL

Server also offers a free express edition, suitable for smaller applications and development environments.

Conversely, MySQL and PostgreSQL are open-source and therefore free to use, making them attractive options for cost-sensitive projects. However, it is important to note that commercial support and enterprise-grade features in open-source RDBMS may still incur costs.

Overall, a comprehensive comparison of these systems' capabilities can be examined by conducting a feature matrix analysis (See Table below):

Table 1.1: Feature comparison among SQL Server, Oracle, MySQL, and PostgreSQL

Feature	SQL Server	Oracle	MySQL	PostgreSQL
In-Memory OLTP	Yes	Yes	Limited	Yes
Always-Encrypted	Yes	TDE (Transparent Data Encryption)	Yes	Yes
Cost	High (Commercial)	High (Commercial)	Low (Open-source)	Low (Open-source)
Active Directory	Yes	Yes	No	No
Community Support	Strong	Moderate	Strong	Strong

This table outlines various feature capabilities amongst SQL Server, Oracle, MySQL, and PostgreSQL, aiding in determining the most appropriate RDBMS for different use cases. Each system has its unique strengths; the choice should align with specific project requirements considering performance, scalability, security, and cost constraints.

1.7 SQL Server and the Relational Model

The relational model, introduced by E. F. Codd in 1970, serves as the foundation for modern relational database management systems (RDBMS) such as SQL Server. Understanding the principles of the relational model is essential for effective database design and implementation in SQL Server. This section delves into how SQL Server integrates and utilizes the relational model, emphasizing its core aspects including tables, keys, relationships, normalization, and constraints.

In the relational model, data is organized into tables (also referred to as relations), each of which consists of rows and columns. Each table represents a distinct type of entity, and the columns within a table represent attributes of that entity type. In SQL Server, tables are created using the CREATE TABLE statement, which specifies the table's name and its columns. Each column is defined by its name, data type, and additional constraints such as NOT NULL or PRIMARY KEY. Below is an example of how a table can be created in SQL Server:

```
CREATE TABLE Employees (
    EmployeeID INT PRIMARY KEY,
    FirstName NVARCHAR(50) NOT NULL,
    LastName NVARCHAR(50) NOT NULL,
    BirthDate DATE,
    HireDate DATE,
    JobTitle NVARCHAR(50)
);
```

Here, the Employees table consists of six columns: EmployeeID, FirstName, LastName, BirthDate, HireDate, and JobTitle. The EmployeeID column is designated as the primary key, ensuring that each employee in the table has a unique identifier.

Keys are a fundamental aspect of the relational model. The primary key uniquely identifies each row within a table, while foreign keys establish relationships between tables. A foreign key in one table corresponds to the primary key in another table, creating a referential link between the two entities. For example, consider a Departments table that maintains information about company departments:

```
CREATE TABLE Departments (
    DepartmentID INT PRIMARY KEY,
    DepartmentName NVARCHAR(50) NOT NULL
);

ALTER TABLE Employees
ADD DepartmentID INT,
FOREIGN KEY (DepartmentID) REFERENCES Departments(DepartmentID);
```

In this example, the Departments table includes a primary key column DepartmentID. The Employees table is then altered to include a DepartmentID column as a foreign key that references the DepartmentID column in the Departments table, establishing a relationship between employees and their respective departments.

Normalization is another key principle of the relational model aimed at reducing redundancy and ensuring data integrity. Normalization involves organizing data into tables and columns following rules known as normal forms. The most commonly adhered to normal forms are the first normal form (1NF), second normal form (2NF), and third normal form (3NF). Let us explain these with the following example.

Assume we have an initial table that stores employee data along with department information:

```
CREATE TABLE EmployeeDepartment (
    EmployeeID INT PRIMARY KEY,
    FirstName NVARCHAR(50) NOT NULL,
    LastName NVARCHAR(50) NOT NULL,
    DepartmentID INT,
    DepartmentName NVARCHAR(50)
);
```

First Normal Form (1NF): A table is in 1NF if all columns contain atomic, indivisible values, and there are no repeating groups. In the EmployeeDepartment table above, each cell contains a single value, satisfying 1NF.

Second Normal Form (2NF): A table is in 2NF if it is in 1NF and all non-key columns are fully functionally dependent on the primary key. To achieve 2NF, we would create separate tables for employees and departments, removing partial dependencies:

```
CREATE TABLE Employees (
    EmployeeID INT PRIMARY KEY,
    FirstName NVARCHAR(50) NOT NULL,
    LastName NVARCHAR(50) NOT NULL
);

CREATE TABLE Departments (
    DepartmentID INT PRIMARY KEY,
    DepartmentName NVARCHAR(50) NOT NULL
);

CREATE TABLE EmployeeDepartments (
    EmployeeID INT,
    DepartmentID INT,
    PRIMARY KEY (EmployeeID, DepartmentID),
    FOREIGN KEY (EmployeeID) REFERENCES Employees(EmployeeID),
    FOREIGN KEY (DepartmentID) REFERENCES Departments(DepartmentID)
);
```

Third Normal Form (3NF): A table is in 3NF if it is in 2NF and all columns are non-transitively dependent on the primary key. This means that any field in a table should not be dependent on another non-key field. In the normalized design above, all tables are in 3NF, as attributes are dependent solely on the primary keys.

Constraints in the relational model ensure data integrity and enforcement of business rules. SQL Server supports various types of constraints including primary key, foreign key, unique, not null, and check constraints. These constraints are specified during table creation or modification and automatically enforced by SQL Server. For instance:

```
CREATE TABLE Projects (
    ProjectID INT PRIMARY KEY,
    ProjectName NVARCHAR(50) NOT NULL,
```

```
    StartDate DATE,
    EndDate DATE,
    CHECK (EndDate > StartDate)
);
```

In this example, a check constraint ensures that the EndDate of a project is always after the StartDate, thus enforcing a business rule at the database level.

SQL Server's adherence to the relational model ensures that it provides a robust platform for data management, emphasizing data integrity, consistency, and ease of access. By leveraging tables, keys, relationships, normalization, and constraints, SQL Server allows efficient organization and retrieval of data, adhering to the core principles established by the relational model.

1.8 Getting Started with SQL Server

To begin utilizing SQL Server, familiarity with the installation process, configuration, and fundamental operations is essential. This section elucidates each of these steps to equip the reader with the foundational tools necessary for effective database management.

1. Installing SQL Server

The initial step involves downloading and installing SQL Server. The installation package can be obtained from the official Microsoft SQL Server website. It is crucial to select the appropriate edition that best suits the intended use case, such as SQL Server Express for lightweight applications or the Enterprise Edition for larger, more complex implementations.

Once the download is complete, execute the installer:

```
SQLServer2019-SSEI-Dev.exe
```

Follow the installation wizard. Key choices include:

- **Feature Selection**: Choose components like Database Engine Services, Analysis Services, and Reporting Services based on your needs.

- **Instance Configuration**: Decide between default instance and named instance. The default instance is accessible via the server name, whereas named instances require server\instance_name format.

- **Server Configuration**: Configure service accounts for SQL Server services. Opt for default settings initially, which can be changed after the installation if necessary.
- **Database Engine Configuration**: Set authentication mode—Windows Authentication or Mixed Mode. Mixed Mode allows both Windows and SQL Server authentication. Create a strong system administrator (sa) password if Mixed Mode is selected.

2. Configuring SQL Server Management Studio (SSMS)

Installing SQL Server Management Studio (SSMS) is recommended for managing SQL Server instances effectively. SSMS is a free, integrated environment for accessing, configuring, managing, administering, and developing all components of SQL Server.

Download and run the SSMS installer:

```
SSMS-Setup-ENU.exe
```

Once installed, launch SSMS and connect to your SQL Server instance by entering the server name, authentication type, and appropriate credentials.

3. Creating a New Database

After successfully connecting to SQL Server through SSMS, the next task is to create a new database. Within SSMS, perform the following steps:

- Right-click on the **Databases** node in the Object Explorer.
- Select **New Database**.
- Enter the database name in the **New Database** dialog box.
- Configure additional settings such as filegroup options, if necessary.
- Click **OK** to create the database.

To verify that the database was created, it should appear under the **Databases** node in Object Explorer.

4. Creating Database Objects

Tables: Tables are fundamental objects in any database. They store data in rows and columns. To create a table:

- Right-click on the newly created database.
- Select **New Table**.
- Define columns by specifying column names, data types, and constraints such as primary key, NOT NULL, and unique constraints.
- Save the table with a relevant name.

Example Script for Creating a Table:

```
CREATE TABLE Employees (
    EmployeeID INT PRIMARY KEY,
    FirstName NVARCHAR(50),
    LastName NVARCHAR(50),
    BirthDate DATE,
    Position NVARCHAR(50)
);
```

Indexing: Indexes improve the speed of data retrieval operations on a database table. Create an index using:

```
CREATE INDEX idx_LastName
ON Employees (LastName);
```

Views: Views are virtual tables based on the result set of an SQL statement. To create a view:

```
CREATE VIEW EmployeeInfo AS
SELECT FirstName, LastName, BirthDate
FROM Employees;
```

5. Inserting Data

To insert data into a table, use the INSERT INTO statement:

```
INSERT INTO Employees (EmployeeID, FirstName, LastName, BirthDate, Position)
VALUES (1, 'John', 'Doe', '1980-01-01', 'Software Developer');
```

6. Querying Data

Data retrieval is done through the SELECT statement. Here is how to retrieve all data from the Employees table:

```
SELECT * FROM Employees;
```

The output of this query will display in a tabular format, showing all columns and rows in the Employees table.

```
EmployeeID | FirstName | LastName | BirthDate | Position
-------------------------------------------------------
   1       |  John     |  Doe     |1980-01-01 | Software Developer
```

7. Backup and Restore

Regular backups are crucial for data recovery and protection. To create a database backup:

- Right-click on the database.
- Select **Tasks** -> **Back Up**.
- Configure the backup settings and destination.
- Click **OK** to perform the backup.

To restore a database backup:

- Right-click on **Databases** in Object Explorer.
- Select **Restore Database**.
- Choose the source of the backup.
- Configure the settings and destination database.
- Click **OK** to restore.

Adequate mastery of these steps provides a robust foundation for managing SQL Server environments effectively.

1.9 Common Use Cases for SQL Server

SQL Server's versatility and robustness have made it a preferred choice for a variety of applications across numerous industries. This section delves into some of the prevalent use cases for SQL Server, highlighting its capabilities in each scenario.

Enterprise Resource Planning (ERP): ERP systems are pivotal in managing day-to-day business operations such as accounting, procurement, project management, and supply chain operations. SQL Server provides a reliable backend for ERP systems owing to its scalability and support for handling large datasets. Its integration with other Microsoft products enhances seamless data flow and integrity across various modules within the ERP system.

Customer Relationship Management (CRM): CRM applications, essential for managing a company's interactions with current and potential customers, benefit significantly from SQL Server. With its robust querying capabilities, SQL Server facilitates efficient data retrieval, thus enabling businesses to gain insights into customer behavior and preferences. The SQL Server Reporting Services (SSRS) also allows companies to generate detailed customer reports, aiding in strategic decision-making.

E-commerce Platforms: E-commerce platforms require databases that can handle high volumes of transactions and user data with minimal downtime. SQL Server's high availability and disaster recovery options, including Always On availability groups and failover clustering, ensure that these platforms remain operational at all times. Additionally, SQL Server's security features, such as encryption and role-based access control, protect sensitive data.

Business Intelligence (BI) and Data Warehousing: SQL Server's integration with SQL Server Integration Services (SSIS), SQL Server Analysis Services (SSAS), and SQL Server Reporting Services (SSRS) make it an excellent choice for BI and Data Warehousing applications. These services allow organizations to extract, transform, and load (ETL) large datasets from various sources, perform complex analyses, and generate comprehensive reports. This enables stakeholders to make data-driven decisions.

Web Applications: Many web applications utilize SQL Server as a backend to store and retrieve user data, session information, and other critical data. Its compatibility with various web technologies and frameworks, such as .NET, PHP, and Python, makes it a versatile option. Features like full-text search and JSON support enhance its capability to handle and query different types of data efficiently.

Healthcare Systems: Healthcare applications, including Electronic Health Records (EHR), require a database system that ensures data integrity, privacy, and compliance with regulations such as HIPAA. SQL Server offers robust encryption mechanisms to protect sensitive patient data and provides auditing features to track data access and modifications. Its ability to handle large volumes of structured and unstructured data makes it suitable for clinical analytics and research.

Finance and Banking: SQL Server is extensively used in the finance and banking sectors due to its ability to execute complex transactions with high reliability and security. It supports ACID (Atomicity, Consistency, Isolation, Durability) properties, which are critical for financial transactions. Features like Transparent Data Encryption (TDE) and dynamic data masking provide an added layer of security to safeguard financial information.

Supply Chain Management: Managing a supply chain involves tracking inventory, orders, suppliers, and shipments. SQL Server's high performance and scalability enable it to handle the extensive data generated by these processes. Its advanced analytics capabilities allow businesses to optimize their supply chains through predictive analytics and real-time data monitoring.

Gaming Industry: Online gaming platforms require real-time transaction processing and high availability to provide a seamless user experience. SQL Server's performance tuning and optimization features, such as indexing and caching, improve query performance and overall responsiveness. Its cloud integration options also allow gaming companies to scale their databases according to user demand.

Government and Public Sector: Government databases often store vast amounts of sensitive information requiring stringent security and compliance standards. SQL Server's comprehensive security features, including encryption, auditing, and fine-grained access control, make it a suitable choice. Moreover, its robust replication and synchronization capabilities ensure data consistency across multiple locations.

Overall, SQL Server's flexibility, performance, and integrated tools make it suitable for a wide range of applications across various industries. Its ability to seamlessly integrate with other Microsoft products and its robust security features further enhance its appeal. The aforementioned use cases exemplify SQL Server's capacity to address the diverse requirements of modern data management.

Chapter 2

Installation and Configuration

This chapter outlines the system requirements and steps for selecting the appropriate edition of SQL Server. It provides a pre-installation checklist, detailed instructions for installation, and guidance for post-installation configuration. Additionally, the chapter covers setting up SQL Server instances, configuring services, using SQL Server Configuration Manager, and basic troubleshooting during the installation process.

2.1 System Requirements

Ensuring that the system meets the necessary requirements is critical for the successful installation and efficient operation of SQL Server. The system requirements encompass hardware specifications, software requirements, and network configurations. Each of these areas must be meticulously evaluated to avoid any disruptions or performance degradation during the lifecycle of SQL Server.

Hardware Requirements

The hardware specifications for SQL Server can vary depending on the edition being installed and the expected workload. However, some general guidelines can be followed.

- **Processor:** SQL Server requires a 1.4 GHz 64-bit processor or faster. A multi-core processor is recommended for improved performance. For enterprise-level applications, processors with higher clock speeds and more cores are beneficial.
- **Memory:** The minimum requirement is 2 GB of RAM. However, 4 GB or more is recommended for optimal performance. For larger databases and heavy queries, increasing the available memory will significantly improve performance.
- **Storage:** A minimum of 6 GB of available hard-disk space is required for the SQL Server installation. It's important to additionally account for the space needed to store databases, logs, and backups. High-speed storage solutions such as SSDs are recommended for intensive read/write operations.
- **Network:** A network adapter appropriate for the type of network to which you want to connect is required. It is also important for the network hardware to support network speeds that do not bottleneck SQL Server performance.
- **Display:** A VGA or higher-resolution monitor is required with a minimum resolution of 1024x768 pixels.

Software Requirements

The operating system and additional software components must be compatible with the SQL Server edition in use. Below are the general software requirements.

- **Operating System:** SQL Server supports various editions of Windows Server and Windows operating systems including Windows Server 2019, Windows Server 2016, and Windows 10. Ensure the latest service packs and updates are installed.
- **.NET Framework:** The installation of .NET Framework 4.6 or higher is required. SQL Server Setup installs necessary .NET components if they are not already part of the system.
- **SQL Server Setup Support Files:** These are required for running the Setup process. They are installed automatically during the installation process.
- **Windows PowerShell:** PowerShell 2.0 or higher must be installed and enabled on the machine.

- **Server Core Support:** While SQL Server can run on Server Core installations of Windows Server, certain features may not be available. Review the specific feature requirements if using Server Core.

Permissions and Privileges

The account used to install SQL Server must have appropriate permissions to access and modify the necessary directories, registries, and services. This generally includes:

- **Administrative Rights:** The installation account should possess administrative rights on the computer where SQL Server is being installed.
- **Service Accounts:** Dedicated domain or local user accounts should be prepared for SQL Server services. These accounts should have minimal permissions initially and will be granted necessary access rights during installation.

Network Configuration

Configuring the network settings is critical for ensuring that SQL Server can communicate effectively in a multi-tier environment.

- **DNS Configuration:** Ensure that the server's DNS settings resolve correctly so that SQL Server can locate and communicate with other network resources.
- **IP Address Configuration:** Assign static IP addresses to avoid any disruptions caused by changes in dynamic IP assignments. For multiple instance installations, different ports must be assigned to each SQL Server instance.
- **Firewall Settings:** Configure the firewall to allow SQL Server traffic. The default instance uses port 1433 for TCP/IP connections, and this must be open along with any other custom ports configured for named instances.

Before proceeding with the installation, double-checking these system requirements ensures a smooth setup process and lays down a firm foundation for the deployment and operation of SQL Server. Each component—hardware, software, permissions, and network—must be assessed and aligned with the requirements and expected usage scenarios of SQL Server. This preparatory step minimizes the risk of encountering performance, compatibility, or security issues post-installation.

2.2 Choosing the Right Edition

Choosing the appropriate SQL Server edition is a crucial step that depends on various factors including budget, required features, performance needs, and intended use cases. Microsoft offers multiple editions, each tailored to specific demands and environments.

SQL Server Editions

- **Enterprise Edition**: Provides comprehensive high-end datacenter capabilities with high availability, advanced security features, extensive BI tools, and performance optimization. Suitable for large-scale applications, this edition supports unlimited CPU cores and memory.
- **Standard Edition**: Balances performance and cost, providing core database, reporting, and analytics capabilities. Supports up to 24 cores and offers many of the essential features needed for most small to medium-sized businesses.
- **Web Edition**: Designed for web hosting environments, offering cost-effective hosting suitable for small to medium web applications. This edition is available via hosting providers and includes necessary web-specific BI tools.
- **Express Edition**: Free to use, catering to small-scale applications and development environments. It has limitations regarding database size (up to 10 GB), memory usage, and CPU cores.
- **Developer Edition**: Mirrors the Enterprise Edition in terms of features, but licensed only for development, testing, and demonstration purposes. It offers a valuable platform for developers to build and test applications.

Licensing Models

- **Per Core Licensing**: Available for Enterprise and Standard editions. This model charges based on the number of cores utilized by the SQL Server. It is advantageous for systems using high-core-count CPUs, providing flexibility and scalability.

- **Server + CAL Licensing (Client Access License)**: Applicable exclusively to the Standard Edition. Under this model, separate licenses are required for the server and each accessing client.

Feature Set Each edition provides a distinct feature set designed to fulfill specific requirements. It is essential to analyze the functionalities offered by different editions and evaluate them against your needs. Below is a summarized comparison highlighting key features:

Feature	Enterprise	Standard	Web	Express	Developer
Max DB Size	Unlimited	524 PB	524 PB	10 GB	Unlimited
Memory (RAM)	OS Max	128 GB	64 GB	1 GB	OS Max
Max Compute Capacity	OS Max	4 Sockets / 24 Cores	4 Sockets / 16 Cores	1 Socket / 4 Cores	OS Max
Always On Availability Groups	Yes (up to 8)	Basic	No	No	Yes
Data Compression	Yes	Yes	No	No	Yes
In-Memory OLTP	Yes	Yes (limited)	No	No	Yes
Advanced Security Features	Yes	Basic	Basic	Basic	Yes
BI and Analytics Tools	Comprehensive	Essential	No	No	Comprehensive

Use Cases Understanding typical use cases for each edition can further aid in making an informed selection:

- **Enterprise Edition**: Suitable for large enterprises requiring maximum performance, scalability, and advanced high-availability features. Example use cases include data warehousing, real-time analytics, and critical transactional processing systems.
- **Standard Edition**: Ideal for medium-sized organizations with moderate transactional workloads and basic analytics needs. Common use cases involve departmental applications, smaller ERPs, and business reporting systems.
- **Web Edition**: Best for small to medium web applications hosted by service providers. Tailored for scenarios where cost-efficiency

is paramount, such as content management systems and e-commerce platforms.

- **Express Edition**: Suitable for small-scale applications, desktop applications, and learning environments. Typical use cases include lightweight data-driven applications and student projects.
- **Developer Edition**: Primarily utilized for developing and testing applications that will be deployed on higher-end SQL Server editions. It is essential for environments focused on developing complex, resource-intensive applications.

Cost Considerations Budget constraints play a significant role in the decision-making process. High-level editions come with correspondingly higher costs, but they include features necessary for handling complex, large-scale operations. Organizations must balance their requirements against the financial implications:

```
-- An illustrative cost estimation query using a hypothetical pricing table

SELECT Edition, Core_Price, Server_Price, CAL_Price
FROM Pricing
WHERE Edition IN ('Enterprise', 'Standard', 'Web');

-- Output
+-----------+------------+------------+------------+
| Edition | Core_Price | Server_Price| CAL_Price |
+-----------+------------+------------+------------+
| Enterprise| $14,256 | N/A | N/A |
| Standard | $3,717 | $931 | $209 |
| Web | $1,543 | N/A | N/A |
+-----------+------------+------------+------------+
```

```
Edition    | Core_Price   | Server_Price   | CAL_Price
Enterprise| $14,256      | N/A            | N/A
Standard  | $3,717       | $931           | $209
Web       | $1,543       | N/A            | N/A
```

Selecting the right SQL Server edition requires a holistic evaluation of the application needs, feature requirements, budget limitations, and expected growth. When carefully matched to the organizational goals and workload demands, the chosen edition can significantly enhance database performance, security, and overall productivity.

2.3 Pre-Installation Checklist

To ensure a smooth installation process of SQL Server, it is essential to follow a comprehensive pre-installation checklist. This checklist helps to verify that all necessary components and configurations are in place before initiating the installation. The following items should be included in the pre-installation checklist:

1. Verify System Requirements:

- **Operating System Compatibility:** Ensure that the operating system version is supported by the SQL Server edition you plan to install. Refer to the official documentation for detailed compatibility matrices.
- **Hardware Specifications:** Verify that the system meets or exceeds the minimum required specifications for CPU, RAM, and disk space. For instance, SQL Server 2019 Standard Edition requires a minimum of 2 GHz 64-bit processor, 2 GB of RAM, and at least 6 GB of available hard disk space.
- **Network Configuration:** Confirm that network settings, including IP addresses and DNS configurations, are correctly set up. Adequate network bandwidth and connectivity are crucial for SQL Server operations, especially in enterprise environments.

2. Ensure Sufficient Disk Space:

- **Database Storage:** Determine the required storage space for databases and logs. Allocate additional space for growth projections based on anticipated data volumes.
- **TempDB:** Adequately size the TempDB files for efficient query processing. Insufficient TempDB space can lead to performance degradation and system errors.
- **Backup Storage:** Identify and provision adequate storage for backups. Ensure that the backup strategy is aligned with organizational recovery objectives.

3. Install Required Software Components:

- **.NET Framework:** Confirm that the necessary version of the .NET Framework is installed. SQL Server setup may require specific .NET Framework versions.
- **Visual C++ Redistributable:** Verify the installation of Visual C++ Redistributable packages needed by SQL Server.

- **PowerShell:** Ensure PowerShell is installed and updated to the required version, as certain SQL Server features depend on it.

4. **Configure Firewall Settings:**

- **SQL Server Ports:** Identify the port numbers used by SQL Server services (default is TCP 1433 for Database Engine). Configure the firewall to allow inbound and outbound traffic on these ports.
- **Named Instances:** If using named instances, identify additional ports or configure dynamic port allocation as necessary.

5. **Review Service Accounts:**

- **Dedicated Service Accounts:** Use separate, dedicated service accounts for SQL Server services to enhance security and manageability.
- **Privileges and Permissions:** Ensure that service accounts have the minimum necessary privileges. Avoid running services under high-privilege accounts such as LocalSystem.

6. **Validate Domain and User Account Settings:**

- **Domain Membership:** Ensure that the server is joined to the appropriate domain if required, and verify domain trust relationships if necessary.
- **User Account Permissions:** Confirm that the user account performing the installation has administrative privileges on the server.

7. **Prepare Environment for High Availability and Disaster Recovery:**

- **Clustering and Always On:** For high availability features such as Failover Clustering or Always On Availability Groups, verify the prerequisite configurations and ensure the availability of necessary hardware and network resources.
- **Backup and Restore Strategy:** Define and document a backup and restore strategy that aligns with business continuity requirements. Test the strategy in a pre-production environment.

8. **Review Compliance and Licensing:**

    - **Licensing Model:** Understand the licensing model for the SQL Server edition being installed. Verify that the appropriate licenses are available and assigned.
    - **Compliance Requirements:** Ensure that the installation and configuration adhere to relevant regulatory and compliance standards.

9. **Plan for Monitoring and Maintenance:**

    - **Monitoring Tools:** Identify and configure monitoring tools to track performance, resource utilization, and health of the SQL Server instance.
    - **Maintenance Plans:** Develop maintenance plans for regular tasks such as backups, index optimization, and integrity checks.

Adhering to this pre-installation checklist significantly reduces the risk of encountering issues during installation and ensures that the SQL Server environment is optimized for performance, security, and reliability from the onset.

2.4 Installing SQL Server

The steps for installing SQL Server are straightforward yet require careful attention to detail to ensure a successful setup. This section covers the detailed, step-by-step process for installing SQL Server, including selecting the installation type, configuring necessary services, specifying authentication modes, and completing the setup.

Begin with launching the SQL Server setup executable. Depending on your source, this might be an executable file that you downloaded from Microsoft's website, or it might be a setup disc.

```
Setup.exe
```

Launching this file will open the SQL Server Installation Center. The Installation Center provides various options, but for a new installation, select New SQL Server stand-alone installation or add features to an existing installation.

1. **New Installation or Add Features:** Click on New SQL Server stand-alone installation or add features to an existing installation.
2. **Product Key:** If required, provide a valid product key. For evaluation or a free edition, select the appropriate option.
3. **License Terms:** Read and accept the license terms to proceed.
4. **Global Rules:** The installer will run a set of checks to ensure your system meets the minimum requirements. Address any warnings or issues before proceeding.
5. **Microsoft Update:** Opt into Microsoft Update to receive updates directly through Windows Update.
6. **Setup Role:** Choose the appropriate role for the installation. Typically, SQL Server Feature Installation will be selected for a new installation.

Feature Selection

In the Feature Selection page, choose the features you want to install. Options may include Database Engine Services, Analysis Services, Reporting Services, etc. Each feature selection can affect the components installed, and you should select only those features necessary for your environment.

- **Database Engine Services**
- **SQL Server Replication**
- **Full-Text and Semantic Extractions for Search**
- **Analysis Services**
- **Reporting Services**
- **Data Quality Services**

Instance Configuration

Specify whether to install SQL Server as a default instance or as a named instance. The default instance uses the instance name MSSQLSERVER, whereas a named instance requires a unique identifier.

- **Default Instance**
  Installation path:
  C:\Program Files\Microsoft SQL Server\MSSQLxx.MSSQLSERVER\
- **Named Instance**
  Installation path:
  C:\Program Files\Microsoft SQL Server\MSSQLxx.<InstanceName>\

Server Configuration

This page allows setting up service accounts and collation configurations:

- **Service Accounts:** Specify the account and password for each SQL Server service. It is advisable to use separate accounts for each service for security and manageability.

```
SQL Server Agent NT Service\SQLSERVERAGENT
SQL Server Database Engine NT Service\MSSQLSERVER
SQL Server Browser NT AUTHORITY\LOCALSERVICE
SQL Server Analysis Services NT Service\MSOLAP\$MSSQLSERVER
SQL Server Reporting Services NT AUTHORITY\NETWORK SERVICE
```

Configure the collation settings for the SQL Server instance. These settings determine how text is sorted and compared, and cannot be easily changed post-installation.

Database Engine Configuration

Define the database engine configuration, including authentication modes and user permissions:

- **Authentication Mode:** Choose between Windows authentication mode and Mixed Mode (SQL Server and Windows Authentication). For broader compatibility, Mixed Mode is generally recommended.
- **SQL Server Administrators:** Specify SQL Server administrators. It is important for maintenance and administration to list at least one SQL Server administrator.

```
Add Current User
```

Data Directories

Configure the directories for various SQL Server data components. Proper directory configuration can improve performance and manageability:

- **Data Root Directory:**

```
C:\Program Files\Microsoft SQL Server\
```

- **User Database Directory:** Set the default directory for user databases.
- **Database Log Directory:** Set the directory for database logs.
- **Backup Directory:** Set the directory for database backups.

Ready to Install

Review the installation settings, including:

- Selected features
- Disk space requirements
- Anything else configured during the setup

If everything is accurate, proceed with the installation:

```
Install
```

```
The installation progress will be displayed, logging the status of each component.
Upon successful completion, a message will indicate that SQL Server has been installed successfully.
You may need to restart your machine to complete the installation process.
```

With SQL Server installed, the next steps involve post-installation configurations, such as configuring server settings and maintenance plans.

2.5 Post-Installation Configuration

Post-installation configuration is a crucial phase in the deployment of SQL Server, aimed at optimizing performance, ensuring security, and preparing the server environment for effective data management operations. This section covers essential tasks and adjustments to be made following the installation process.

1. Verification of Installation

Firstly, verifying the installation ensures that SQL Server has been installed correctly and is functioning as expected. Open the SQL Server Management Studio (SSMS) and connect to the SQL Server instance. Run the following query to check the version and edition of SQL Server:

```
SELECT @@VERSION;
```

The output should give you details about the SQL Server version, edition, and other relevant information.

2. Configure Server Authentication Mode

SQL Server can operate in two authentication modes: Windows Authentication mode and Mixed Mode (Windows Authentication and SQL Server Authentication). To change the authentication mode:

- Open SSMS and connect to the server.
- In Object Explorer, right-click the server name and select Properties.
- In the Server Properties dialog box, click Security.
- Under Server authentication, select the desired authentication mode (Windows Authentication mode or SQL Server and Windows Authentication mode).
- Click OK and restart the SQL Server service for changes to take effect.

3. Setup SQL Server Agent

SQL Server Agent is responsible for executing scheduled tasks such as backups and maintenance plans. To configure SQL Server Agent:

- In SSMS, connect to the SQL Server instance.
- Expand the SQL Server Agent node in Object Explorer.
- Right-click Jobs to create new scheduled tasks or manage existing ones.

Ensure the SQL Server Agent service is running by navigating to Services in the SQL Server Configuration Manager and starting the SQL Server Agent service if it isn't already running.

4. Configure TempDB Database

The TempDB database is a global resource for all users connected to the SQL Server instance. Proper configuration of TempDB ensures optimal performance. Key considerations include the number of data files, file growth settings, and initial size.

- Open SSMS and connect to the server.
- Execute the following query to review the current TempDB configuration:

```
USE tempdb;
GO
EXEC sp_spaceused;
GO
```

- To modify the TempDB, execute:

```
ALTER DATABASE tempdb
MODIFY FILE (NAME = 'tempdev', SIZE = 1024MB, FILEGROWTH = 256MB);
ALTER DATABASE tempdb
MODIFY FILE (NAME = 'templog', SIZE = 512MB, FILEGROWTH = 128MB);
GO
```

For multiple data files, add file specifications accordingly.

5. Configuring Database Mail

Database Mail allows SQL Server to send email notifications. To configure Database Mail:

- Open SSMS and connect to the SQL Server instance.
- Expand the Management node, right-click Database Mail, and select Configure Database Mail.
- Follow the wizard to set up a new mail profile and account.

Once configured, test the mail setup by sending a test email through SSMS.

```
EXEC msdb.dbo.sp_send_dbmail
    @profile_name = 'YourProfileName',
    @recipients = 'your.email@example.com',
    @subject = 'Test Email',
    @body = 'This is a test email from SQL Server.';
```

6. SQL Server Performance Tuning

Performance tuning is essential to optimize SQL Server performance. Initial tuning steps include:

- **Max Degree of Parallelism (MAXDOP)**: Specifies the number of processors that SQL Server can use in parallel. Adjust this setting based on your workload type.
- **Optimize for Ad Hoc Workloads**: Reduces memory usage for single-use ad hoc queries.
- **Cost Threshold for Parallelism**: Sets the cost threshold at which SQL Server creates parallel execution plans.

Using SSMS, these configurations can be updated by executing:

```
EXEC sp_configure 'show advanced options', 1;
RECONFIGURE;
EXEC sp_configure 'max degree of parallelism', 4; -- Change as necessary
RECONFIGURE;
EXEC sp_configure 'optimize for ad hoc workloads', 1;
RECONFIGURE;
EXEC sp_configure 'cost threshold for parallelism', 50; -- Change as necessary
RECONFIGURE;
```

7. Security Configuration

Configuring security includes setting up logins, roles, and permissions. Ensure that the sa account is disabled or its password is strong if using Mixed Mode authentication. Create necessary logins and assign appropriate roles and permissions using the following commands:

```
CREATE LOGIN TestUser WITH PASSWORD = 'StrongPassword1!';
CREATE USER TestUser FOR LOGIN TestUser;
EXEC sp_addrolemember 'db_datareader', 'TestUser';
EXEC sp_addrolemember 'db_datawriter', 'TestUser';
```

Regularly review and update security settings to maintain compliance and protect against unauthorized access.

8. Enable SQL Server Error and Usage Reporting

Enabling error and usage reporting helps in troubleshooting and improving SQL Server by sending error reports and usage data to Microsoft. This setting can be enabled during SQL Server setup or by using SSMS post-installation:

- In SSMS, connect to the SQL Server instance.

- Navigate to Properties of the SQL Server instance.
- Under the Error and Usage Reporting tab, select relevant options to send data for error reporting and usage analysis.

Maintaining a well-configured SQL Server environment post-installation ensures stability, optimal performance, and secure operations, fulfilling organizational data management requirements effectively.

2.6 Setting Up SQL Server Instances

Setting up SQL Server instances is a critical task in database administration, as it allows multiple, separate environments to run on a single machine. Each instance operates independently, enabling distinct configurations and security settings. This section will guide you through the process of setting up SQL Server instances, covering both the conceptual and practical aspects.

Instance Types and Naming Conventions

SQL Server supports two types of instances: **default** and **named**. The default instance is accessed through the server name alone, while named instances require the server name followed by a backslash and the instance name (e.g., ServerName\InstanceName). Ensuring proper naming conventions can enhance manageability and readability. Typically, instance names are chosen based on their purpose, such as DEV, TEST, or PROD.

Installation of a New Instance

To install a new SQL Server instance, follow these steps:

1. Launch the SQL Server Installation Center from the setup executable.
2. Click on the **New SQL Server stand-alone installation or add features to an existing installation** option.
3. In the **Product Key** dialog, enter your product key, or proceed with the default setting if you are using an Evaluation or Express edition.
4. Accept the license terms on the **License Terms** page and click **Next**.

5. The **Global Rules** page will check for potential issues that could cause installation failures. Ensure all checks are passed before moving forward.
6. On the **Microsoft Update** page, choose whether to include SQL Server updates through Microsoft Update, then click **Next**.
7. The **Install Setup Files** page downloads and installs necessary setup files. After completion, click **Next**.
8. On the **Installation Type** page, select **Perform a new installation of SQL Server 2019**, and click **Next**.
9. On the **Instance Configuration** page, choose **Named instance** and enter the desired instance name.

```
ExampleInstance
```

10. Click **Next** to proceed. The **Disk Space Requirements** page will validate that there is sufficient space on the selected drives.
11. In the **Server Configuration** page, specify the SQL Server services accounts. Use a separate account for each service for security reasons.

SQL Server Agent	NT SERVICE\SQLAgent$ExampleInstance
SQL Server Database Engine	NT SERVICE\MSSQL$ExampleInstance

12. In the **Collation** tab, set the Database Engine's collation, which determines the default sort order and comparison rules in the database.
13. The **Database Engine Configuration** page requires setting the authentication mode (Windows Authentication Mode or Mixed Mode). If Mixed Mode is selected, specify a strong password for the SQL Server system administrator (**sa**) account.
14. Add SQL Server administrators by clicking the **Add Current User** or adding specific domain users.

```
MYDOMAIN\SQLAdmin
```

15. Configure SQL Server directories on the **Data Directories** tab. It's recommended to separate data, log, and backup directories for performance and manageability.

16. The **TempDB** tab allows configuration of the TempDB data and log file sizes and growth settings. Best practices involve multiple data files and configured autogrowth settings.

17. On the **MaxDOP** tab, configure the Maximum Degree of Parallelism to optimize CPU usage.

18. Review the **Ready to Install** page, which summarizes the selected configurations. Click **Install** to start the instance installation.

```
Starting SQL Server instance installation...
Configuring services and directories...
Instance installation complete.
```

Post-Installation Tasks

After instance installation, verify connectivity and performance by performing the following tasks:

- Connect to the instance using SQL Server Management Studio (SSMS) by specifying the server name and instance name.

```
Server name: MyServer\ExampleInstance
```

- Execute test queries to confirm instance functionality.
- Apply the latest SQL Server updates and service packs.
- Configure instance-level security settings, including firewalls and SQL Server permissions.

Establishing a naming convention and configuring instances appropriately enhances the manageability of your SQL Server environment. Following the detailed installation process ensures that each instance operates optimally and securely.

2.7 Configuring SQL Server Services

Configuring SQL Server services is pivotal for optimal performance, security, and manageability of your SQL Server environment. Proper configuration ensures that services run efficiently, with appropriate privileges and resource permissions, thereby minimizing potential vulnerabilities and performance bottlenecks.

SQL Server services can be managed using various tools, such as SQL Server Configuration Manager, Windows Services, and command-line utilities like sqlcmd. This section focuses on using the SQL Server Configuration Manager due to its integrated approach and specialized options for SQL Server.

1. SQL Server Configuration Manager Overview

SQL Server Configuration Manager is a Microsoft Management Console (MMC) snap-in tool used for managing SQL Server services. It provides a consolidated view of all SQL Server-related services and allows for starting, stopping, pausing, resuming, and configuring these services.

2. Accessing SQL Server Configuration Manager

To access SQL Server Configuration Manager:

1. Press Windows+R to open the Run dialog.
2. Type SQLServerManager13.msc (for SQL Server 2016) or SQLServerManager14.msc (for SQL Server 2017), based on your installed version.
3. Press Enter.

3. SQL Server Service Components

SQL Server Configuration Manager lists several components, each serving a specific purpose:

- **SQL Server (MSSQLSERVER)**: The core database engine service.
- **SQL Server Agent (MSSQLSERVER)**: Handles scheduled tasks and automation.
- **SQL Server Browser**: Manages incoming connections and directs them to the correct SQL Server instance.
- **SQL Server Reporting Services (MSSQLSERVER)**: Generates and manages reports.

- **SQL Server Integration Services**: Manages data integration tasks.

4. Configuring SQL Server Services

Standard steps for configuring any SQL Server service are as follows:

1. **Right-click on the service**: From the SQL Server Configuration Manager console, right-click on the service you wish to configure.
2. **Select Properties**: A dialog box appears with multiple tabs.
3. **General Tab**: Offers a brief overview of the service status and allows for starting and stopping the service.
4. **Log On Tab**: Allows you to define the service account. It is recommended to use a low-privilege, dedicated local or domain account.
5. **Service Tab**: Enables you to configure parameters such as start-up type (Automatic, Manual, Disabled).
6. **Dependencies Tab**: Lists system components that depend on the service, as well as services that this one depends on.

5. Example: Configuring SQL Server Service Account

Assigning a dedicated service account enhances security. Follow these steps to configure the service account for SQL Server (MSSQLSERVER):

```
# Starting Configuration Manager
1. sqlservermanager14.msc

# Navigating to the service
2. Select SQL Server Services from the left pane
3. Right-click SQL Server (MSSQLSERVER) and select Properties

# Setting up the Log On account
4. Navigate to the Log On tab
5. Select This account: and provide credentials for the dedicated account
6. Click Apply and OK
```

Changes typically require you to restart the service. Restart by right-clicking the service again and selecting Restart.

6. SQL Server Agent Configuration

SQL Server Agent plays a critical role in automating administrative tasks. Proper configuration ensures that scheduled jobs execute reliably. Key areas include:

- **Service Account**: Set a dedicated, low-privilege account.
- **Job Execution Permissions**: Ensure jobs have necessary permissions without compromising security.
- **Alerts and Notifications**: Configure email or event log notifications for job statuses.

7. Using Command Line for Service Configuration

For advanced users, the command-line utility sqlcmd enables configuration through scripts. This is particularly useful for automated deployments:

```
# Checking the status of SQL Server service
sqlcmd -S .\texttt{INSTANCE\_NAME} -Q "EXEC xp_servicecontrol '
    QUERYSTATE', 'SQL Server (MSSQLSERVER)'"

# Starting SQL Server service
sqlcmd -S .\texttt{INSTANCE\_NAME} -Q "EXEC xp_servicecontrol 'START', 'SQL
    Server (MSSQLSERVER)'"
```

8. Monitoring and Maintenance

Regular monitoring of SQL Server services ensures ongoing reliability. Key practices include:

- **Logs Review**: Regularly review SQL Server logs for potential issues.
- **Performance Metrics**: Use Performance Monitor to evaluate CPU, memory usage, and disk I/O.
- **Backup Configurations**: Ensure service configurations are backed up regularly as part of your disaster recovery plan.

Implementing these practices creates a robust, secure, and efficient SQL Server environment.

2.8 Using SQL Server Configuration Manager

SQL Server Configuration Manager is an essential tool for managing the various services and network protocols associated with SQL Server.

This utility allows you to configure server and client network protocols, administer SQL Server services, manage server aliases, and set startup parameters. Proper configuration can enhance SQL Server performance and security.

To begin with SQL Server Configuration Manager, follow these steps:

- Open the tool: On a Windows operating system, navigate to Start → All Programs → Microsoft SQL Server → Configuration Tools → SQL Server Configuration Manager.

The Configuration Manager interface (Figure **??**) is organized into several key areas: SQL Server Services, SQL Server Network Configuration, and SQL Native Client Configuration.

SQL Server Services: This area allows you to manage SQL Server-related services, including starting, stopping, and configuring the services. It includes SQL Server Database Engine, SQL Server Agent, SQL Server Browser, and other components such as SQL Server Analysis Services (if installed).

- To start or stop a service, right-click on the service name and select the desired action (Start, Stop, Pause, Resume, Restart).
- To configure a service, right-click on the service name and choose Properties. You can set the service account, update recovery options, and configure advanced settings through this dialog.

SQL Server Network Configuration: This section is crucial for configuring the network interface through which SQL Server communicates. It includes both server and client configuration nodes.

- **Protocols for *InstanceName***: Manage the network protocols that SQL Server instances use. Common protocols are shared memory, named pipes, and TCP/IP.
- To enable or disable a protocol, select Protocols for InstanceName, right-click on a protocol (e.g., TCP/IP), and select either Enable or Disable.
- For protocol-specific settings, right-click on a protocol and select Properties.

- **TCP/IP Properties**: Configure IP addresses, TCP ports, and listen behavior. This step is critical for setting up remote connections.

SQL Native Client Configuration:

- *Client Protocols*: Configure protocols used by SQL Server clients.
- *Aliases*: Set up server aliases to simplify client connections. An alias allows clients to connect using an alias name instead of the actual server name.

Here, we look at examples of configuring specific settings:

```
# Steps to enable TCP/IP Protocol:
1. Open SQL Server Configuration Manager.
2. Navigate to 'SQL Server Network Configuration' -> 'Protocols for <InstanceName>'.

3. Right-click on 'TCP/IP' and select 'Enable'.
4. Confirm the protocol change and restart the SQL Server service if prompted.

# Configuring TCP/IP Properties:
1. Right-click on 'TCP/IP' within the 'Protocols for <InstanceName>' node.
2. Select 'Properties'.
3. Navigate to the 'IP Addresses' tab.
4. Configure the TCP Port for desired IP Address (e.g., 1433 for default instances).
```

Execution of the above configuration will allow SQL Server to listen to connections on the specified TCP port, facilitating remote connectivity.

```
Output:
TCP/IP protocol for SQL Server instance <InstanceName> is now enabled. Configured to listen on port 1433.
```

Service Accounts Configuration: The service account configuration plays a crucial role in SQL Server security and functionality. Modify service accounts as follows:

- Open SQL Server Configuration Manager.
- Under the SQL Server Services node, right-click on the service (e.g., SQL Server (MSSQLSERVER)) and select Properties.
- Navigate to the Log On tab.
- Specify the desired account and password for the service. Options include Local System, Network Service, or a specific user account.
- After specifying the account, click OK and restart the service to enact changes.

Service account configuration must adhere to the principle of least privilege. Use dedicated accounts with minimal permissions to enhance security.

In the next segment, we examine common scenarios and troubleshooting steps:

```
# Checking Service Status:
1. Open a command prompt.
2. Execute the command:
   sc query MSSQLSERVER

# Verifying Network Configuration:
1. Execute the SQL Server Network Utility application.
2. Verify that the server is listening on the correct IP settings and ports.

# Checking SQL Server Error Logs:
1. Navigate to SQL Server Error Log location.
2. Open the current log file for detailed service start-up and connection information.
```

The provided troubleshooting commands and steps aid in verifying and rectifying common configuration-related issues.

By leveraging SQL Server Configuration Manager, administrators can fine-tune service settings, optimize network protocols, and secure SQL Server instances effectively. Proper use of this tool is pivotal for maintaining a secure and efficient SQL Server environment.

2.9 Basic Troubleshooting During Installation

During the installation of SQL Server, encountering issues is not uncommon. Effective troubleshooting requires a systematic approach to identify and resolve problems. This section details common installation issues and their resolutions to facilitate a successful setup process.

One common hurdle includes service startup failures. If a SQL Server service fails to start, it is essential to examine the error log files. These logs provide diagnostic information that can reveal configuration mismatches, port conflicts, or missing components.

```
-- Locate the SQL Server error log file, typically found in the default installation
    directory:
C:\Program Files\Microsoft SQL Server\MSSQL15.MSSQLSERVER\MSSQL\Log\
    ERRORLOG
```

SQL Server setup errors often manifest due to inadequate system resources. Verify that the server meets the minimum hardware and software requirements, as specified in the "System Requirements" section. Insufficient disk space and memory can particularly hinder the installation process. Use the Windows System Information tool to check resource availability:

```
-- Access Windows System Information
msinfo32
```

Careful inspection of the system event logs also provides insights into any hardware or OS-related issues that could impede SQL Server installation. Access these logs via the Event Viewer.

```
-- Open the Event Viewer to review system and application logs
eventvwr
```

Another frequent issue is permission-related errors. Ensure the account running the SQL Server installation has administrative privileges on the system. This account should also have necessary permissions on the directories specified for data, logs, and backups.

```
-- Check effective permissions for the user account:
CACLS "C:\Program Files\Microsoft SQL Server" /E /G [Domain\User]:F
```

Conflicts with existing SQL Server instances can also cause complications. If multiple instances are present, ensure that each instance is assigned a unique instance ID and distinct port numbers to prevent conflicts.

```
-- Verify instance names and ports:
SELECT instance_name, port
FROM sys.dm_tcp_listener_states;
```

Component compatibility is another critical area. Ensure that all SQL Server components and the operating system are compatible with each other. Check the SQL Server version's supported operating system documentation.

Antivirus software can sometimes interfere with the SQL Server installation. Temporarily disable any active antivirus or security software that might block the setup process.

```
-- Example command to temporarily disable Windows Defender:
Set-MpPreference -DisableRealtimeMonitoring \$true
```

Network settings and firewall configurations may block SQL Server connections. Ensure that necessary TCP/IP ports are open and that SQL Server Browser services are enabled to allow remote connections.

```
-- Enabling TCP/IP and setting ports:
```

```
exec sp_configure 'show advanced options', 1;
RECONFIGURE;
exec sp_configure 'remote admin connections', 1;
RECONFIGURE;
```

In scenarios where setup files are corrupted, it is advisable to re-download the SQL Server installation media. Always verify the integrity of the setup files using checksums or hash values provided on the official download page.

For SQL Server installations that fail during the setup process, checking the detailed setup logs can be highly informative. These logs are located in the system's setupbootstrap\Log directory.

```
-- Path to SQL Server setup logs:
C:\Program Files\Microsoft SQL Server\150\Setup Bootstrap\Log\Summary.txt
```

It is also effective to use the SQL Server Setup Support Rules to check for potential issues proactively. Run these rules directly from the setup media:

```
-- Command to run Setup Support Rules
Setup.exe /ACTION=INSTALL /Q="Checks only"
```

Performing installations in a clean boot environment can eliminate software conflicts. To clean boot, disable all non-essential services and startup programs:

```
-- Steps to perform a clean boot in Windows:
msconfig
-- Navigate to the Services tab and select "Hide all Microsoft services", then disable the
      remaining services.
```

By systematically addressing these potential issues, you can effectively troubleshoot and resolve common problems that might arise during the SQL Server installation process.

Chapter 3

SQL Server Management Studio (SSMS)

This chapter introduces SQL Server Management Studio (SSMS), covering its installation and interface overview. It details setting up your workspace, connecting to SQL Server instances, and navigating the Object Explorer. The chapter also explains using the Query Editor, managing databases and objects, executing queries and scripts, customizing the SSMS environment, and basic troubleshooting within SSMS.

3.1 Introduction to SQL Server Management Studio (SSMS)

SQL Server Management Studio (SSMS) is a comprehensive integrated environment designed to manage and administer SQL Server instances. It provides tools and functionalities essential for configuring, monitoring, and administering instances of SQL Server and databases. SSMS is an indispensable tool for database administrators, developers, and data professionals due to its robust feature set and user-friendly interface. This section will introduce the fundamental components and purposes of SSMS, emphasizing its relevance and applications.

Core Components of SSMS:

SSMS consists of several core components, each serving a distinct purpose:

- **Object Explorer:** This tool provides a hierarchical interface to view and manage all objects within a SQL Server instance, including databases, tables, views, stored procedures, and more.
- **Query Editor:** A powerful interface for writing, executing, and debugging Transact-SQL (T-SQL) queries. It includes features such as syntax highlighting, code completion, and error detection.
- **Properties Window:** Displays detailed properties and settings of selected objects, facilitating quick edits and configurations.
- **Solution Explorer:** Organizes database-related projects and files for easy access and management.
- **Template Explorer:** Provides a collection of pre-written scripts for common database tasks, which can be customized and reused.

Purpose and Functionality:

SSMS serves a variety of purposes vital to the management and development of SQL Server databases:

- **Database Administration:** SSMS allows administrators to create, alter, and drop databases, back up and restore databases, manage security settings, and configure server options.
- **Development:** Developers can use SSMS to write and test T-SQL queries, stored procedures, functions, and triggers. The Query Editor's debugging tools help in identifying and resolving issues within scripts.
- **Monitoring:** Monitoring features include viewing active connections, locks, and performance metrics. The Activity Monitor tool provides real-time insights into server performance and resource usage.
- **Configuration:** Administering SQL Server configurations such as setting server properties, managing linked servers, and configuring SQL Server Agent jobs.

- **Data Tools Integration:** SSMS seamlessly integrates with SQL Server Data Tools (SSDT), enabling advanced data modeling, integration, and deployment capabilities.

User Interface Overview:

The SSMS user interface is designed to be intuitive and accessible, with several key areas:

- **Menus and Toolbars:** Situated at the top of the interface, menus provide access to all SSMS functionalities, while toolbars offer quick shortcuts to frequently used commands.
- **Object Explorer:** Located on the left side by default, this pane is the primary navigation tool for browsing and managing SQL Server objects.
- **Query Editor Window:** Centered in the interface, the Query Editor is where users write and execute SQL queries.
- **Output Panel:** Positioned typically at the bottom, it displays messages, errors, and query results.

Capabilities of SSMS:

SSMS extends beyond basic administrative and development functionalities. Key capabilities include:

- **Scripting:** Generate T-SQL scripts for database objects and actions, which can be used for automation and replication of environments.
- **Data Import/Export:** Tools for importing and exporting data between SQL Server and various file formats, aiding data migration and transformation tasks.
- **Reports:** Built-in reporting features to create and run custom reports on server activity, performance, and usage.
- **Data Analysis:** Integration with SQL Server Analysis Services (SSAS) for multidimensional analysis and data mining capabilities.

SSMS is continually evolving, with updates that introduce new features, enhance existing tools, and improve overall user experience. Regular updates ensure compatibility with the latest SQL Server versions and enhance performance and reliability.

Understanding SSMS's foundational components, interface, and functionalities is essential before delving into more advanced topics. The streamlined and integrated design of SSMS makes it a powerful tool for efficiently managing and developing SQL Server databases, catering to the diverse needs of database professionals.

3.2 Installing SSMS

To begin interfacing with SQL Server, it is imperative to have the SQL Server Management Studio (SSMS) installed on your machine. SSMS serves as the primary tool for managing SQL Server instances, ranging from database creation to advanced performance tuning. The following steps detail the installation process of SSMS on a Windows operating system to ensure a proper setup.

Step 1: Downloading SSMS

First, visit the official Microsoft website to download the latest version of SSMS. Navigate to the SSMS download page using URL https://docs.microsoft.com/en-us/sql/ssms/download-sql-server-management-studio-ssms. Microsoft frequently updates SSMS, so it is essential to download the latest release to benefit from all improvements and bug fixes. Upon reaching the download page, click on the download link corresponding to the latest SSMS version.

Step 2: Running the Installer

Locate the downloaded executable file (typically named SSMS-Setup-ENU.exe) in your downloads folder. Run the installer by double-clicking the executable file. You may receive a User Account Control (UAC) prompt asking for permission to allow the application to make changes to your device. Click **Yes** to proceed.

Step 3: Installation Process

The SSMS installation wizard starts, presenting you with an initial welcome screen. Click **Install** to commence the installation. By default, SSMS will be installed in the C:Program Files (x86)Microsoft SQL Server Management Studio 18 directory, but you can change the destination folder if needed.

The installation process involves several steps, including the extraction of installation files and setting up the necessary components. The wizard automatically handles these steps and presents status updates during the installation. Depending on your system specifications and network speed, this process could take several minutes.

Step 4: Completing the Installation

Once the installation is complete, the installation wizard will display a completion screen indicating that SSMS has been successfully installed. Click **Close** to exit the installer. SSMS is now available for use. You can verify the installation by searching for "SQL Server Management Studio" in the Windows Start menu.

Step 5: Launching SSMS

Open SQL Server Management Studio by clicking its icon in the Start menu. The first time SSMS is launched, it may take a few extra moments to initialize its components and settings. Subsequently, SSMS will start more quickly.

Ensure that SSMS opens correctly and that the interface is fully operational. If you face any issues, consult the troubleshooting resources available on the official Microsoft documentation site or forums.

System Requirements and Compatibility

Before proceeding with the installation, it is crucial to ensure that your system meets the necessary requirements. The following are the minimum system requirements for installing SSMS:

- **Operating System:** Windows 8.1 (64-bit), Windows 10 (64-bit), Windows Server 2012 (64-bit), Windows Server 2016 (64-bit), or later versions.
- **Memory:** Minimum of 2 GB of RAM (4 GB or more recommended).
- **Disk Space:** At least 1.5 GB of available space.
- **.NET Framework:** .NET Framework 4.7.2 or later.
- **Processor:** 1.8 GHz or faster, dual-core or higher.

Using a system that meets or exceeds these requirements ensures optimal performance and minimizes potential issues during installation and usage.

Command Line Installation

While the graphical installation process is straightforward, SSMS can also be installed via the command line for silent or automated deployments. This is particularly useful for scripting installations across multiple machines or integrating the installation into a larger setup process. The command line for installing SSMS with default settings is:

```
SSMS-Setup-ENU.exe /Passive /NoRestart
```

The /Passive switch performs the installation without user interaction, and the /NoRestart switch prevents the installer from restarting the system automatically. It is advisable to verify and test these command-line installations in a non-production environment to ensure they meet organizational policies and deployment standards.

Having SSMS installed sets a solid foundation for managing SQL Server instances efficiently. The subsequent sections will explore how to set up your workspace, connect to SQL Server instances, and begin utilizing SSMS's numerous features for database management.

3.3 Overview of SSMS Interface

SQL Server Management Studio (SSMS) is an integrated environment for managing any SQL infrastructure, from SQL Server to Azure SQL Database. The primary components of the SSMS interface include the menu bar, toolbar, Object Explorer, properties window, Solution Explorer, Template Explorer, Query Editor, and various other tool windows. Each element within the SSMS interface is designed to maximize productivity and streamline database management and development processes.

The Menu Bar at the top of the SSMS window provides access to various commands and functions through a set of menus such as File, Edit, View, Tools, Debug, Window, and Help. These menus house numerous commands for performing tasks such as creating new database objects, connecting to database servers, configuring SSMS settings, and accessing help documentation.

Directly below the menu bar, the Toolbar offers quick access to commonly used commands, represented by icons for actions like connecting to a server, creating new queries, executing scripts, and saving files. Users can also customize the toolbar to include preferred commands for enhanced efficiency.

The Object Explorer is one of the most critical components of the SSMS interface. It displays a hierarchical view of server instances, databases, and their objects, such as tables, views, stored procedures, and functions. The Object Explorer enables easy navigation and management of database objects. Here's an example showing how to connect to a server and explore its objects:

```
-- Connect to the server
SELECT @@SERVERNAME AS 'Server Name';

-- Retrieve a list of databases on the server
SELECT name AS 'Database Name'
FROM sys.databases
WHERE state_desc = 'ONLINE';
```

The Properties Window provides detailed information about selected objects in the Object Explorer. For instance, when a database object such as a table or stored procedure is selected, the properties window displays properties and settings such as the object's name, schema, creation date, and other pertinent attributes.

The Solution Explorer assists in managing project files and scripts within SSMS. It is especially useful when working with SQL Server Data Tools (SSDT) projects, allowing users to organize, access, and deploy multiple scripts effectively.

The Template Explorer contains a collection of script templates for various database tasks, such as creating indexes or executing stored procedures. These templates provide a standardized starting point for common tasks, reducing the effort required to write scripts from scratch. An example template for creating a new table might look like:

```
-- Template for creating a new table
CREATE TABLE [schema\_name].[table\_name]
(
    column1 datatype PRIMARY KEY,
    column2 datatype,
    column3 datatype
);
```

The Query Editor is the primary workspace for writing, testing, and running T-SQL scripts and queries. It provides features such as syntax highlighting, IntelliSense, and code formatting to aid in script development. For example, the Query Editor allows users to write and execute T-SQL statements like:

```
-- Example query in Query Editor
SELECT TOP 10 *
```

```
FROM [database\_name].[schema\_name].[table\_name];
```

Results from executed queries are displayed in the Results Pane, where data can be viewed in a tabular format, SQL messages, and execution plans can be analyzed. Data from results can be easily exported to various formats such as CSV or Excel.

Additional tool windows such as Error List, Output, and Registered Servers also contribute to a comprehensive development and management environment. The Error List displays syntax errors and warnings from query execution, the Output window logs the actions performed within SSMS, and the Registered Servers window allows users to manage multiple server connections efficiently.

Customization of the SSMS interface is attainable through various options, such as docking and auto-hiding windows, or modifying font sizes and colors to suit user preferences. This flexibility ensures that SSMS can be tailored to fit individual workflows, enhancing overall user experience and productivity.

Understanding the components and functionalities of the SSMS interface provides a solid foundation for leveraging the tool effectively, facilitating efficient database management and development tasks.

3.4 Setting Up Your Workspace

Setting up your workspace in SQL Server Management Studio (SSMS) is a crucial step to ensure an efficient and effective database management experience. A well-configured workspace streamlines your interactions with SQL Server and enhances your productivity by providing quick access to essential tools and resources.

Configuring the Environment

Upon launching SSMS, the first window that surfaces is the *Connect to Server* dialog. This initial interface allows you to establish a connection to your SQL Server instance. Ensure that the correct server type, server name, and authentication method are selected. Clicking *Connect* logs you into the SQL Server instance, opening the SSMS main interface.

Docking and Floating Windows

SSMS is designed with a series of dock-able windows that can be repositioned based on user preference. Windows such as *Object Explorer*, *Properties*, and *Solution Explorer* can be docked on the sides of the main window or floated freely for multi-monitor setups. To dock a window, click and drag its title bar to the desired area; a positioning overlay will assist in docking. To float a window, select the title bar, drag it away from the main window, and release it.

```
-- Adjusting the size of the Object Explorer window
-- Accessibility improves if the window is large enough
-- to display all relevant database objects.
```

Customizing Toolbars

Toolbars in SSMS can be customized to display a variety of buttons for quick access to frequently used commands. Right-clicking on an existing toolbar opens a menu where additional toolbars can be enabled or disabled. For example, enabling the *Database Diagram Toolbar* provides direct access to tools for creating and modifying database diagrams. Press the *Customize* option to modify the toolbars further, allowing you to add or remove specific commands as necessary.

Setting Up Keyboard Shortcuts

Keyboard shortcuts significantly enhance efficiency by allowing quick execution of common tasks. Navigate to *Tools* → *Options* → *Environment* → *Keyboard* to customize shortcuts. Assign meaningful shortcuts to commands frequently used, such as opening a new query window, executing scripts, or connecting to a server. Below is an example of setting a shortcut for opening a new query window.

```
-- Navigate to Tools -> Options -> Environment -> Keyboard
-- Under Keyboard, assign 'Ctrl + N' to open a new query window
```

Tailoring the Query Editor

The Query Editor is a vital component of SSMS for writing and executing SQL code. Configure it to enhance code readability and facilitate ease of use. Under *Tools* → *Options* → *Text Editor*, settings such as font size, text color, and line numbering can be adjusted. For instance, increasing the font size and enabling line numbers can help in navigating and debugging scripts.

```
-- Navigate to Tools -> Options -> Text Editor -> All Languages
-- Set line numbers to be visible and increase font size to 12
```

Using Templates and Solution Explorer

Templates in SSMS provide pre-defined SQL scripts for creating database objects and performing common tasks. Access templates via *View → Template Explorer*. You can create custom templates by saving frequently used scripts into the Template Explorer, which is particularly useful for repetitive tasks.

The Solution Explorer organizes projects, queries, and scripts, making them easily accessible. Adding solutions and projects through *File → New → Project* allows better management and categorization of scripts. This organization is instrumental for extensive development environments where multiple scripts are utilized.

```
-- Navigate to File -> New -> Project
-- Select SQL Server -> SQL Server Project
-- Name the project and add it to a new solution
```

Configuring Execution Settings

Lastly, configure the settings related to script execution to enhance control over query results. Access *Tools → Options → Query Execution* to configure various options such as SET STATISTICS TIME/IO, which provides performance statistics post-query execution.

```
-- Navigate to Tools -> Options -> Query Execution
-- Enable SET STATISTICS TIME and IO settings
```

A meticulously configured SSMS workspace contributes significantly to seamless and efficient database management. Establishing a personalized workspace setup bridges the gap between complex query executions and user productivity, ensuring an optimized interaction with SQL Server.

3.5 Connecting to SQL Server Instances

Establishing a connection to a SQL Server instance is a fundamental procedure that is indispensable for performing any database operations within SQL Server Management Studio (SSMS). This section delineates the step-by-step process required to connect to a SQL Server instance and includes detailed configurations and options available within the connection dialog. It also addresses common connection issues and their resolutions.

Upon launching SSMS, the first interaction typically involves the Connect to Server dialog box. This dialog box prompts the user to specify the server type, server name, and authentication method. Understanding each component of this dialog box is pivotal for establishing a successful connection.

Server Type: SQL Server provides several types of servers, including:

- **Database Engine**: The core service for storing, processing, and securing data.
- **Analysis Services**: For Online Analytical Processing (OLAP) and data mining tasks.
- **Reporting Services**: For creating, managing, and delivering reports.
- **Integration Services**: For data integration and workflow applications.

For most database operations, the **Database Engine** option is selected.

Server Name: The server name specifies the instance of SQL Server to which you are connecting. This can be a local or remote SQL Server instance and must be identifiable by a valid network name. The syntax for server names can take several forms:

- **Local Server**: When SQL Server is installed on the local machine, you can use (local) or localhost.
- **Named Instances**: For named instances, use the format servername\instancename, e.g., MyServer\SQLEXPRESS.
- **Remote Server**: For remote servers, provide the full network name or IP address.

It is essential to ensure that the SQL Server instance is accessible and that the network configurations permit remote connections if applicable.

Authentication: SSMS supports two primary authentication modes:

- **Windows Authentication**: Uses the current user's Windows credentials. This is often the default for environments integrated with Active Directory.
- **SQL Server Authentication**: Requires a user-provided SQL Server username and password. This method is used when SQL Server is configured to allow traditional SQL login methods.

Select the appropriate authentication method based on the server configuration and user permissions.

Example of using Windows Authentication:

```
Server type: Database Engine
Server name: localhost
Authentication: Windows Authentication
```

Example of using SQL Server Authentication:

```
Server type: Database Engine
Server name: MyServer\SQLEXPRESS
Authentication: SQL Server Authentication
Login: sa
Password: ********
```

After filling out the required fields, clicking on the Connect button initiates the connection to the SQL Server instance.

Common Connection Issues and Resolutions:

- **Network-related or instance-specific error**: Ensure the SQL Server is running, and the instance name is correct. Verify that the SQL Server Browser service is running.
- **Login failed for user**: Confirm that the login credentials are correct and that the user has permission to connect to the database engine.
- **Server does not exist or access denied**: Check network connectivity, firewall settings, and ensure that SQL Server is configured to allow remote connections.

Using T-SQL to Connect: While SSMS GUI provides an intuitive way to connect to SQL Server instances, connections can also be established using Transact-SQL (T-SQL). This method is particularly useful for automating tasks or scripting.

Consider the following example, which utilizes the sqlcmd utility to connect to a SQL Server instance:

```
sqlcmd -S MyServer\SQLEXPRESS -U sa -P MyPassword
```

The -S flag specifies the server name, -U denotes the username, and -P indicates the password for SQL Server Authentication.

Upon successful connection, the SQL Server instance is accessible for executing various database operations, including but not limited to, querying data, managing database objects, and administering users and permissions.

Integrating this knowledge ensures a robust understanding of how to connect to SQL Server instances, forming the foundation for effectively utilizing SQL Server Management Studio in further sections.

3.6 Navigating Object Explorer

Object Explorer is a crucial feature of SQL Server Management Studio (SSMS) that provides a hierarchical view of the database objects within a server instance. It facilitates tasks such as managing databases, exploring table structures, viewing stored procedures, and more. Using Object Explorer effectively is essential for database administration and development.

The Object Explorer is typically located on the left-side pane of the SSMS interface. It is divided into several key nodes:

- Registered Servers
- Database Engine
- Analysis Services
- Reporting Services
- Integration Services
- SQL Server Agent

These nodes allow users to manage various components of SQL Server seamlessly.

Starting with Database Engine

To begin exploring the vast capabilities of Object Explorer, double-click the Database Engine node. This action will expand the node and display the server instances you are connected to. Each server instance will have a tree structure where database objects are organized systematically.

Within a server instance, there are multiple sub-nodes including:

- Databases

- Security
- Server Objects
- Replication
- Management
- SQL Server Agent

Databases Node

Expanding the Databases node reveals all the databases present within that server instance. For each database, there are several sub-level nodes:

- Tables
- Views
- Stored Procedures
- Functions
- Synonyms
- Programmability
- Service Broker
- Storage
- Security

By expanding any database, you can see its complete structure. For instance, clicking on the Tables node lists all the tables within the selected database. Right-clicking on a table provides various options, such as Select Top 1000 Rows, Edit Top 200 Rows, Script Table as, and more.

Security Node

The Security node under each database allows managing users, roles, and schemas peculiar to that database. Here, you can find essential security-related elements, including:

- Users
- Roles

- Schemas
- Asymmetric Keys
- Certificates
- Symmetric Keys
- Audits

Managing permissions and configuring security settings are vital tasks for database administrators to ensure data protection and compliance.

Server Objects Node

The Server Objects node comprises items that are common across the server instance, such as Backup Devices, Endpoints, Linked Servers, and Triggers. Each of these items serves significant roles:

- Backup Devices store backup files.
- Endpoints enable communications between SQL Server instances and other network protocols.
- Linked Servers allow execution of commands against OLE DB data sources on different servers.
- Triggers define automated responses to server-level events.

Replication and Management Nodes

The Replication node handles configuration and monitoring of replication processes, essential for data distribution across multiple databases or locations. This includes elements like Local Publications, Subscriptions, and Distributor properties.

The Management node offers tools for managing facets of the server, including:

- Maintenance Plans
- SQL Server Logs
- Policy Management
- Data Collection
- Resource Governor

Maintenance Plans guide administrators in automating routine tasks such as backups, index reorganizations, and updating statistics.

SQL Server Agent Node

The SQL Server Agent facilitates job scheduling and automation. Expanding this node reveals sub-nodes like Jobs, Alerts, Operators, and Error Logs. Right-clicking a job provides options for executing, modifying, and viewing job history.

Interacting with Object Explorer

Interacting with Object Explorer often involves context menus invoked by right-clicking any object. For instance, right-clicking the Tables subnode under a database and selecting New Table brings up the table designer interface for creating new tables. Right-clicking a specific table and choosing Design allows modifications to table schema.

Object Explorer integrates with other SSMS features like Query Editor. You can drag and drop objects from Object Explorer into Query Editor to quickly reference them in SQL queries. For example:

```
-- Suppose we drag a table named Employees into the Query Editor
SELECT * FROM dbo.Employees;
```

The above operation auto-generates the table reference, streamlining the query writing process.

Navigating and utilizing Object Explorer efficiently aids in managing SQL Server instances and databases, providing an indispensable toolkit for database administrators and developers.

3.7 Using Query Editor

The Query Editor in SQL Server Management Studio (SSMS) is a robust and versatile tool for creating and running Transact-SQL (T-SQL) scripts and queries. Its usability and powerful features make it indispensable for database administrators and developers. The Query Editor supports syntax highlighting, IntelliSense, code snippets, and provides various utilities to enhance your productivity when writing and debugging SQL code.

Running a query begins with launching the Query Editor. This is achieved by selecting the *New Query* button from the toolbar or navigating through *File → New → Query with Current Connection*.

```
-- This query selects all records from the Products table
SELECT * FROM Products;
```

Syntax Highlighting and IntelliSense:

The Query Editor includes syntax highlighting to improve readability, enabling quick identification of different elements such as keywords, functions, and identifiers. IntelliSense assists by providing code suggestions and automatic completions as you type, reducing syntactical errors and speeding up script writing.

```
-- Start typing the SELECT statement and IntelliSense provides suggestions
SELECT ProductName, UnitPrice FROM Products WHERE ProductID = 1;
```

Code Snippets:

Code snippets are reusable blocks of T-SQL code that can be quickly inserted into your script through the Query Editor. Common snippets include table creation, stored procedure templates, and view definitions. To insert a snippet, use the *Ctrl + K, Ctrl + X* shortcut, or right-click within the editor and select *Insert Snippet* from the context menu.

```
-- Code snippet for creating a new table
CREATE TABLE NewTable (
    ID INT PRIMARY KEY,
    Column1 NVARCHAR(50),
    Column2 NVARCHAR(50)
);
```

Executing Queries:

To execute a query, click the *Execute* button or press *F5*. The results are displayed in the *Results* pane, which can show data in grid format or as text. You can also capture execution messages related to the T-SQL script in the *Messages* pane.

```
-- Query to select specific columns from the Categories table
SELECT CategoryID, CategoryName FROM Categories;
```

```
Results:
+------------+-----------------+
| CategoryID | CategoryName    |
+------------+-----------------+
| 1          | Beverages       |
| 2          | Condiments      |
+------------+-----------------+
```

Query Execution Plan:

The Query Editor allows you to view the execution plan of your queries, providing insight into how SQL Server processes them. This is essential in optimizing query performance. To display the estimated execution plan, click on *Display Estimated Execution Plan* or press *Ctrl + L*.

```
-- Example of a query to analyze its execution plan
SELECT OrderID, ProductID, Quantity
FROM [Order Details]
WHERE Quantity > 5;
```

```
Execution Plan:
-- The graphical execution plan displays the sequence of operations SQL Server uses
```

Query Templates:

SSMS provides built-in query templates that contain boilerplate code structures for common tasks such as creating databases, tables, and stored procedures. These templates can be accessed via *File → New → Template Explorer*.

```
-- Example of a stored procedure template
CREATE PROCEDURE uspGetEmployee
    @EmployeeID INT
AS
BEGIN
    SELECT FirstName, LastName, Title
    FROM Employees
    WHERE EmployeeID = @EmployeeID;
END;
```

Debugging Support:

The Query Editor also includes debugging support. You can set breakpoints, step through T-SQL code, and inspect variables. This aids in identifying and resolving logic errors in complex scripts. To start debugging, use *Debug → Start Debugging* or press *Alt + F5*.

```
-- Example script to debug
DECLARE @Counter INT = 1;
WHILE @Counter <= 10
BEGIN
    PRINT 'Counter Value: ' + CAST(@Counter AS NVARCHAR(10));
    SET @Counter = @Counter + 1;
END;
```

```
Debugging Output:
Counter Value: 1
Counter Value: 2
Counter Value: 3
...
Counter Value: 10
```

Utilizing the robust features of the Query Editor in SSMS optimizes the scripting and query execution processes, substantially enhancing efficiency and productivity in managing SQL Server databases.

3.8 Managing Databases and Objects

Managing databases and objects within SQL Server Management Studio (SSMS) is a fundamental skill for database administrators and developers. This section explores various tasks associated with database management, including creating, modifying, and deleting databases, as well as managing database objects such as tables, views, stored procedures, and triggers.

Creating a Database

To create a new database in SSMS, open the Object Explorer. Right-click the Databases node, and select New Database... from the context menu. This action opens the New Database dialog box, where several attributes of the database can be specified:

- Database Name: Specifies the name of the new database.
- Owner: Optionally, specify the owner of the database.
- Files: Define the logical and physical names, file sizes, and growth parameters for the Primary data file and Log file.
- Options: Here, set database options such as recovery model, compatibility level, and collation.
- Filegroups: Create secondary filegroups if needed for better database management.

After setting the desired attributes, click OK to create the database. The new database appears in the Object Explorer under the Databases node.

Modifying a Database

Modifying an existing database involves altering its properties or schema. In the Object Explorer, right-click the database you wish to modify and select Properties. This opens the Database Properties dialog box. Here you can make changes to:

- General: Change the database owner or modify file properties.
- Options: Adjust database options like auto-growth, recovery model, or compatibility level.

- Files: Modify file sizes, add or remove database files, and adjust file growth parameters.
- Filegroups: Reconfigure filegroups or add new ones.
- Permissions: Modify database-level security by adding/removing users or roles and adjusting permissions.

Make the necessary changes and click OK to apply them.

Deleting a Database

To delete a database, right-click the target database in the Object Explorer and select Delete. Confirm the action in the Delete Object dialog box. Ensure that you check the Close existing connections option if there are active connections to the database to avoid errors during the deletion process. Click OK to delete the database.

Managing Tables

Tables are fundamental database objects that store data in rows and columns. To create a new table, expand the Databases node in Object Explorer, navigate to the desired database, right-click Tables, and select New Table.

```
CREATE TABLE Employee (
    EmployeeID INT PRIMARY KEY,
    FirstName NVARCHAR(50),
    LastName NVARCHAR(50),
    BirthDate DATE,
    JobTitle NVARCHAR(50)
);
```

The Table Designer allows defining columns and specifying data types, constraints, and indexes. After setting up the table, save it by choosing Save from the File menu or by right-clicking and selecting Save Table.

To modify an existing table, right-click the table under the Tables node and select Design. This opens the Table Designer where columns, data types, constraints, and indexes can be added, modified, or removed.

Deleting a table is straightforward; right-click the table and select Delete, then confirm the action.

Managing Views

Views are virtual tables that represent the result set of a stored query. To create a new view, expand the Views node under the desired database, right-click it, and choose New View.... Use the Query Designer to build the view.

```
CREATE VIEW EmployeeDetails AS
SELECT
    EmployeeID,
    FirstName,
    LastName,
    JobTitle
FROM Employee
WHERE JobTitle = 'Manager';
```

Save the view by selecting Save from the File menu. To modify an existing view, right-click the view and choose Design. To delete a view, right-click it and select Delete, then confirm.

Managing Stored Procedures Stored procedures are compiled SQL statements that can include logic and control-of-flow constructs. Create a new stored procedure by expanding the Programmability node, then Stored Procedures, and right-click New Stored Procedure.

```
CREATE PROCEDURE GetEmployeeByID
    @EmployeeID INT
AS
BEGIN
    SELECT
        EmployeeID,
        FirstName,
        LastName,
        BirthDate,
        JobTitle
    FROM Employee
    WHERE EmployeeID = @EmployeeID;
END;
```

To modify a stored procedure, right-click the procedure and select Modify. Make the necessary changes and execute the script to update it. To delete a procedure, right-click and choose Delete, then confirm.

Managing Triggers

Triggers are special types of stored procedures that automatically execute when specified database events occur. To create a trigger, use the following SQL template within a new query window:

```
CREATE TRIGGER trgAfterInsertEmployee
ON Employee
FOR INSERT
AS
BEGIN
    INSERT INTO AuditLog (LogText)
    SELECT 'New employee inserted with ID: ' + CAST(EmployeeID AS NVARCHAR)

    FROM Inserted;
END;
```

To view or modify a trigger, expand the Tables node, find the table, expand it to see Triggers, right-click the trigger, and select Modify. Deleting a trigger can be done similarly by right-clicking it and choosing Delete, then confirming the action.

Correct management of databases and objects in SSMS ensures optimal performance and data integrity, supporting the essential functions of modern databases.

3.9 Executing Queries and Scripts

When working with SQL Server Management Studio (SSMS), one of the essential tasks is executing queries and scripts. Understanding how to run these and interpret their results is fundamental for database management, analysis, and development.

Executing queries involves writing and running SQL statements that perform tasks such as data retrieval, insertion, updating, and deletion. Scripts extend this concept by allowing multiple SQL statements to be executed sequentially or conditionally. In this section, we will delve into the mechanics of running these commands within SSMS.

Writing and Executing Queries

To write and execute a query:

- Open SSMS and connect to the appropriate SQL Server instance.
- Open a new Query Editor window by clicking on the New Query button on the toolbar.
- Ensure the correct database context is selected by choosing the database from the dropdown list in the Query Editor toolbar.
- Type your SQL query in the Query Editor window. An example query for retrieving data from a table named Employees might look like this:

```
SELECT * FROM Employees;
```

- Execute the query by clicking the Execute button or pressing F5.

Upon execution, the results are displayed in the Results pane beneath the Query Editor. The Messages tab will show any informational messages, errors, or warnings returned during query execution, alongside the time taken and the number of rows affected.

Working with Scripts

Scripts in SSMS are text files containing sequences of SQL statements. These are often used to perform bulk operations, such as setting up databases or batch processing data. To execute a script:

- Open a new Query Editor window.
- Write or paste the SQL script into the editor. For example:

```
USE AdventureWorks;
GO

-- Update employee records
UPDATE Employees
SET Title = 'Senior Engineer'
WHERE EmployeeID = 10;
GO

-- Insert a new employee
INSERT INTO Employees (FirstName, LastName, Title)
VALUES ('Jane', 'Doe', 'Junior Engineer');
GO

-- Retrieve updated records
SELECT * FROM Employees;
GO
```

- Execute the script by pressing F5 or clicking the Execute button.

In this script, the USE statement changes the database context to AdventureWorks. The GO statements act as batch separators allowing SSMS to process the script as a series of independent statements.

Parameterization and Variables in Scripts

Scripts frequently use variables and parameters to make them more flexible and reusable. In Transact-SQL (T-SQL), variables are declared using the DECLARE statement, assigned values with SET, and employed in expressions or statements. For example:

```
DECLARE @EmployeeID INT;
SET @EmployeeID = 10;

SELECT * FROM Employees
WHERE EmployeeID = @EmployeeID;
```

Executing the above script will retrieve information for the employee with ID 10. Using variables helps avoid hardcoding values and improves script maintainability.

Error Handling in Scripts

Robust scripts should incorporate error handling to ensure smooth execution. T-SQL provides TRY...CATCH constructs for this purpose:

```
BEGIN TRY
    -- Try to divide by zero to cause an error
    SELECT 1 / 0;
END TRY
BEGIN CATCH
    -- Handle the error
    SELECT ERROR_MESSAGE() AS ErrorMessage;
END CATCH;
```

In the above script, the error caused by dividing by zero is caught in the CATCH block, and the error message is retrieved and displayed.

Viewing Execution Plans

Understanding how SQL Server executes queries can optimize performance. SQL Server provides execution plans that graphically display the data retrieval methods chosen by the SQL Server query optimizer. To view an execution plan:

- Type a query in the Query Editor window.
- Click the Display Estimated Execution Plan button or press Ctrl + L. This shows a graphical representation without executing the query.
- Click Include Actual Execution Plan or press Ctrl + M and then execute the query. This displays an execution plan for the executed query.

Execution plans can highlight areas of inefficiency, such as missing indexes or costly operations, enabling you to adjust your queries for optimal performance.

Utilizing Tab Completion and IntelliSense

SSMS provides features like tab completion and IntelliSense to enhance scripting efficiency:

- **Tab Completion**: Start typing the name of a database object (e.g., table, column), then press Tab to auto-complete the name.

- **IntelliSense**: As you type, a list of suggestions appears, including tables, views, columns, and functions, which can be selected to auto-complete your text.

These features aid in reducing syntax errors and speeding up script writing.

Through SSMS, effectively executing queries and scripts involves understanding minor nuances and features. This empowers users to manage and manipulate databases with precision, automate repetitive tasks, and implement sophisticated data operations seamlessly.

3.10 Customizing SSMS Environment

SQL Server Management Studio (SSMS) offers a robust set of customization options to tailor the user interface and functionality to better suit individual user preferences and workflows. These customizations can enhance productivity and streamline tasks by providing a user experience that aligns better with specific needs and habits. This section delves into various aspects of customizing the SSMS environment.

Customizing the Layout

SSMS allows users to customize the layout of tool windows to create a more efficient workspace. Users can dock, float, hide, and pin windows such as the Object Explorer, Solution Explorer, and Properties window.

To dock a window, click and hold its title bar, then drag it to any edge of the SSMS interface until a docking guide appears. Release the mouse button to dock the window at the desired location. To float a window so that it remains independent of the main SSMS window, drag it to a position where no docking guide appears and release. Floating windows can be relocated to secondary monitors for an expanded workspace.

Modifying Fonts and Colors

SSMS enables users to change the fonts and colors of various text elements within the interface. To modify these settings, navigate to **Tools** → **Options** → **Environment** → **Fonts and Colors**.

Users can select from a variety of pre-defined color schemes or create custom schemes to improve readability and reduce eye strain. The settings under **Show settings for:** allow users to customize the appearance of text in different parts of SSMS, such as the text editor, results grid, and IntelliSense.

```
-- Example of changing font size for readability
SELECT FirstName, LastName
FROM Employees
WHERE Department = 'Sales';
```

Configuring Keyboard Shortcuts

SSMS supports custom keyboard shortcuts to enhance navigation and functionality. To customize keyboard shortcuts, go to **Tools** → **Options** → **Environment** → **Keyboard**. Here, users can view all existing keyboard shortcuts and assign new ones.

Assign keyboard shortcuts to frequently used commands to enhance efficiency. For instance, setting a shortcut for running a query or opening a new query window can save time.

Creating Custom Menus and Toolbars

SSMS allows users to create custom menus and toolbars to group frequently used commands together for easier access. To customize menus and toolbars, go to **Tools** → **Customize**. Users can add or remove commands, create new toolbars, and rearrange the order of existing commands.

Using Macros

Macros in SSMS can automate repetitive tasks, saving significant time and effort. Users can record sequences of actions and replay them as needed. To record a macro, navigate to **Tools** → **Macros** → **Record TemporaryMacro**. After recording the desired actions, users can save and assign macros to keyboard shortcuts for quick access.

```
-- Example of a simple macro for inserting a comment header
/* ------ New Query ------ */
-- Developer: [Your Name]
-- Date: [Current Date]
-- Description: [Short Description]
```

Setting Environment Options

SSMS offers various environment options to customize the behavior and appearance of the tool. Access these settings by navigating to **Tools** → **Options**. Explore different categories such as **Startup**, **Projects and Solutions**, **Text Editor**, and **SQL Server Object Explorer** to configure options that match your workflow.

Users can adjust settings such as query execution results display (text, grid, or file), default encoding for script files, error and warning levels, among others. Fine-tuning these options can result in an SSMS environment that significantly enhances user productivity.

Customizing Templates

SSMS provides a set of predefined templates for common SQL operations, available under the **View** → **Template Explorer**. Users can edit these templates or create new ones to standardize and speed up the development process.

To create or modify templates, simply right-click within Template Explorer and select the appropriate option. Organize templates into folders for easy access. Templates can include placeholders for dynamic content, which SSMS will prompt users to replace upon insertion.

```
-- Template for creating a new stored procedure
CREATE PROCEDURE [dbo].[ProcedureName]
AS
BEGIN
    -- Insert logic here
END;
```

Customizing IntelliSense

IntelliSense can significantly enhance code writing efficiency by providing code completion, parameter information, and quick information on database objects. Customize IntelliSense settings by navigating to **Tools** → **Options** → **Text Editor** → **Transact-SQL** → **IntelliSense**.

Options include enabling or disabling IntelliSense, auto list members, parameter information, and highlighting related keywords. Users can also configure suggestions delay and manage code snippets to further personalize IntelliSense behavior.

Customizing these facets of SSMS helps create an environment that supports and accelerates daily SQL Server administration and development activities.

3.11 Basic Troubleshooting in SSMS

When working with SQL Server Management Studio (SSMS), encountering issues is inevitable. This section outlines fundamental troubleshooting techniques to diagnose and resolve common problems within SSMS. These methods can help maintain seamless operations of your SQL Server environment, ensuring efficient database management.

1. Connection Issues:

One of the most common problems users face is failing to connect to a SQL Server instance. To address this, ensure that the SQL Server service is running. Use the Services application on Windows to verify the status of SQL Server (MSSQLSERVER) and SQL Server Agent (SQLSERVERAGENT). If these services are stopped, start them.

Check the server name and instance name. Ensure it matches the format *server\instance*. For local servers, try using *(local)* or *.* as the server name. Also, confirm that the SQL Server browser service is running, which is necessary for named instance connections.

Verify network issues by pinging the server:

```
ping servername
```

2. Login Issues:

Another frequent issue is authentication failures. If you're using SQL Server Authentication, ensure the login credentials are correct. For Windows Authentication, ensure your Windows account has the necessary permissions. If login issues persist, check the server's error log for detailed messages.

To access the error log through SSMS:

- Expand the Management node in Object Explorer.
- Expand SQL Server Logs.
- Double-click the Current log to open it.

3. Query Performance:

When experiencing slow query performance, first analyze the execution plan. Right-click on the query and select Display Estimated Execution Plan. This plan graphically displays how SQL Server executes the query, highlighting potential bottlenecks.

To improve performance, consider adding indexes, optimizing query syntax, and updating statistics. For example, to create an index:

```
CREATE INDEX idx_column_name
ON table_name (column_name);
```

To update statistics:

```
UPDATE STATISTICS table_name;
```

4. Deadlocks:

Deadlocks can occur when two or more tasks permanently block each other. To detect and troubleshoot deadlocks, enable trace flags to capture deadlock information. Use the following SQL command:

```
DBCC TRACEON (1204, 1222, -1);
```

This command enables deadlock tracing, providing valuable information in the error log.

5. Transaction Log Issues:

A common issue faced by DBAs is a full transaction log. Regularly backing up the transaction log can prevent this. To manually back up:

```
BACKUP LOG database_name
TO DISK = 'path_to_backup_file';
```

Additionally, monitor the log file size using:

```
DBCC SQLPERF(LOGSPACE);
```

This command provides an overview of the space used by transaction logs.

6. Missing Data or Objects:

If data or objects are missing, ensure you are connected to the correct database and instance. Verify the user's permissions and review recent transactions. Restore from a backup if necessary.

To restore a database:

```
RESTORE DATABASE database_name
FROM DISK = 'path_to_backup_file';
```

7. Configuration Issues:

Misconfigurations can cause various issues. Use the SQL Server Configuration Manager to inspect and adjust settings. Common properties to check include memory allocation, max degree of parallelism, and network protocols.

8. SQL Server Agent Jobs:

To troubleshoot SQL Server Agent jobs that fail to execute, review the job history for error messages. Check the SQL Server Agent logs found in:

- SQL Server Agent → Error Logs

Additionally, verify that the jobs have appropriate permissions and resources.

System Health Monitoring:

Regularly monitor system health using Dynamic Management Views (DMVs) to identify potential issues. For instance:

```
SELECT *
FROM sys.dm_os_performance_counters;
```

This DMV provides performance counter information directly from the SQL Server instance.

Effective troubleshooting in SSMS requires a combination of technical know-how and systematic diagnostics. By understanding and implementing these fundamental techniques, you can resolve common issues and maintain robust SQL Server operations efficiently.

Chapter 4

Basic SQL Queries

This chapter covers fundamental SQL and T-SQL concepts, starting with database schema and table basics. It provides instructions for writing simple SELECT statements, filtering data with the WHERE clause, and sorting results using ORDER BY. The chapter also discusses aggregate functions, grouping data with GROUP BY, joining tables with JOIN, using subqueries, handling NULL values, and modifying data with INSERT, UPDATE, and DELETE operations.

4.1 Introduction to SQL and T-SQL

Structured Query Language (SQL) is a standardized language used to interact with relational database management systems (RDBMS). Its primary function is to enable the retrieval, manipulation, and management of data stored within relational databases. SQL has become the cornerstone of modern database interactions due to its declarative nature, straightforward syntax, and powerful capabilities.

Transact-SQL (T-SQL) is an extension of SQL that is specific to Microsoft SQL Server. It incorporates additional features that enable more complex operations and procedural programming capabilities. Understanding both SQL and T-SQL is crucial for efficiently managing and querying databases hosted on SQL Server.

SQL consists of several types of statements, each serving a different purpose. These statements fall into different categories, typically defined as Data Query Language (DQL), Data Manipulation Language (DML), Data Definition Language (DDL), and Data Control Language (DCL).

- Data Query Language (DQL): Primarily involves SELECT statements, used for querying the database to retrieve data.
- Data Manipulation Language (DML): Includes INSERT, UPDATE, DELETE, and MERGE statements, which are used to modify data within the database.
- Data Definition Language (DDL): Comprises CREATE, ALTER, DROP, and TRUNCATE statements, which are used to define and modify database schema objects such as tables, indexes, and views.
- Data Control Language (DCL): Encompasses GRANT, REVOKE, and DENY statements, which manage permissions and access control for database users.

SQL standard syntax consists of a set of well-defined commands and clauses. A basic understanding of the following elements is essential before diving into actual queries:

- Keywords: Reserved words that have special meaning in SQL, such as SELECT, INSERT, UPDATE, DELETE, WHERE, FROM, JOIN, etc.
- Identifiers: Names given to various database objects such as tables, columns, and indexes.
- Literals: Constants or fixed data values that are used directly in SQL statements, such as numbers, strings, and dates.
- Operators: Symbols that specify an operation to be performed, such as arithmetic operators (+, -, *, /) and comparison operators (=, <>, >, <).

Consider the following SQL statement:

```
SELECT first_name, last_name, email
FROM employees
WHERE department_id = 10;
```

In this example:

- SELECT: A keyword used to specify the columns to retrieve.
- first_name, last_name, email: Identifiers representing the columns to be included in the result.
- FROM: A keyword that specifies the table from which to retrieve the data.
- employees: An identifier referring to the table storing employee data.
- WHERE: A keyword used to filter the rows based on a specified condition.
- department_id = 10: A condition that filters results to include only employees in department 10.

T-SQL extends the capabilities of standard SQL with additional procedural programming constructs, such as variables, control-of-flow language (like IF...ELSE, WHILE loops), and error handling (using TRY...CATCH). These features elevate T-SQL beyond simple data retrieval and manipulation, allowing for more sophisticated logical operations and administrative tasks.

An example of a T-SQL script demonstrating variable usage and control-of-flow:

```
DECLARE @EmployeeID INT;
SET @EmployeeID = 101;

IF @EmployeeID IS NOT NULL
BEGIN
    SELECT first_name, last_name, email
    FROM employees
    WHERE employee_id = @EmployeeID;
END
ELSE
BEGIN
    PRINT 'Employee ID is NULL';
END
```

In this T-SQL script:

- DECLARE @EmployeeID INT; Declares a variable named @EmployeeID with an integer data type.
- SET @EmployeeID = 101; Assigns the value 101 to the variable @EmployeeID.

- IF @EmployeeID IS NOT NULL: A control-of-flow statement that checks if @EmployeeID is not NULL.
- BEGIN...END: Keywords that group a series of statements to be executed together if the IF condition is true.
- SELECT...: Retrieves employee details if the condition is met.
- ELSE: Designates the block of code to execute if the IF condition is not met.
- PRINT...: Outputs a message if @EmployeeID is NULL.

A thorough comprehension of SQL and T-SQL serves as the backbone for database management and operational efficiency in SQL Server environments. Mastery of these languages ensures optimized data retrieval, robust data manipulation, and secure database administration.

4.2 Database Schema and Table Basics

A database schema is a blueprint of the database structure that defines the organization of data as a blueprint or framework. It encompasses the definitions of tables, views, indexes, and the relationships between these entities. Schemas provide a high-level overview of the database, serving as a guide for database design and maintenance. It's essential to understand schema concepts to efficiently manage and interact with databases.

Tables are the fundamental units in a database schema. They are composed of rows and columns where each column has a defined data type. The table structure enforces data integrity and allows for efficient querying and data management. To illustrate, consider the following SQL command to create a table:

```
CREATE TABLE Employees (
    EmployeeID INT PRIMARY KEY,
    FirstName VARCHAR(50),
    LastName VARCHAR(50),
    BirthDate DATE,
    HireDate DATE,
    Email VARCHAR(100)
);
```

This command creates a table named Employees with six columns: EmployeeID, FirstName, LastName, BirthDate, HireDate, and Email. The

EmployeeID column is designated as the primary key, ensuring each row in the table can be uniquely identified.

In databases, each column within a table must adhere to a defined **Data Type**. Data types specify the kind of data that can be stored in each column, ensuring consistency and preventing invalid data entries. Some commonly used data types include:

- INT for integer values.
- VARCHAR(n) for variable-length string data.
- DATE for dates.
- DECIMAL(p, s) for fixed-point numerical values.
- BIT for boolean values.

To optimize query performance and enforce data integrity, **Constraints** are utilized within tables. Constraints define rules that the data in the table must adhere to. Examples of constraints include:

- PRIMARY KEY - ensures that a column or a set of columns uniquely identifies each row.
- FOREIGN KEY - enforces a link between columns in two tables, maintaining referential integrity.
- UNIQUE - ensures all values in a column are unique across the table.
- CHECK - enforces a condition that each row in the table must satisfy.
- NOT NULL - ensures that a column cannot have NULL values.

Here is an example demonstrating a table with multiple constraints:

```
CREATE TABLE Orders (
    OrderID INT PRIMARY KEY,
    OrderDate DATE NOT NULL,
    CustomerID INT,
    TotalAmount DECIMAL(10, 2) CHECK (TotalAmount > 0),
    CONSTRAINT FK_Customer FOREIGN KEY (CustomerID) REFERENCES
        Customers(CustomerID)
);
```

In this Orders table, OrderID is the primary key, OrderDate cannot be null, TotalAmount must be greater than zero, and CustomerID is a foreign key referencing the CustomerID in the Customers table.

Tables can be **Normalized** to minimize redundancy and dependency by organizing fields and table relations. Normalization involves splitting a large table into smaller tables and defining relationships to ensure that each piece of data is stored only once. The normal forms, from first (1NF) to fifth (5NF), serve as a guideline for the normalization process.

Indexes are used to speed up the retrieval of rows by utilizing a pointer mechanism. Indexes improve the efficiency of queries by reducing the amount of data pages that need to be scanned. They can be created on one or more columns of a table, and typical index types include:

- Clustered Index - sorts and stores the data rows of the table based on the index key.
- Non-Clustered Index - contains a pointer to the data rows instead of sorting and storing the data.

Here is an example of creating an index on the Email column of the Employees table:

```
CREATE INDEX IDX_Email ON Employees (Email);
```

Understanding database schemas and table basics, including data types, constraints, normalization, and indexes, forms the foundation for efficient database design and querying. This knowledge is essential for creating robust, scalable, and high-performance databases.

4.3 Writing Simple SELECT Statements

The SELECT statement is fundamental to SQL (Structured Query Language) as it allows data retrieval from one or multiple tables. The basic syntax for a SELECT statement is straightforward and forms the foundation for more complex queries.

```
SELECT column1, column2, ...
FROM table\_name;
```

Here, column1, column2, etc., represent the column names from which you want to fetch data. The FROM clause specifies the table containing these columns. Consider an example with a table named Employees. The table schema is as follows:

| EmployeeID | FirstName | LastName | Department | Salary |

To select all columns from the Employees table, the query would be:

```
SELECT *
FROM Employees;
```

The * symbol is a wildcard character that represents all columns. This query retrieves all rows from the Employees table and all columns for each row. The output might look something like this:

EmployeeID	FirstName	LastName	Department	Salary
1	John	Doe	Sales	60000
2	Jane	Smith	HR	50000
3	Michael	Brown	IT	75000

Sometimes, it is necessary to retrieve specific columns rather than all columns in the table. This can be accomplished by explicitly listing the desired columns:

```
SELECT FirstName, LastName
FROM Employees;
```

The result of this query will display only the FirstName and LastName columns:

FirstName	LastName
John	Doe
Jane	Smith
Michael	Brown

For more sophisticated queries, it is common to rename columns using aliasing for clarity, especially when calculations or joins are involved. Aliasing is achieved using the AS keyword:

```
SELECT FirstName AS "First Name", LastName AS "Last Name"
FROM Employees;
```

The output will include the new column headers "First Name" and "Last Name":

First Name	Last Name
John	Doe
Jane	Smith
Michael	Brown

To illustrate, let us consider using expressions or functions within the SELECT statement. Suppose we want to calculate the annual salary of each employee from their monthly salary, assuming the Salary column stores monthly values:

```
SELECT FirstName, LastName, Salary * 12 AS "Annual Salary"
FROM Employees;
```

Resultantly, the output table will display the calculated "Annual Salary" for each employee:

```
| FirstName | LastName | Annual Salary |
|-----------|----------|---------------|
| John      | Doe      | 720000        |
| Jane      | Smith    | 600000        |
| Michael   | Brown    | 900000        |
```

A fundamental feature of SQL is the ability to eliminate duplicate records. Suppose our Employees table contains multiple entries for the same department, and we want to list unique departments. We employ the DISTINCT keyword:

```
SELECT DISTINCT Department
FROM Employees;
```

This query ensures that only unique departments are displayed. The resulting output could be:

```
| Department |
|------------|
| Sales      |
| HR         |
| IT         |
```

Effective use of the SELECT statement is essential for data querying, providing the basis for interacting with and extracting meaningful information from databases. Each element, from selecting specific columns to aliasing and using the DISTINCT keyword, adds clarity and specificity to the data retrieval process, ultimately facilitating more advanced SQL operations and analyses.

4.4 Filtering Data with WHERE Clause

Filtering data in SQL is a fundamental aspect of querying databases. The WHERE clause is instrumental in this process, enabling the retrieval of specific subsets of data based on specified conditions. The WHERE clause can be applied to SELECT, UPDATE, DELETE, and INSERT INTO statements. In this section, we will consider the use of the WHERE clause in the context of SELECT queries, elucidating its syntax, usage, and various applications.

The basic structure of a SELECT statement with the WHERE clause is as follows:

```
SELECT column1, column2, ...
FROM table_name
WHERE condition;
```

The condition in the WHERE clause is an expression that returns a Boolean value (TRUE or FALSE). Only rows for which the condition evaluates to TRUE are included in the result set.

Consider a table named Employees with the following structure:

EmployeeID	Name	Department	Salary
1	John Doe	HR	50000
2	Jane Smith	IT	60000
3	Robert Brown	Finance	55000
4	Emma Wilson	IT	70000
5	Olivia Johnson	HR	45000

To filter employees in the IT department, the SQL query using the WHERE clause would be:

```
SELECT EmployeeID, Name, Salary
FROM Employees
WHERE Department = 'IT';
```

The output from executing this query would be:

```
EmployeeID | Name        | Salary
-----------|-------------|-------
2          | Jane Smith  | 60000
4          | Emma Wilson| 70000
```

The condition Department = 'IT' ensures that only rows with the department set as 'IT' are returned.

WHERE clauses support various operators for constructing conditions. These include comparison operators, logical operators, and other operators such as BETWEEN, IN, and LIKE.

Comparison Operators

Comparison operators compare expressions for equality or inequality:

- = equal to
- <> or != not equal to
- > greater than
- < less than
- >= greater than or equal to
- <= less than or equal to

For instance, to find employees with a salary greater than 55000:

```
SELECT EmployeeID, Name, Department
FROM Employees
WHERE Salary > 55000;
```

This would yield:

```
EmployeeID | Name        | Department
-----------|------------|-----------
2          | Jane Smith | IT
4          | Emma Wilson| IT
```

Logical Operators

Logical operators, such as AND, OR, and NOT, allow combining multiple conditions.

To find employees who are in the IT department and have a salary greater than 55000:

```
SELECT EmployeeID, Name
FROM Employees
WHERE Department = 'IT' AND Salary > 55000;
```

The result is:

```
EmployeeID | Name
-----------|------------
2          | Jane Smith
4          | Emma Wilson
```

Conversely, to find employees who are either in the HR department or have a salary less than 50000:

```
SELECT EmployeeID, Name, Department
FROM Employees
WHERE Department = 'HR' OR Salary < 50000;
```

This returns:

```
EmployeeID | Name           | Department
-----------|---------------|------------
1          | John Doe       | HR
5          | Olivia Johnson| HR
```

To negate a condition, the NOT operator can be used. For example, to find employees not in the IT department:

```
SELECT EmployeeID, Name, Department
FROM Employees
WHERE NOT Department = 'IT';
```

The result will be:

```
EmployeeID | Name          | Department
-----------|---------------|------------
1          | John Doe      | HR
3          | Robert Brown  | Finance
5          | Olivia Johnson| HR
```

Other Operators

The BETWEEN operator is useful for specifying a range to filter records. To find employees with a salary between 45000 and 60000:

```
SELECT EmployeeID, Name, Salary
FROM Employees
WHERE Salary BETWEEN 45000 AND 60000;
```

The results will include:

```
EmployeeID | Name         | Salary
-----------|--------------|-------
1          | John Doe     | 50000
2          | Jane Smith   | 60000
3          | Robert Brown| 55000
5          | Olivia Johnson | 45000
```

The IN operator checks for values within a specified set. To find employees who belong to the HR or Finance departments:

```
SELECT EmployeeID, Name
FROM Employees
WHERE Department IN ('HR', 'Finance');
```

This will yield:

```
EmployeeID | Name
-----------|--------
1          | John Doe
3          | Robert Brown
5          | Olivia Johnson
```

The LIKE operator is employed for pattern matching with wildcard characters. The percent sign (%) represents zero or more characters, and the underscore (_) represents a single character. To find employees whose names start with 'J':

```
SELECT EmployeeID, Name
FROM Employees
WHERE Name LIKE 'J%';
```

The output will be:

```
EmployeeID | Name
-----------|--------
1          | John Doe
2          | Jane Smith
```

Combining these operators can refine data filtering, catering to complex query requirements. Understanding and effectively applying the

WHERE clause enhances the precision of data retrieval, serving as a crucial skill in advancing SQL proficiency.

4.5 Sorting Results with ORDER BY

The ORDER BY clause in SQL is utilized to arrange the output records of a query in a specific sequence. This clause is pivotal for users who require a sorted dataset, whether in ascending or descending order, tailored to the unique demands of their analysis or reporting tasks.

The syntax for sorting the results using the ORDER BY clause is straightforward. It adheres to the following structure:

```
SELECT column1, column2, ...
FROM table\_name
ORDER BY column1 [ASC|DESC], column2 [ASC|DESC], ...;
```

The ORDER BY clause comes at the end of the SELECT statement. By default, the sorting order is ascending, but it can be explicitly set to descending using the DESC keyword. Multiple columns can be specified for sorting, introducing a primary and secondary sorting order.

For example, consider the following table, Employees:

```
+----+-----------+--------+-----------+
| ID | Name      | Salary | Department|
+----+-----------+--------+-----------+
|  1 | Alice     | 70000  | HR        |
|  2 | Bob       | 50000  | Marketing |
|  3 | Charlie   | 60000  | IT        |
|  4 | David     | 55000  | Marketing |
|  5 | Eve       | 90000  | IT        |
|  6 | Frank     | 45000  | HR        |
+----+-----------+--------+-----------+
```

To retrieve a list of employees sorted by their salary in ascending order, the SQL query would be:

```
SELECT ID, Name, Salary, Department
FROM Employees
ORDER BY Salary ASC;
```

The output will be:

```
+----+--------+--------+-----------+
| ID | Name   | Salary | Department|
+----+--------+--------+-----------+
|  6 | Frank  | 45000  | HR        |
|  2 | Bob    | 50000  | Marketing |
|  4 | David  | 55000  | Marketing |
|  3 | Charlie| 60000  | IT        |
|  1 | Alice  | 70000  | HR        |
|  5 | Eve    | 90000  | IT        |
+----+--------+--------+-----------+
```

For descending order, modify the query as follows:

```
SELECT ID, Name, Salary, Department
FROM Employees
ORDER BY Salary DESC;
```

The output changes accordingly:

```
+----+--------+--------+-----------+
| ID | Name   | Salary | Department|
+----+--------+--------+-----------+
|  5 | Eve    | 90000  | IT        |
|  1 | Alice  | 70000  | HR        |
|  3 | Charlie| 60000  | IT        |
|  4 | David  | 55000  | Marketing |
|  2 | Bob    | 50000  | Marketing |
|  6 | Frank  | 45000  | HR        |
+----+--------+--------+-----------+
```

For elucidating sorting on multiple columns, suppose arranging the employees first by Department and then by Salary in ascending order within each department:

```
SELECT ID, Name, Salary, Department
FROM Employees
ORDER BY Department ASC, Salary ASC;
```

The output will be:

```
+----+--------+--------+-----------+
| ID | Name   | Salary | Department|
+----+--------+--------+-----------+
|  6 | Frank  | 45000  | HR        |
|  1 | Alice  | 70000  | HR        |
|  3 | Charlie| 60000  | IT        |
|  5 | Eve    | 90000  | IT        |
|  2 | Bob    | 50000  | Marketing |
|  4 | David  | 55000  | Marketing |
+----+--------+--------+-----------+
```

If the requirement is to sort the employees by Department in descending order and then by Salary in ascending order within each department, the query should be:

```
SELECT ID, Name, Salary, Department
FROM Employees
ORDER BY Department DESC, Salary ASC;
```

The result will rearrange accordingly:

```
+----+--------+--------+-----------+
| ID | Name   | Salary | Department|
+----+--------+--------+-----------+
|  2 | Bob    | 50000  | Marketing |
|  4 | David  | 55000  | Marketing |
|  3 | Charlie| 60000  | IT        |
|  5 | Eve    | 90000  | IT        |
|  6 | Frank  | 45000  | HR        |
|  1 | Alice  | 70000  | HR        |
+----+--------+--------+-----------+
```

Sorting can also incorporate derived columns or expressions. For example, if the query necessitates sorting by the length of the Name field:

```
SELECT ID, Name, Salary, Department
FROM Employees
ORDER BY LEN(Name) ASC;
```

The output will reorder based on the length of the names:

```
+----+--------+--------+-----------+
| ID | Name   | Salary | Department|
+----+--------+--------+-----------+
|  1 | Alice  | 70000  | HR        |
|  2 | Bob    | 50000  | Marketing |
|  4 | David  | 55000  | Marketing |
|  5 | Eve    | 90000  | IT        |
|  6 | Frank  | 45000  | HR        |
|  3 | Charlie| 60000  | IT        |
+----+--------+--------+-----------+
```

Similarly, one can specify complex expressions within the ORDER BY clause. For example, sorting by the absolute difference between each employee's salary and a benchmark value (e.g., 60000):

```
SELECT ID, Name, Salary, Department
FROM Employees
ORDER BY ABS(Salary - 60000) ASC;
```

This will sort based on how close or far each salary is from 60000:

```
+----+--------+--------+-----------+
| ID | Name   | Salary | Department|
+----+--------+--------+-----------+
|  3 | Charlie| 60000  | IT        |
|  4 | David  | 55000  | Marketing |
|  1 | Alice  | 70000  | HR        |
|  2 | Bob    | 50000  | Marketing |
|  5 | Eve    | 90000  | IT        |
|  6 | Frank  | 45000  | HR        |
+----+--------+--------+-----------+
```

The ORDER BY clause is vital for deriving meaningful insights and presenting data logically. It provides powerful mechanisms to impose order and structure, enhancing the interpretability and utility of query results.

4.6 Using Aggregate Functions

In SQL, aggregate functions are used to perform calculations on a set of values to return a single value. These functions operate on a collection of values from a column in a table and provide insights by summarizing data. Aggregate functions are commonly used in data analysis, reporting, and producing summary statistics. SQL Server supports several aggregate functions such as COUNT, SUM, AVG, MIN, and MAX.

COUNT Function

The COUNT function returns the number of rows in a table or the number of non-NULL values in a column. It can be used in two forms: COUNT (*) and COUNT(column_name). The former counts all rows, whereas the latter counts non-NULL values in the specified column.

```
-- Count all rows in the Employees table
SELECT COUNT(*)
FROM Employees;

-- Count non-NULL values in the Department column
SELECT COUNT(Department)
FROM Employees;
```

The result of the first query is the total number of rows in the Employees table. The second query returns the number of non-NULL entries in the Department column.

SUM Function

The SUM function calculates the total sum of a numeric column. It is particularly useful for financial and statistical data.

```
-- Calculate the total salary of all employees
SELECT SUM(Salary)
FROM Employees;
```

This query computes the sum of all salaries recorded in the Employees table.

AVG Function

The AVG function returns the average value of a numeric column. It is used to find the mean value.

```
-- Calculate the average salary of all employees
SELECT AVG(Salary)
FROM Employees;
```

This query calculates the average salary of employees by summing all salaries and dividing by the number of employees with non-NULL salaries.

MIN and MAX Functions

The MIN and MAX functions are used to find the minimum and maximum values in a column, respectively.

```
-- Find the minimum salary of all employees
SELECT MIN(Salary)
FROM Employees;

-- Find the maximum salary of all employees
SELECT MAX(Salary)
FROM Employees;
```

The first query returns the smallest salary value from the Employees table, and the second query returns the largest salary value.

Consider the following example table Employees:

```
+----+--------+----------+
| ID | Name   | Salary   |
+----+--------+----------+
|  1 | John   | 80000    |
|  2 | Alice  | 60000    |
|  3 | Bob    | 75000    |
|  4 | Carol  | 82000    |
|  5 | Dave   | 72000    |
+----+--------+----------+
```

Applying the aggregate functions to this table:

```
SELECT COUNT(*), SUM(Salary), AVG(Salary), MIN(Salary), MAX(Salary)
FROM Employees;
```

The results are:

```
+----------+------------+-------------+------------+------------+
| COUNT(*) | SUM(Salary)| AVG(Salary)  | MIN(Salary)| MAX(Salary)|
+----------+------------+-------------+------------+------------+
|    5     | 369000     |    73800    |    60000   |   82000    |
+----------+------------+-------------+------------+------------+
```

These computations are instrumental in obtaining meaningful insights from datasets, such as understanding the distribution of salaries within an organization.

Using Aggregate Functions with GROUP BY

While aggregate functions can be used on their own to summarize data, they can also be combined with the GROUP BY clause to perform calculations on partitions of the dataset. This combination allows aggregation of data across groups, providing deeper analytical capabilities.

```
-- Calculate the average salary for each department
SELECT Department, AVG(Salary)
```

```
FROM Employees
GROUP BY Department;

-- Count employees in each department
SELECT Department, COUNT(*)
FROM Employees
GROUP BY Department;
```

In the first query, the average salary is calculated for each department. The second query counts the number of employees in each department. This grouping of data enables more granular analysis by breaking down the statistics into meaningful subsets.

Proficiency in utilizing aggregate functions effectively enhances the ability to derive significant conclusions from datasets, making them a powerful tool in SQL for data analysis and reporting.

4.7 Grouping Data with GROUP BY

The GROUP BY clause is an essential component in SQL that allows users to aggregate data and produce summaries. This clause frequently pairs with aggregate functions such as SUM, AVG, MAX, MIN, and COUNT to perform calculations on sets of rows that share a common characteristic.

When using the GROUP BY clause, SQL groups the result set by one or more columns. The rows within each group become the input for the aggregate functions. The syntax for GROUP BY is straightforward:

```
SELECT column\_name1, aggregate\_function(column\_name2)
FROM table\_name
GROUP BY column\_name1;
```

Consider the following example to illustrate its usage. Assume a table named Sales containing the following columns: ProductID, ProductName, Category, QuantitySold, and SaleDate. If we want to calculate the total quantity sold for each product, the query would be:

```
SELECT ProductName, SUM(QuantitySold) AS TotalQuantitySold
FROM Sales
GROUP BY ProductName;
```

Here is how the table might look before the grouping:

```
+-----------+-------------+----------+-------------+------------+
| ProductID | ProductName | Category | QuantitySold | SaleDate |
+-----------+-------------+----------+-------------+------------+
|    1      |  Widget A   | Widgets  |     10      | 2023-01-01 |
|    2      |  Gadget B   | Gadgets  |     15      | 2023-01-02 |
|    1      |  Widget A   | Widgets  |     5       | 2023-01-03 |
|    3      | Thingamajig| Things   |     7       | 2023-01-03 |
|    2      |  Gadget B   | Gadgets  |     10      | 2023-01-05 |
+-----------+-------------+----------+-------------+------------+
```

By executing the above GROUP BY query, the result will be:

```
+-------------+------------------+
| ProductName | TotalQuantitySold |
+-------------+------------------+
|  Widget A   |       15         |
|  Gadget B   |       25         |
| Thingamajig |        7         |
+-------------+------------------+
```

This query groups the rows by ProductName and calculates the total quantity sold for each product.

The GROUP BY clause can also be used with multiple columns. For instance, if we wanted to calculate the total quantity sold per product within each category, we could use:

```
SELECT Category, ProductName, SUM(QuantitySold) AS TotalQuantitySold
FROM Sales
GROUP BY Category, ProductName;
```

Executing this query on the initial table would result in:

```
+----------+-------------+------------------+
| Category | ProductName | TotalQuantitySold |
+----------+-------------+------------------+
| Widgets |  Widget A   |       15         |
| Gadgets |  Gadget B   |       25         |
| Things   | Thingamajig |       7          |
+----------+-------------+------------------+
```

It's important to note that when including columns in the SELECT statement that are not aggregated, they must appear in the GROUP BY clause. This ensures that the SQL engine understands how to group rows before applying aggregate functions.

Moreover, GROUP BY can be extended with the HAVING clause to filter groups based on aggregate function results. Unlike the WHERE clause which filters individual rows, HAVING filters groups. For example, if we need groups where the total quantity sold exceeds 10:

```
SELECT Category, ProductName, SUM(QuantitySold) AS TotalQuantitySold
FROM Sales
GROUP BY Category, ProductName
HAVING SUM(QuantitySold) > 10;
```

On execution, this query would return:

```
+----------+-------------+------------------+
| Category | ProductName | TotalQuantitySold |
+----------+-------------+------------------+
| Widgets |  Widget A  |      15         |
| Gadgets |  Gadget B  |      25         |
+----------+-------------+------------------+
```

This result set excludes the Thingamajig product because its total quantity sold does not exceed 10.

In SQL Server, attention should also be given to NULL values in grouping columns. NULLs are treated as a distinct group. For example, given the table Employees with columns DepartmentID and Salary, the query may look like:

```
SELECT DepartmentID, AVG(Salary) AS AverageSalary
FROM Employees
GROUP BY DepartmentID;
```

If some employees do not belong to any department (indicated by NULL DepartmentID), they will be aggregated into a separate group where DepartmentID is NULL.

GROUP BY enhances SQL's ability to summarize data efficiently. The correct application of this clause contributes significantly to data analysis, enabling the creation of reports and data insights that offer meaningful information. Understanding its syntax and operation, along with combining it with aggregate functions and the HAVING clause, equips the user with powerful tools for database querying.

4.8 Joining Tables with JOIN

In relational database systems, it is common to have data distributed across multiple tables. To retrieve meaningful insights and cohesive information, it is crucial to combine data from these separate tables. This is achieved through the SQL JOIN clause. The JOIN operation is fundamental in SQL, enabling the merging of rows from two or more tables based on a related column.

Consider two tables, Employees and Departments. The Employees table holds information about the employees, and the Departments table contains details about the departments within an organization:

```
Employees:
+----+--------+---------+---------+
| ID | Name   | Salary  | DeptID  |
+----+--------+---------+---------+
| 1  | Alice  | 60000   | 2       |
| 2  | Bob    | 50000   | 1       |
| 3  | Carol  | 70000   | 3       |
| 4  | David  | 80000   | 2       |
+----+--------+---------+---------+

Departments:
+----+-------------+
| ID | Department  |
+----+-------------+
| 1  | HR          |
| 2  | IT          |
| 3  | Sales       |
+----+-------------+
```

To compile a report that includes employee names along with their corresponding department names, we need to join these tables on a common field; in this case, DeptID from the Employees table and ID from the Departments table.

The most straightforward way to achieve this is through an INNER JOIN, which returns rows that have matching values in both tables:

```
SELECT Employees.Name, Departments.Department
FROM Employees
INNER JOIN Departments
ON Employees.DeptID = Departments.ID;
```

The result set:

```
+--------+-------------+
| Name   | Department  |
+--------+-------------+
| Alice  | IT          |
| Bob    | HR          |
| Carol  | Sales       |
| David  | IT          |
+--------+-------------+
```

The INNER JOIN selects records that have matching values in both tables. If a record in the Employees table has a DeptID that does not exist in the Departments table, that record will be excluded from the result set.

Other types of JOINs include:

- LEFT JOIN (or LEFT OUTER JOIN)
- RIGHT JOIN (or RIGHT OUTER JOIN)
- FULL JOIN (or FULL OUTER JOIN)
- CROSS JOIN

- SELF JOIN

A LEFT JOIN returns all records from the left table (Employees), and the matched records from the right table (Departments). If no match is found, NULL values are returned for columns from the right table:

```
SELECT Employees.Name, Departments.Department
FROM Employees
LEFT JOIN Departments
ON Employees.DeptID = Departments.ID;
```

If the Departments table does not include a matching ID for a given DeptID in the Employees table, the department name for those records will be NULL. The result set now includes all employees, irrespective of whether their department information is available:

```
+--------+-------------+
| Name   | Department  |
+--------+-------------+
| Alice  | IT          |
| Bob    | HR          |
| Carol  | Sales       |
| David  | IT          |
+--------+-------------+
```

A RIGHT JOIN, conversely, ensures all records from the right table are returned, with matching rows from the left table. If there is no match, the result is NULL for left table columns:

```
SELECT Employees.Name, Departments.Department
FROM Employees
RIGHT JOIN Departments
ON Employees.DeptID = Departments.ID;
```

A FULL JOIN returns all records when there is a match in either left (Employees) or right (Departments) table records. If no match is found, NULL values are filled in:

```
SELECT Employees.Name, Departments.Department
FROM Employees
FULL JOIN Departments
ON Employees.DeptID = Departments.ID;
```

```
+--------+-------------+
| Name   | Department  |
+--------+-------------+
| Alice  | IT          |
| Bob    | HR          |
| Carol  | Sales       |
| David  | IT          |
+--------+-------------+
```

A CROSS JOIN returns the Cartesian product of the two tables, i.e., all possible combinations of rows. Use this with caution, as it can generate a large number of rows:

```
SELECT Employees.Name, Departments.Department
FROM Employees
CROSS JOIN Departments;
```

A SELF JOIN is a regular join but the table is joined with itself. This can be useful for evaluating hierarchical relationships within a single table. For instance, if you need to list employees along with their direct supervisor from the same Employees table, you can use a SELF JOIN:

```
SELECT e1.Name AS Employee, e2.Name AS Supervisor
FROM Employees e1
INNER JOIN Employees e2
ON e1.SupervisorID = e2.ID;
```

Understanding these various JOIN operations permits robust data querying capabilities, essential for analyzing related data spanning multiple relational tables. This knowledge is pivotal for constructing complex queries that synthesize comprehensive insights from disparate data sources within a relational database system.

4.9 Using Subqueries

Subqueries, also known as inner queries or nested queries, are an essential feature in SQL Server for executing complex operations. They allow for the embedding of a query within another query, thereby enabling more sophisticated data manipulation and retrieval. Subqueries can be utilized in various parts of an SQL statement, including the SELECT clause, WHERE clause, and FROM clause. Understanding the different ways to implement subqueries will significantly enhance the flexibility and functionality of your SQL queries.

Subqueries can be categorized primarily into two types: correlated and non-correlated subqueries. A non-correlated subquery operates independently of the outer query, whereas a correlated subquery depends on the outer query for its values.

Non-correlated subqueries are straightforward to understand and implement. Consider the following example that retrieves the names of employees who have a salary greater than the average salary of all employees in the company:

```
SELECT EmployeeName
FROM Employees
WHERE Salary > (SELECT AVG(Salary) FROM Employees);
```

In this case, the subquery (SELECT AVG(Salary) FROM Employees) calculates the average salary of all employees. The outer query then compares each employee's salary with this average value and returns the names of employees whose salary exceeds the average.

Another typical use of subqueries is in the SELECT clause to derive complex calculations or additional data for each row of the main query. An example of such a subquery is as follows:

```
SELECT EmployeeName, Salary,
       (SELECT AVG(Salary)
        FROM Employees) AS AverageSalary
FROM Employees;
```

Here, the subquery calculates the average salary and includes it as a constant value in each row of the main query result set.

Correlated subqueries are more intricate, involving a reference to columns in the outer query. These subqueries are evaluated once for each row processed by the outer query. For instance, if you wish to find employees whose salary is higher than the average salary in their respective departments, you can write:

```
SELECT EmployeeName, Salary
FROM Employees e1
WHERE Salary > (SELECT AVG(Salary)
                FROM Employees e2
                WHERE e1.DepartmentID = e2.DepartmentID);
```

In this example, the subquery (SELECT AVG(Salary) FROM Employees e2 WHERE e1.DepartmentID = e2.DepartmentID) calculates the average salary for the department of each row in the outer query. The correlation occurs because the subquery references e1.DepartmentID, thereby making the subquery's result dependent on the outer query's current row.

Subqueries can also be used within the FROM clause to create a derived table. This allows the use of intermediate results within larger queries, as demonstrated in the following example:

```
SELECT DepartmentID, AVG(Salary) AS DepartmentAvgSalary
FROM (SELECT DepartmentID, Salary
     FROM Employees) AS EmployeeSubquery
GROUP BY DepartmentID;
```

In this case, the subquery (SELECT DepartmentID, Salary FROM Employees) is treated as a table (named EmployeeSubquery) and grouped by DepartmentID to compute the average salary for each department.

It is essential to understand that properly optimizing subqueries is crucial for performance, especially in correlated subqueries where the inner query executes multiple times. SQL Server's execution plan can help identify performance bottlenecks associated with subqueries.

Furthermore, logical operators such as IN, ANY, ALL, and EXISTS can be effectively utilized with subqueries to perform advanced conditional checks. For example, find employees who work on at least one project in the 'Development' department:

```
SELECT EmployeeName
FROM Employees
WHERE EmployeeID IN (SELECT EmployeeID
                     FROM Projects
                     WHERE Department = 'Development');
```

In this example, the subquery selects EmployeeIDs from the Projects table where the department is 'Development'. The outer query retrieves the names of employees matching these EmployeeIDs.

Using subqueries proficiently requires a strong grasp of SQL fundamentals and practice. Mastering subqueries will enable you to write more precise and high-performing SQL statements, enhancing your ability to handle complex data manipulation tasks with efficiency.

4.10 Working with NULL Values

In SQL, the concept of NULL represents a missing or undefined value in a database table. It is crucial to understand that NULL is not equivalent to zero or an empty string; rather, it signifies the absence of any value. Proper handling of NULL values is essential for accurate data retrieval and manipulation, as NULL can affect query results and their interpretation.

When retrieving data from a table, we can use the IS NULL and IS NOT NULL predicates to filter rows containing NULL values. Consider the following table named Employees:

```
CREATE TABLE Employees (
    EmployeeID INT PRIMARY KEY,
    FirstName NVARCHAR(50),
    LastName NVARCHAR(50),
    Department NVARCHAR(50),
    ManagerID INT
);
```

Assume we have the following data inserted into the Employees table:

```
INSERT INTO Employees (EmployeeID, FirstName, LastName, Department,
      ManagerID) VALUES
(1, 'John', 'Doe', 'Engineering', NULL),
(2, 'Jane', 'Smith', 'Marketing', 1),
(3, 'Emily', 'Jones', 'Engineering', 1),
(4, 'Michael', 'Brown', 'Sales', NULL),
(5, 'Anna', 'Davis', 'Marketing', 2);
```

To find all employees who do not have a manager assigned, we write the following query:

```
SELECT EmployeeID, FirstName, LastName
FROM Employees
WHERE ManagerID IS NULL;
```

Executing this query will return:

```
+------------+-----------+----------+
| EmployeeID | FirstName | LastName |
+------------+-----------+----------+
| 1          | John      | Doe      |
| 4          | Michael   | Brown    |
+------------+-----------+----------+
```

Conversely, to find employees who have a manager, the query would be:

```
SELECT EmployeeID, FirstName, LastName
FROM Employees
WHERE ManagerID IS NOT NULL;
```

Running this query yields:

```
+------------+-----------+----------+
| EmployeeID | FirstName | LastName |
+------------+-----------+----------+
| 2          | Jane      | Smith    |
| 3          | Emily     | Jones    |
| 5          | Anna      | Davis    |
+------------+-----------+----------+
```

It is essential to remember that NULL values affect aggregate functions. For example, the COUNT() function does not include NULL values in its count. Consider the query:

```
SELECT COUNT(ManagerID) AS NonNullManagers
FROM Employees;
```

This query counts only rows where ManagerID is not NULL and returns:

```
+----------------+
| NonNullManagers|
+----------------+
| 3              |
+----------------+
```

However, to count all rows, regardless of NULL values, use COUNT(*):

```
SELECT COUNT(*) AS TotalEmployees
FROM Employees;
```

Executing the above query provides:

```
+---------------+
| TotalEmployees|
+---------------+
| 5             |
+---------------+
```

Furthermore, when performing comparisons, SQL treats NULL as unknown, impacting the results of equality and inequality conditions. Instead of using $= \text{NULL}$, which is invalid, employ IS NULL:

```
SELECT EmployeeID, FirstName, LastName
FROM Employees
WHERE ManagerID = NULL;
```

This query returns no rows because the condition $\text{ManagerID} = \text{NULL}$ never evaluates to true. Proper syntax is critical:

```
SELECT EmployeeID, FirstName, LastName
FROM Employees
WHERE ManagerID IS NULL;
```

To address NULL values in results, use functions like COALESCE or ISNULL. The COALESCE function returns the first non-NULL value in a list of arguments:

```
SELECT
    EmployeeID,
    FirstName,
    LastName,
    COALESCE(ManagerID, 0) AS ManagerID
FROM Employees;
```

This query substitutes any NULL ManagerID with 0:

```
+------------+-----------+----------+-----------+
| EmployeeID | FirstName | LastName | ManagerID |
+------------+-----------+----------+-----------+
| 1          | John      | Doe      | 0         |
| 2          | Jane      | Smith    | 1         |
| 3          | Emily     | Jones    | 1         |
| 4          | Michael   | Brown    | 0         |
| 5          | Anna      | Davis    | 2         |
+------------+-----------+----------+-----------+
```

Similarly, the ISNULL function can replace NULL values with a specified value, but note that it is specific to SQL Server:

```
SELECT
    EmployeeID,
    FirstName,
    LastName,
```

```
    ISNULL(ManagerID, 0) AS ManagerID
FROM Employees;
```

These tools for handling NULL values enable SQL developers to craft robust queries that account for incomplete data, ensuring accurate and meaningful results. Proper understanding and utilization of these concepts are key to effective database management and data retrieval.

4.11 Modifying Data with INSERT, UPDATE, DELETE

Modifying data within an SQL Server database encompasses the fundamental operations of inserting new records, updating existing ones, and deleting those no longer needed. These operations are executed via the INSERT, UPDATE, and DELETE statements respectively. This section delves into the syntax and usage of these statements, presenting various examples to elucidate their application.

INSERT Statement

The INSERT statement adds new rows of data to a table. It follows two primary forms: specifying values directly or taking values from another table.

- *Inserting Direct Values*

  The basic syntax for inserting direct values is:

  ```
  INSERT INTO table_name (column1, column2, column3, ...)
  VALUES (value1, value2, value3, ...);
  ```

  For example, to insert a new employee into the Employees table:

  ```
  INSERT INTO Employees (EmployeeID, FirstName, LastName, BirthDate)
  VALUES (2315, 'John', 'Doe', '1984-07-15');
  ```

  If all columns are to be inserted and values are provided for each column, the column names can be omitted:

  ```
  INSERT INTO Employees
  VALUES (2316, 'Jane', 'Smith', '1990-03-22');
  ```

- *Inserting Data from Another Table*

  Data can also be inserted by selecting rows from another table:

```
INSERT INTO Employees (EmployeeID, FirstName, LastName, BirthDate)
SELECT EmployeeID, FirstName, LastName, BirthDate
FROM TempEmployees
WHERE EmploymentStatus = 'Active';
```

This command copies active employees from the TempEmployees table to the Employees table.

UPDATE Statement

The UPDATE statement modifies existing data within a table. It can update one or multiple columns for all or a subset of rows based on a specified condition.

The basic syntax is:

```
UPDATE table_name
SET column1 = value1, column2 = value2, ...
WHERE condition;
```

For instance, to correct the birthdate of the employee with EmployeeID 2315:

```
UPDATE Employees
SET BirthDate = '1984-07-16'
WHERE EmployeeID = 2315;
```

Multiple columns can be updated simultaneously. For instance, updating the last name and birthdate:

```
UPDATE Employees
SET LastName = 'Dane', BirthDate = '1985-08-20'
WHERE EmployeeID = 2315;
```

Without a WHERE clause, all rows in the table are updated, which can be risky:

```
UPDATE Employees
SET Status = 'Inactive';
```

This statement sets the Status column to 'Inactive' for every record in the Employees table.

DELETE Statement

The DELETE statement removes rows from a table based on a specified condition.

The basic syntax is:

```
DELETE FROM table_name
WHERE condition;
```

For example, to delete a specific employee from the Employees table:

```
DELETE FROM Employees
WHERE EmployeeID = 2315;
```

Another example demonstrates deleting all inactive employees:

```
DELETE FROM Employees
WHERE Status = 'Inactive';
```

Like the UPDATE statement, omitting the WHERE clause in a DELETE statement removes all rows:

```
DELETE FROM Employees;
```

This operation should be performed with caution.

Transaction Control

Execution of data modification statements often entails transaction control to ensure database integrity. SQL Server supports the use of transactions, allowing groups of statements to execute in an all-or-nothing fashion through the BEGIN TRANSACTION and COMMIT or ROLLBACK statements.

An example of utilizing a transaction to delete and insert operations is illustrated below:

```
BEGIN TRANSACTION;
BEGIN TRY
    DELETE FROM Employees
    WHERE EmployeeID = 2310;

    INSERT INTO Employees (EmployeeID, FirstName, LastName, BirthDate)
    VALUES (2318, 'Alice', 'Wonderland', '1989-02-14');

    COMMIT;
END TRY
BEGIN CATCH
    ROLLBACK;
    PRINT 'Transaction failed!';
END CATCH;
```

Transactions safeguard against partial changes by grouping operations and reverting changes if an error occurs. This example demonstrates removing an employee and inserting another only if both operations succeed; otherwise, all changes are undone. The BEGIN TRY and BEGIN CATCH blocks handle exceptions effectively.

These modification operations form the basis of dynamic and responsive database manipulation, essential for maintaining up-to-date and accurate data, adhering to ACID (Atomicity, Consistency, Isolation,

Durability) principles which are foundational to reliable database management.

Chapter 5

Advanced SQL Queries

This chapter delves into advanced SQL querying techniques, including complex JOIN operations and advanced subqueries. It covers the use of Common Table Expressions (CTEs), window functions, and pivot and unpivot operations. The chapter also explores dynamic SQL, views, performance tuning for queries, handling large datasets, recursive queries, using temporary tables and table variables, and error handling in SQL queries.

5.1 Complex JOIN Operations

SQL JOIN operations are fundamental to extracting related data from multiple tables within a database. In this section, we will explore complex join operations, including various join types and their applications. By understanding and implementing these advanced techniques, one can optimize queries to efficiently handle intricate data relationships.

JOIN operations can be categorized into several types:

- INNER JOIN
- LEFT JOIN (or LEFT OUTER JOIN)
- RIGHT JOIN (or RIGHT OUTER JOIN)
- FULL JOIN (or FULL OUTER JOIN)
- CROSS JOIN

- SELF JOIN

INNER JOIN retrieves records from multiple tables where the joined fields have matching values. It is the most commonly used join type.

```
SELECT A.*, B.*
FROM TableA A
INNER JOIN TableB B
ON A.id = B.id;
```

This query will only return rows where id matches in both TableA and TableB.

LEFT JOIN retrieves all records from the left table (TableA) and the matched records from the right table (TableB). If no match is found, NULL values are returned for columns from the right table.

```
SELECT A.*, B.*
FROM TableA A
LEFT JOIN TableB B
ON A.id = B.id;
```

This query will return all rows from TableA, with matched rows from TableB. If there are no matches, columns for TableB will show NULL.

RIGHT JOIN retrieves all records from the right table (TableB) and the matched records from the left table (TableA). Like LEFT JOIN, if no match is found, NULL values are returned for columns from the left table.

```
SELECT A.*, B.*
FROM TableA A
RIGHT JOIN TableB B
ON A.id = B.id;
```

This query will return all rows from TableB, with matched rows from TableA. If there are no matches, columns for TableA will show NULL.

FULL JOIN retrieves all records when there is a match in either left (TableA) or right table (TableB). If there is no match, NULL values are included in the results wherever no corresponding match is found.

```
SELECT A.*, B.*
FROM TableA A
FULL JOIN TableB B
ON A.id = B.id;
```

This query will return all rows from both TableA and TableB, including all unmatched rows with NULL values filled in for each table as necessary.

CROSS JOIN returns the Cartesian product of the two tables being joined. This means each row from the first table is combined with all rows in the second table.

```
SELECT A.*, B.*
FROM TableA A
CROSS JOIN TableB B;
```

This will generate a result set that includes every combination of rows from TableA and TableB.

SELF JOIN is a regular join but the table is joined with itself. It is useful for finding hierarchical relationships or comparing rows within the same table.

```
SELECT A.*, B.*
FROM TableA A
INNER JOIN TableA B
ON A.related\_id = B.id;
```

This query joins TableA with itself, matching rows based on a relationship between related_id in A and id in B.

To illustrate practical applications of these joins, consider the following advanced example involving multiple join types:

```
SELECT E.employee\_id, E.name, M.name AS manager\_name, D.department\
    _name
FROM Employees E
LEFT JOIN Employees M ON E.manager\_id = M.employee\_id
INNER JOIN Departments D ON E.department\_id = D.department\_id;
```

In this query, employees are joined with their managers using a LEFT JOIN (if an employee has no manager, the result will include NULL for manager_name). Additionally, employees are matched with their respective departments using an INNER JOIN, ensuring only those associated with a valid department are included.

When dealing with complex joins, it is crucial to carefully consider the order and logic of joins to ensure efficient and accurate query results. Furthermore, understanding the potential impacts on performance, especially with large datasets, guides the selection of appropriate join strategies. One may utilize query execution plans to analyze and fine-tune the database queries, ensuring optimization and efficiency.

The correct employment of these advanced join operations enhances the ability to query relational databases in powerful and flexible ways.

5.2 Advanced Subqueries

Subqueries, also known as inner queries or nested queries, are a form of a query embedded within another SQL query. They can be placed in various clauses of an SQL statement, such as the SELECT, FROM, WHERE, and HAVING clauses. Advanced subqueries extend their basic usages and delve into more complex scenarios, improving data retrieval and manipulation efficiency by structuring queries in nuanced ways.

Advanced subqueries empower SQL users to conduct more sophisticated data analysis and complex query formulations. Four primary types of advanced subqueries are correlated subqueries, subqueries in the FROM clause (inline views or derived tables), subqueries with EXISTS/NOT EXISTS, and subqueries used in the SELECT clause.

- **Correlated Subqueries**

A correlated subquery is a type of subquery that references columns from the outer query. The subquery is executed repeatedly, once for each row processed by the outer query. Consequently, the correlated subquery depends on the outer query for its values.

Consider the following example:

```
SELECT e1.EmployeeID, e1.EmployeeName
FROM Employees e1
WHERE e1.Salary > (SELECT AVG(e2.Salary)
                   FROM Employees e2
                   WHERE e2.DepartmentID = e1.DepartmentID);
```

In the above query, the subquery:

```
(SELECT AVG(e2.Salary)
 FROM Employees e2
 WHERE e2.DepartmentID = e1.DepartmentID)
```

is executed for each employee (e1) and retrieves the average salary of employees in the relevant department. This subquery's results are then employed to filter out employees earning more than the departmental average salary.

- **Subqueries in the FROM Clause**

Using subqueries in the FROM clause allows complex computations or intermediate results to be organized into reusable, logical blocks of code known as derived tables or inline views.

Example:

```
SELECT d.DepartmentName, t.AverageSalary
FROM Departments d,
     (SELECT DepartmentID, AVG(Salary) AS AverageSalary
      FROM Employees
      GROUP BY DepartmentID) t
WHERE d.DepartmentID = t.DepartmentID;
```

The subquery inside the FROM clause:

```
(SELECT DepartmentID, AVG(Salary) AS AverageSalary
 FROM Employees
 GROUP BY DepartmentID)
```

calculates the average salary for each department. This derived table t is subsequently joined with the Departments table.

- **EXISTS and NOT EXISTS Subqueries**

Subqueries can also employ the EXISTS and NOT EXISTS operators, which test for the presence or absence of rows returned by the subquery. EXISTS effectively halts execution once a matching row is found, which can be more efficient than other approaches.

Example:

```
SELECT EmployeeID, EmployeeName
FROM Employees e
WHERE EXISTS (SELECT 1
              FROM TrainingSessions t
              WHERE t.EmployeeID = e.EmployeeID
              AND t.SessionDate > '2023-01-01');
```

In this query, the EXISTS subquery checks if any training sessions occurred for each employee after January 1, 2023. If so, the main query returns the employee's details.

Conversely, NOT EXISTS can exclude certain rows based on the absence of records in a related subquery:

```
SELECT EmployeeID, EmployeeName
FROM Employees e
WHERE NOT EXISTS (SELECT 1
                  FROM Terminations t
                  WHERE t.EmployeeID = e.EmployeeID);
```

The above query retrieves employees who have no termination records, using the subquery to validate the absence.

- **Subqueries within the SELECT Clause**

Subqueries can be utilized within the SELECT clause to generate scalar values utilized as columns in the result set, enhancing computation without multiple joins or aggregations.

Example:

```
SELECT e.EmployeeID, e.EmployeeName,
       (SELECT COUNT(*)
        FROM Orders o
        WHERE o.EmployeeID = e.EmployeeID) AS OrderCount
FROM Employees e;
```

Here, the subquery:

```
(SELECT COUNT(*)
 FROM Orders o
 WHERE o.EmployeeID = e.EmployeeID)
```

returns the total number of orders processed by each employee, presenting the count as a column alongside employee details.

Advanced subqueries serve as a pivotal component for writing expressive and efficient SQL queries, enabling intricate logical flows and condition validation. Proper utilization of these techniques significantly enhances data manipulation capabilities, contributing to robust and optimized database interactions.

5.3 Common Table Expressions (CTEs)

Common Table Expressions (CTEs) are a powerful and versatile feature in SQL that enhance the readability and maintainability of queries. CTEs provide a way to create temporary result sets that can be referenced within a SELECT, INSERT, UPDATE, or DELETE statement. They are defined using the WITH clause, which precedes the main query.

The basic syntax for defining a CTE is as follows:

```
WITH cte_name (column1, column2, ...)
AS
(
    -- CTE Query
    SELECT ...
)
SELECT ...
FROM cte_name;
```

In this structure, the CTE is named cte_name, and it comprises one or more columns specified within parentheses. The CTE query enclosed in parentheses generates the temporary result set which can subsequently be queried.

CTEs are particularly useful for breaking down complex queries into manageable parts, enabling the reuse of result sets within a query, and enhancing recursive query capabilities. They can also improve code readability, given that they self-describe parts of a query that would otherwise be nested and difficult to understand.

Example 1: Basic CTE Usage

Consider a scenario where we need to compute the average salary for each department within a company:

```
WITH avg_salaries AS
(
    SELECT
        department_id,
        AVG(salary) AS avg_salary
    FROM employees
    GROUP BY department_id
)
SELECT
    department_id,
    avg_salary
FROM avg_salaries;
```

This example demonstrates defining a CTE named avg_salaries, which calculates the average salary for each department. The main query then selects from this CTE.

Example 2: Recursive CTEs

One of the most powerful features of CTEs is their ability to handle recursive queries, which are useful for hierarchical data such as organizational structures or graph data. The syntax for a recursive CTE includes an anchor member that forms the base result set and a recursive member that references the CTE itself.

```
WITH RECURSIVE cte_name AS
(
    -- Anchor member
    SELECT ...
    UNION ALL
    -- Recursive member
    SELECT ...
    FROM cte_name
    WHERE ...
)
SELECT ...
FROM cte_name;
```

Example 3: Recursive CTE to Traverse a Hierarchical Relationship

Suppose we have an employee hierarchy and want to retrieve all subordinates of a given employee, including their hierarchical levels:

```
WITH RECURSIVE EmployeeHierarchy AS
(
    -- Anchor member: Retrieve the root employee
    SELECT
        employee_id,
        manager_id,
        employee_name,
        0 AS hierarchical_level
    FROM employees
    WHERE manager_id IS NULL

    UNION ALL

    -- Recursive member: Retrieve subordinates
    SELECT
        e.employee_id,
        e.manager_id,
        e.employee_name,
        eh.hierarchical_level + 1
    FROM employees e
    INNER JOIN EmployeeHierarchy eh
        ON e.manager_id = eh.employee_id
)
SELECT
    employee_id,
    manager_id,
    employee_name,
    hierarchical_level
FROM EmployeeHierarchy;
```

In this scenario, the CTE EmployeeHierarchy starts with the root employee (those with no manager, indicated by manager_id IS NULL). The recursive member selects employees managed by those already in the CTE, incrementing the hierarchical level with each recursion.

Example 4: Multiple CTEs in a Query

CTEs can be defined in sequence, with each CTE building upon the previous ones. This can be particularly useful when dealing with interdependent queries.

```
WITH DepartmentSalary AS
(
    SELECT
        department_id,
        SUM(salary) AS total_salary
    FROM employees
    GROUP BY department_id
),

DepartmentCount AS
(
    SELECT
```

```
        department_id,
        COUNT(*) AS num_employees
    FROM employees
    GROUP BY department_id
)

SELECT
    ds.department_id,
    ds.total_salary,
    dc.num_employees
FROM DepartmentSalary ds
JOIN DepartmentCount dc
    ON ds.department_id = dc.department_id;
```

In this example, the first CTE DepartmentSalary calculates the total salary for each department, while the second CTE DepartmentCount counts the number of employees per department. The main query then joins these two CTEs to obtain a combined result.

CTEs contribute significantly to code clarity and maintenance, affording an elegant solution for nested subqueries and complex data retrievals. The recursive capabilities further enhance their suitability for hierarchical data processing, making them an essential tool in the repertoire of an SQL practitioner.

5.4 Window Functions

Window functions in SQL are powerful tools that allow for the performance of calculations across sets of table rows that are somehow related to the current row. They are often used for running totals, moving averages, and ranking operations. Unlike aggregate functions, window functions do not cause rows to become grouped into a single output row, and each row retains its separate identity.

A window function is made up of three main components:

- The function itself, such as RANK(), ROW_NUMBER(), SUM(), etc.
- The OVER() clause, which defines the window of rows to be considered.
- An optional PARTITION BY clause, used to break the result set into partitions to which the function is applied independently.

Consider the following basic structure of a window function:

```
SELECT
    column_name,
    aggregate_function() OVER (PARTITION BY column1 ORDER BY column2)
FROM
    table_name;
```

ROW_NUMBER()

This function assigns a unique sequential integer to rows within a partition of a result set, starting with one for the first row in each partition.

```
SELECT
    column_name,
    ROW_NUMBER() OVER (PARTITION BY partition_column ORDER BY
        order_column) AS row_num
FROM
    table_name;
```

RANK() and DENSE_RANK()

Both functions add a unique rank number to the rows within the partition. The difference is that RANK() might leave gaps in the ranking sequence when there are ties, whereas DENSE_RANK() does not.

```
SELECT
    column_name,
    RANK() OVER (PARTITION BY partition_column ORDER BY order_column)
        AS rank_num,
    DENSE_RANK() OVER (PARTITION BY partition_column ORDER BY
        order_column) AS dense_rank_num
FROM
    table_name;
```

SUM() and AVG() as Window Functions

These aggregate functions can also be applied as window functions to calculate sums or averages over the specified window.

```
SELECT
    column_name,
    SUM(value_column) OVER (PARTITION BY partition_column ORDER BY
        order_column ROWS BETWEEN UNBOUNDED PRECEDING AND
        CURRENT ROW) AS running_sum,
    AVG(value_column) OVER (PARTITION BY partition_column) AS average_value
FROM
    table_name;
```

OVER() Clause Details

The OVER() clause may include the following elements:

- PARTITION BY clause: Defines the partition for the window function.

- ORDER BY clause: Specifies the order of the rows in each partition.
- ROWS or RANGE: These keywords specify limits for the window frame relative to the current row.

Here is an example using all these elements:

```
SELECT
    column_name,
    SUM(value_column) OVER (PARTITION BY partition_column ORDER BY
        order_column
    ROWS BETWEEN 1 PRECEDING AND 1 FOLLOWING) AS moving_sum
FROM
    table_name;
```

To see the effect of each window function, consider the following table sales:

SaleID	Product	SaleDate	SaleAmount
1	A	2023-01-01	100
2	B	2023-01-02	150
3	A	2023-01-03	200
4	A	2023-01-04	100
5	B	2023-01-05	300

Using the ROW_NUMBER() and SUM() functions:

```
SELECT
    Product,
    SaleDate,
    SaleAmount,
    ROW_NUMBER() OVER (PARTITION BY Product ORDER BY SaleDate) AS
        RowNum,
    SUM(SaleAmount) OVER (PARTITION BY Product ORDER BY SaleDate) AS
        RunningTotal
FROM
    sales;
```

The output will be:

```
Product SaleDate   SaleAmount RowNum RunningTotal
A       2023-01-01 100        1      100
A       2023-01-03 200        2      300
A       2023-01-04 100        3      400
B       2023-01-02 150        1      150
B       2023-01-05 300        2      450
```

The use of window functions enhances the flexibility and power of SQL queries, providing functionality that goes beyond standard aggregation and filtering. Proper understanding and implementation of window functions can significantly simplify complex analytical queries and performance metrics in SQL Server.

5.5 Pivot and Unpivot Operations

Pivot and unpivot operations in SQL Server are powerful techniques for transforming data from row-oriented to column-oriented formats and vice versa. These operations are essential for preparing datasets for reporting and analysis, making them an indispensable tool for advanced SQL querying.

The PIVOT operator aggregates data and then re-orients the rows into columns, providing a cross-tabular view of the data. The basic syntax for a pivot operation involves specifying the aggregation function, the values to be aggregated, and the resulting columns.

Below is an example illustrating the use of the PIVOT operator. Consider a table named Sales that records quarterly sales for different products:

```
CREATE TABLE Sales (
    ProductID INT,
    Quarter VARCHAR(2),
    SalesAmount DECIMAL(10, 2)
);
```

The data in this table might look like this:

```
ProductID  | Quarter | SalesAmount
-----------|---------|------------
1          | Q1      | 12000.00
1          | Q2      | 15000.00
1          | Q3      | 13000.00
1          | Q4      | 14000.00
2          | Q1      | 9000.00
2          | Q2      | 9500.00
2          | Q3      | 8900.00
2          | Q4      | 12000.00
```

To pivot this data, use the following SQL query:

```
SELECT *
FROM (
    SELECT ProductID, Quarter, SalesAmount
    FROM Sales
) AS SourceTable
PIVOT (
    SUM(SalesAmount)
    FOR Quarter IN ([Q1], [Q2], [Q3], [Q4])
) AS PivotTable;
```

The resulting pivoted data would be:

```
ProductID  |    Q1    |    Q2    |    Q3    |    Q4
-----------|----------|----------|----------|----------
1          | 12000.00 | 15000.00 | 13000.00 | 14000.00
2          |  9000.00 |  9500.00 |  8900.00 | 12000.00
```

In the query, SUM(SalesAmount) specifies the aggregation function to sum the sales for each quarter for each product. The FOR Quarter IN ([Q1], [Q2], [Q3], [Q4]) clause defines the columns to be created in the pivoted table.

Conversely, the UNPIVOT operator transforms columns back into rows. This operation is useful for normalizing denormalized data or preparing data for processing.

For example, consider the pivoted data above when stored back into a table named QuarterlySales:

```
CREATE TABLE QuarterlySales (
    ProductID INT,
    Q1 DECIMAL(10, 2),
    Q2 DECIMAL(10, 2),
    Q3 DECIMAL(10, 2),
    Q4 DECIMAL(10, 2)
);
```

To unpivot this data back into its original row format, use the following query:

```
SELECT ProductID, Quarter, SalesAmount
FROM (
    SELECT ProductID, Q1, Q2, Q3, Q4
    FROM QuarterlySales
) AS SourceTable
UNPIVOT (
    SalesAmount
    FOR Quarter IN ([Q1], [Q2], [Q3], [Q4])
) AS UnpivotTable;
```

The transformed (unpivoted) data would look like this:

```
ProductID  | Quarter | SalesAmount
-----------|---------|------------
1          | Q1      | 12000.00
1          | Q2      | 15000.00
1          | Q3      | 13000.00
1          | Q4      | 14000.00
2          | Q1      |  9000.00
2          | Q2      |  9500.00
2          | Q3      |  8900.00
2          | Q4      | 12000.00
```

In the UNPIVOT query, SalesAmount defines the value to extract from the specified column list, and FOR Quarter IN ([Q1], [Q2], [Q3], [Q4]) defines the columns to be unpivoted.

Understanding the behavior and application of pivot and unpivot operations is crucial for comprehensive data manipulation. The ability to interchange between row-based and column-based structures using these operators allows for greater flexibility in data presentation and analysis, enabling more complex queries and insights.

5.6 Dynamic SQL

Dynamic SQL enables the construction and execution of SQL statements dynamically at runtime. This capability is valuable when the full form of an SQL query cannot be decided until the actual execution. Dynamic SQL allows for more flexible application development and provides a mechanism to construct complex queries based on input parameters or conditions that may not be predetermined. However, great care must be taken to avoid SQL injection vulnerabilities.

The EXEC and sp_executesql commands are primarily used for executing dynamic SQL in SQL Server.

EXEC command: The EXEC command can be used to execute dynamically built SQL strings. The basic syntax is as follows:

```
EXEC('sql_string')
```

Consider an example where we want to retrieve data from a table based on a column name provided at runtime:

```
DECLARE @columnName NVARCHAR(50)
SET @columnName = 'LastName'
EXEC('SELECT ' + @columnName + ' FROM Employees')
```

This code concatenates the column name into the SQL string and executes it. While EXEC is simple to use, it does not support parameterization, which can open up vulnerabilities to SQL injection attacks.

sp_executesql command: The sp_executesql procedure offers a more secure alternative, allowing parameterized queries. The basic syntax for sp_executesql is:

```
sp_executesql
    @sql_string,
    @parameter_definition,
    @parameter_value_1,
    @parameter_value_2, ...
```

In this scenario, @sql_string contains the dynamic query, @parameter_definition specifies the parameter type definitions, and the subsequent arguments provide parameter values.

Consider modifying the earlier example using sp_executesql:

```
DECLARE @SQLString NVARCHAR(500)
```

```
DECLARE @ParmDefinition NVARCHAR(500)
DECLARE @columnName NVARCHAR(50)

SET @columnName = 'LastName'
SET @SQLString = N'SELECT ' + @columnName + ' FROM Employees'
SET @ParmDefinition = N'@columnName NVARCHAR(50)'

EXEC sp_executesql @SQLString, @ParmDefinition, @columnName = @columnName
```

Dynamic SQL Execution with Parameters: An advantage of sp_executesql over EXEC is that it allows you to use parameters within the statement, increasing security and efficiency. Here is a parameterized query example:

```
DECLARE @EmpID INT
SET @EmpID = 1

EXEC sp_executesql
     N'SELECT FirstName, LastName
       FROM Employees
       WHERE EmployeeID = @EmpID',
     N'@EmpID INT',
     @EmpID = @EmpID
```

This code dynamically constructs the SQL statement safely by passing @EmpID as a parameter.

- **Practical Considerations**

- **Advantages:**
  - Flexibility to build and execute complex queries on the fly.
  - Ability to handle variable database objects and data sets more dynamically.
  - Enhanced security through parameterization when using sp_executesql.

- **Disadvantages:**
  - Code complexity can increase, making maintenance harder.
  - Potential performance overhead if overused or misused.
  - Risk of SQL injection attacks if inputs are not properly sanitized.

To mitigate risks:

- Always use parameterized queries with sp_executesql.

- Avoid concatenating user inputs directly into the SQL strings.
- Use proper validation and sanitization mechanisms for inputs.

- **SQL Injection Prevention**

SQL injection is a critical security vulnerability that arises when attackers can manipulate SQL queries by injecting malicious SQL code. Dynamic SQL increases the risk if not handled carefully. To prevent SQL injection:

- Avoid using EXEC with concatenated user input.
- Use sp_executesql with proper parameterization.
- Implement rigorous input validation.

For example, the insecure dynamic SQL:

```
DECLARE @userInput NVARCHAR(50)
SET @userInput = '''; DROP TABLE Employees; --'
EXEC('SELECT * FROM Employees WHERE FirstName = ''' + @userInput + '''')
```

This could be exploited by an attacker to drop the Employees table. Instead, use:

```
DECLARE @SQLString NVARCHAR(500)
DECLARE @ParmDefinition NVARCHAR(500)
DECLARE @userInput NVARCHAR(50)
SET @userInput = 'John'

SET @SQLString = N'SELECT * FROM Employees WHERE FirstName =
    @FirstName'
SET @ParmDefinition = N'@FirstName NVARCHAR(50)'

EXEC sp_executesql @SQLString, @ParmDefinition, @FirstName = @userInput
```

This ensures safer execution by properly handling user input through parameters.

Dynamic SQL, when used judiciously and with proper security measures, can greatly enhance the flexibility and power of database applications. Its prudent use, especially with sp_executesql, can help leverage complex queries and variable dataset operations while maintaining security and performance.

5.7 Using Views

Views in SQL Server are virtual tables representing the result of a stored query. They provide a level of abstraction and encapsulation over the underlying table structures. A view does not store data itself but rather stores a SQL query that can be executed to retrieve the desired data.

The basic syntax for creating a view is as follows:

```
CREATE VIEW view\_name AS
SELECT column1, column2, ...
FROM table\_name
WHERE condition;
```

Once created, a view can be queried like a regular table:

```
SELECT * FROM view\_name;
```

Benefits of Using Views:

- **Simplicity:** Views simplify complex queries by encapsulating them. Instead of writing complex joins and filters repeatedly, you can encapsulate them in a view and query the view.
- **Security:** Views can be used to restrict access to data by exposing only specific columns or rows to users, improving data security.
- **Consistency:** By centralizing complex queries, views ensure that changes in business logic need to be made in one place only, maintaining consistency.
- **Abstraction:** Views provide an abstraction layer, hiding the complexity of the underlying database schema from the end users.

Examples of Views in Practice: Consider a database with the following tables: Employees and Departments. The Employees table has columns EmployeeID, Name, DepartmentID, and Salary. The Departments table consists of DepartmentID and DepartmentName.

To create a view that joins these tables to display employee names along with their department names, use the following SQL:

```
CREATE VIEW EmployeeDepartmentView AS
SELECT e.EmployeeID, e.Name, d.DepartmentName, e.Salary
FROM Employees e
JOIN Departments d ON e.DepartmentID = d.DepartmentID;
```

To query this view:

```
SELECT * FROM EmployeeDepartmentView;
```

This query returns:

```
EmployeeID | Name       | DepartmentName | Salary
------------------------------------------------
1          | John Doe   | HR             | 50000
2          | Jane Smith| IT             | 60000
```

Updating Views: Views can be updatable if certain conditions are met. This means you can issue an INSERT, UPDATE, or DELETE statement against the view. However, not all views are updatable. For instance, a view that involves a join between multiple tables might not be updatable unless specific rules (such as unique rows in underlying join) are held.

Consider a simplified view on a single table:

```
CREATE VIEW EmployeeView AS
SELECT EmployeeID, Name, Salary
FROM Employees;
```

An update can be performed on this view:

```
UPDATE EmployeeView
SET Salary = 55000
WHERE EmployeeID = 1;
```

Indexed Views: SQL Server allows the creation of indexed views for performance optimization. Indexed views store the result set physically, which can significantly improve query performance, especially for complex aggregations and joins. To create an index on a view, the view must first be created with the SCHEMABINDING option, ensuring that the underlying table schema cannot be changed without first dropping the view.

```
CREATE VIEW IndexedEmployeeView WITH SCHEMABINDING AS
SELECT EmployeeID, Name, Salary
FROM dbo.Employees;
GO
CREATE UNIQUE CLUSTERED INDEX IX\_IndexedEmployeeView ON
    IndexedEmployeeView(EmployeeID);
```

Dropping Views: A view can be removed from the database using the DROP VIEW statement.

```
DROP VIEW view\_name;
```

For instance, to drop the EmployeeDepartmentView:

```
DROP VIEW EmployeeDepartmentView;
```

Views are essential in SQL Server for abstraction, security, and query simplification. They encapsulate complex queries and provide a level of security by exposing only necessary data. Indexing views can further enhance performance for large datasets and complex operations.

5.8 Performance Tuning for Queries

Performance tuning is a critical skill for database administrators and developers aiming to optimize SQL queries for faster and more efficient data retrieval. This section discusses various techniques and best practices for enhancing query performance in SQL Server.

To begin with, understanding query execution plans is fundamental. SQL Server provides execution plans as a roadmap to how queries are executed. Analyzing these plans helps identify potential performance bottlenecks. The execution plan can be accessed using the SET SHOWPLAN_XML, SET SHOWPLAN_ALL, or SET STATISTICS_PROFILE commands before executing a query.

```
-- This command displays a graphical execution plan.
SET SHOWPLAN_XML ON;
GO

-- Your query here
SELECT * FROM Sales.SalesOrderDetail WHERE ProductID = 900;
GO

SET SHOWPLAN_XML OFF;
GO
```

Indexes play a vital role in speeding up data retrieval. Indexing creates a structured path to the data, reducing the number of rows SQL Server must scan. However, poorly designed indexes can degrade performance. A balanced approach by using clustered and non-clustered indexes appropriately is necessary.

Consider the following example where a non-clustered index is created to speed up queries filtering on the LastName column in the Person.Person table:

```
-- Creating a non-clustered index on LastName
CREATE NONCLUSTERED INDEX IX\_Person\_LastName
ON Person.Person (LastName);
```

In situations where multiple indexes exist, SQL Server may use the least optimal one. Updating statistics frequently ensures the query optimizer has current information to make accurate decisions.

```
-- Updating statistics on a specific table
UPDATE STATISTICS Sales.SalesOrderDetail;
```

Joins, especially complex ones involving many tables, can heavily impact performance. Rewriting queries to reduce the number of JOIN operations or employing EXISTS instead of inefficient joins can provide significant improvements.

```
-- Using EXISTS instead of JOIN for better performance
SELECT ProductID
FROM Production.Product p
WHERE EXISTS(
    SELECT 1
    FROM Sales.SalesOrderDetail sod
    WHERE sod.ProductID = p.ProductID
);
```

Another effective technique is query refactoring. Queries can often be rewritten in a more efficient manner. For instance, avoid using functions on columns in WHERE clauses as it can prevent the use of indexes, leading to full table scans.

```
-- Avoiding functions on columns in the WHERE clause
-- Less efficient:
SELECT * FROM Sales.SalesOrderDetail
WHERE YEAR(OrderDate) = 2023;

-- More efficient:
SELECT * FROM Sales.SalesOrderDetail
WHERE OrderDate >= '2023-01-01'
  AND OrderDate < '2024-01-01';
```

Furthermore, utilizing temporary tables and derived tables can reduce the complexity of large queries. Breaking down a complex query into simpler, intermediate steps stored in temporary tables can lead to better performance.

```
-- Using a temporary table
SELECT ProductID, SUM(OrderQty) AS TotalQty
INTO #TempTable
FROM Sales.SalesOrderDetail
GROUP BY ProductID;

SELECT ProductID, TotalQty
FROM #TempTable
WHERE TotalQty > 100;
```

Reviewing and adjusting query hints is another method to improve performance for specific queries. Query hints alter the default behavior of the query optimizer.

```
-- Using a query hint to force a particular join type
SELECT a.ProductID, b.OrderQty
FROM Production.Product AS a
INNER MERGE JOIN Sales.SalesOrderDetail AS b
ON a.ProductID = b.ProductID;
```

Parallelism in SQL Server can optimize performance by using multiple processors for query execution. However, excessive parallelism can lead to resource contention. Configuring the Cost Threshold for Parallelism and Max Degree of Parallelism settings judiciously matches the workload and hardware capabilities.

It's crucial to monitor performance over time using tools like SQL Server Profiler, Extended Events, and Performance Monitor. These diagnostic tools enable the identification of long-running queries and other performance-related issues.

The query performance tuning process involves continuous monitoring, analysis, and adjustment. Regularly reviewing query performance and making necessary adjustments ensures optimal database operations and responsiveness.

```
Output of a well-tuned query:
Query execution successfully completed in 200 milliseconds.
```

Additionally, maintaining and tuning the SQL Server environment by regularly updating statistics, rebuilding indexes, and ensuring adequate hardware resources is indispensable for sustained performance improvements.

5.9 Handling Large Datasets

Handling large datasets efficiently is crucial for maintaining optimal performance and ensuring accurate, timely query results. Several strategies can be employed to address the challenges posed by large datasets, including indexing, partitioning, and utilizing appropriate SQL Server features.

Indexing is a foundational technique that improves the performance of queries by reducing the amount of data SQL Server needs to scan. Clustered indexes define the physical order of data in a table, improving the speed of data retrieval for large datasets. Non-clustered indexes provide a logical ordering independent of the physical storage of the data and can significantly speed up queries involving specific columns.

```
CREATE CLUSTERED INDEX IX_Example ON LargeTable(ColumnA);
```

Partitioning allows large tables and indexes to be divided into smaller, more manageable pieces called partitions. SQL Server can process queries more efficiently by working on smaller sets of data. Partitioning can be based on various criteria, such as range or list values.

```
-- Define a partition function
CREATE PARTITION FUNCTION PartitionFunctionExample(int)
AS RANGE LEFT FOR VALUES (10, 20, 30);

-- Define a partition scheme
CREATE PARTITION SCHEME PartitionSchemeExample
AS PARTITION PartitionFunctionExample ALL TO ([PRIMARY]);

-- Create a partitioned table
CREATE TABLE PartitionedLargeTable
(
    ColumnA int PRIMARY KEY,
    ColumnB varchar(255)
)
ON PartitionSchemeExample(ColumnA);
```

SQL Server provides tools like **BULK INSERT** and **BULKCOLLECT** to handle large volumes of data efficiently. Bulk loading operations bypass the traditional logging mechanisms for each row, which accelerates the data import process.

```
BULK INSERT LargeTable
FROM 'C:\\Data\\LargeFile.csv'
WITH
(
    FIELDTERMINATOR = ',',
    ROWTERMINATOR = '\n',
    FIRSTROW = 2
);
```

Batch Processing helps in dealing with large datasets by breaking down the transactions into smaller, more manageable batches. This method is beneficial for operations like bulk updates or deletes, minimizing the log space usage and the risk of lock contention.

```
DECLARE @BatchSize INT = 1000;

WHILE (1=1)
BEGIN
    DELETE TOP (@BatchSize) FROM LargeTable
    WHERE SomeColumn = 'SomeValue';

    IF @@ROWCOUNT < @BatchSize BREAK;
END;
```

Utilizing **Compression** can reduce the physical storage requirements and potentially improve query performance. SQL Server offers row-level and page-level compression, both of which can be applied to tables and indexes.

```
ALTER TABLE LargeTable
REBUILD PARTITION = ALL
WITH (DATA_COMPRESSION = ROW);
```

Parallel Execution leverages multiple CPU cores to process queries simultaneously, reducing execution time. SQL Server's query optimizer automatically determines when to use parallel execution based on query complexity and available resources.

```
OPTION (MAXDOP 4);
```

Data Archiving entails moving historical data that is infrequently accessed to an archive table or database, reducing the load on the primary database. Data archiving can utilize partitioning schemes or dedicated archive databases.

SQL Server also provides several DMVs (Dynamic Management Views) and functions that can be instrumental in monitoring and tuning query performance for large datasets. Examples include sys.dm_exec_query_stats, sys.dm_exec_sql_text, and sys.dm_exec_query_plan, which provide insights into query execution plans, statistics, and performance metrics.

```
SELECT TOP 10
    qs.sql_handle,
    qs.execution_count,
    qs.total_worker_time,
    qs.total_elapsed_time,
    SUBSTRING(st.text, (qs.statement_start_offset/2) + 1,
        ((CASE statement_end_offset
            WHEN -1 THEN DATALENGTH(st.text)
            ELSE qs.statement_end_offset
        END - qs.statement_start_offset)/2) + 1) AS query_text
FROM sys.dm_exec_query_stats qs
CROSS APPLY sys.dm_exec_sql_text(qs.sql_handle) st
ORDER BY qs.total_worker_time DESC;
```

Efficient **Query Optimization** strategies also play a pivotal role in handling large datasets. Techniques such as avoiding SELECT *, preferring joins over subqueries, and ensuring appropriate indexing can make substantial differences in query performance.

Properly managing large datasets is a multifaceted task that requires a combination of appropriate database design, configuration, and ongoing maintenance. By integrating these strategies, SQL Server can handle large datasets more efficiently and maintain optimal performance.

5.10 Recursive Queries

Recursive queries in SQL are a powerful feature that allows for the hierarchical or recursive processing of data. This technique is particularly useful for querying hierarchical relationships such as organizational structures, bill of materials, or graph structures like network paths. In SQL Server, Common Table Expressions (CTEs) are often employed to implement recursive queries.

A recursive CTE consists of three main components:

- An initial query, known as the anchor member.
- A recursive query, which must reference the CTE itself.
- A termination check to prevent infinite recursion, often achieved with a condition.

To define a recursive CTE, use the WITH clause, followed by the CTE's name and the definition. Let us consider an example of an organizational hierarchy where each employee reports to a manager. A recursive query can be used to list all employees under a specific manager.

```
WITH EmployeeHierarchy AS (
    -- Anchor member
    SELECT
        EmployeeID,
        EmployeeName,
        ManagerID,
        0 AS Level
    FROM Employees
    WHERE ManagerID IS NULL

    UNION ALL

    -- Recursive member
    SELECT
        e.EmployeeID,
        e.EmployeeName,
        e.ManagerID,
        eh.Level + 1 AS Level
    FROM Employees e
    INNER JOIN EmployeeHierarchy eh ON e.ManagerID = eh.EmployeeID
)
SELECT
    EmployeeID,
    EmployeeName,
    ManagerID,
    Level
FROM EmployeeHierarchy;
```

In this example, the EmployeeHierarchy CTE starts with the anchor member, which retrieves the root employees (those without a manager).

The recursive member joins the Employees table with the EmployeeHierarchy CTE on the ManagerID column. The recursion proceeds by incrementally increasing the Level until no more records satisfy the join condition.

```
Output:
EmployeeID | EmployeeName | ManagerID | Level
-----------|--------------|-----------|-------
1          | John Doe     | NULL      | 0
2          | Jane Smith   | 1         | 1
3          | Emily Jones  | 2         | 2
```

Another common use for recursive queries is in processing hierarchical data stored in a graph structure. Consider a table representing a directory structure, where each directory may have multiple subdirectories. A recursive query can traverse the entire directory hierarchy.

```
WITH DirectoryHierarchy AS (
    -- Anchor member
    SELECT
        DirectoryID,
        DirectoryName,
        ParentDirectoryID,
        0 AS Level
    FROM Directories
    WHERE ParentDirectoryID IS NULL

    UNION ALL

    -- Recursive member
    SELECT
        d.DirectoryID,
        d.DirectoryName,
        d.ParentDirectoryID,
        dh.Level + 1 AS Level
    FROM Directories d
    INNER JOIN DirectoryHierarchy dh ON d.ParentDirectoryID = dh.DirectoryID
)
SELECT
    DirectoryID,
    DirectoryName,
    ParentDirectoryID,
    Level
FROM DirectoryHierarchy;
```

This query's recursive logic follows the same principles outlined earlier. The anchor member identifies root directories, and the recursive member joins directories with their parent directories, extending the hierarchy level-by-level.

```
Output:
DirectoryID | DirectoryName | ParentDirectoryID | Level
------------|---------------|-------------------|-------
1           | Root          | NULL              | 0
2           | SubDir1       | 1                 | 1
3           | SubDir2       | 1                 | 1
4           | SubSubDir1    | 2                 | 2
```

When working with recursive CTEs, it is crucial to ensure proper termination of recursion to prevent infinite loops. SQL Server imposes a default recursion limit of 100 levels, but this can be modified using the MAXRECURSION query hint.

```
OPTION (MAXRECURSION 200);
```

This hint specifies the maximum number of recursion levels allowed. If the recursion limit is reached without termination, SQL Server will raise an error.

Recursive queries are versatile and can be applied to various real-world scenarios requiring the traversal of hierarchical data. Their ability to express complex relationships succinctly and efficiently makes them an essential tool in advanced SQL querying.

5.11 Using Temporary Tables and Table Variables

Temporary tables and table variables play a significant role in SQL Server when dealing with intermediate result sets, complex operations, or enhancing the performance of query processing through temporary storage of data. This section elucidates how to use these tools effectively, emphasizing their distinctions, creation, and applicable scenarios.

Temporary tables are similar to regular tables but are stored in the tempdb database. They can be local or global. Local temporary tables are accessible only within the session that created them, whereas global temporary tables are accessible to all sessions.

To create a local temporary table, utilize the following structure:

```
CREATE TABLE #LocalTempTable (
    Column1 INT,
    Column2 NVARCHAR(50),
    Column3 DATETIME
);
```

A global temporary table is defined similarly but with two hash signs:

```
CREATE TABLE ##GlobalTempTable (
    Column1 INT,
    Column2 NVARCHAR(50),
    Column3 DATETIME
);
```

Temporary tables can then be populated and manipulated like regular tables within the scope of their visibility:

```
INSERT INTO #LocalTempTable (Column1, Column2, Column3)
VALUES (1, 'Example', GETDATE());

SELECT * FROM #LocalTempTable;

DROP TABLE #LocalTempTable;
```

Table variables offer an alternative to temporary tables, declared using the DECLARE statement and prefixed with an at sign @. They are stored in memory, making them more efficient for smaller datasets and operations confined to the batch or stored procedure scope.

Here is how to declare and use a table variable:

```
DECLARE @TableVar TABLE (
    Column1 INT,
    Column2 NVARCHAR(50),
    Column3 DATETIME
);

INSERT INTO @TableVar (Column1, Column2, Column3)
VALUES (2, 'Data', GETDATE());

SELECT * FROM @TableVar;
```

Unlike temporary tables, table variables do not require explicit dropping, as they are automatically deallocated at the end of the batch or stored procedure.

When to use temporary tables versus table variables hinges on several factors:

- **Scope:** Temporary tables can persist across batches, whereas table variables are restricted to the scope within which they are declared.
- **Indexes:** You can create indexes on temporary tables but not on table variables directly (except implicitly through primary or unique constraints).
- **Statistics:** Temporary tables maintain statistics necessary for optimizing query plans, while table variables do not, potentially causing suboptimal performance for large datasets.
- **Transaction Logging:** Modifications to temporary tables are logged in the transaction log, potentially impacting performance under heavy writes. Table variables have less logging overhead.

- **Complex Operations:** For complex operations like joins with large datasets, temporary tables often perform better due to their ability to maintain statistics and indexes.

An example scenario illustrating a complex operation using a temporary table is as follows. Assume we have multiple steps in a process requiring intermediate result sets for clarity and separation of operations:

```
CREATE TABLE #EmployeeSales (
    EmployeeID INT,
    TotalSales MONEY
);

INSERT INTO #EmployeeSales (EmployeeID, TotalSales)
SELECT EmployeeID, SUM(SalesAmount)
FROM Sales
GROUP BY EmployeeID;

-- Additional processing on the intermediate results
UPDATE e
SET e.Bonus = es.TotalSales * 0.1
FROM Employees e
INNER JOIN #EmployeeSales es
ON e.EmployeeID = es.EmployeeID;

SELECT * FROM Employees;

DROP TABLE #EmployeeSales;
```

In this example, #EmployeeSales is a temporary table storing aggregated sales data per employee. This intermediate result is later utilized to update the Employees table with calculated bonuses.

When performance or memory footprint is a concern, table variables can be beneficial. For instance:

```
DECLARE @EmployeeSales TABLE (
    EmployeeID INT,
    TotalSales MONEY
);

INSERT INTO @EmployeeSales (EmployeeID, TotalSales)
SELECT EmployeeID, SUM(SalesAmount)
FROM Sales
GROUP BY EmployeeID;

-- Additional processing on the intermediate results
UPDATE e
SET e.Bonus = es.TotalSales * 0.1
FROM Employees e
INNER JOIN @EmployeeSales es
ON e.EmployeeID = es.EmployeeID;

SELECT * FROM Employees;
```

Here, the table variable @EmployeeSales serves the same purpose but without the overhead of explicit management and cleanup. However, this approach may not scale as well with larger datasets due to the lack of indexing and statistics.

Comprehending the nuanced differences between temporary tables and table variables enables a database developer or administrator to make informed decisions, achieving optimal performance and efficient resource utilization within SQL Server environments.

5.12 Error Handling in SQL Queries

In SQL Server, robust error handling mechanisms are crucial for building reliable and maintainable database applications. Error handling ensures that unexpected conditions can be managed gracefully, providing meaningful feedback and maintaining data integrity. This section overviews various methods and best practices for handling errors in SQL queries.

BEGIN...END Blocks and Error Handling

The most basic form of error handling uses the BEGIN...END block to manage the flow of T-SQL statements:

```
BEGIN
    -- Check if the table exists
    IF OBJECT_ID('Sales.OrderDetails', 'U') IS NOT NULL
    BEGIN
        SELECT * FROM Sales.OrderDetails;
    END
    ELSE
    BEGIN
        PRINT 'Table does not exist.';
    END
END
```

This structure allows for conditional checks and executes different blocks of code based on the condition's evaluation.

TRY...CATCH Blocks

The TRY...CATCH construct provides more advanced error handling in SQL Server. It allows embedding error checking directly within T-SQL code, making it possible to capture and handle errors gracefully:

```
BEGIN TRY
    -- Intentionally cause a divide by zero error
    SELECT 1 / 0;
END TRY
BEGIN CATCH
    SELECT
```

```
        ERROR\_NUMBER() AS ErrorNumber,
        ERROR\_MESSAGE() AS ErrorMessage,
        ERROR\_SEVERITY() AS ErrorSeverity,
        ERROR\_STATE() AS ErrorState,
        ERROR\_LINE() AS ErrorLine,
        ERROR\_PROCEDURE() AS ErrorProcedure;
END CATCH;
```

In this example, the BEGIN TRY block contains the code that may cause an error. If an error occurs, the control transfers to the BEGIN CATCH block, where various system functions like ERROR_NUMBER(), ERROR_MESSAGE(), ERROR_SEVERITY(), ERROR_STATE(), ERROR_LINE(), and ERROR_PROCEDURE() provide details about the error. These functions can be used to log errors or return meaningful messages to the application.

Transaction Handling

Handling errors in transaction management is vital to ensure data consistency. The following example demonstrates handling errors within a transaction using TRY...CATCH:

```
BEGIN TRANSACTION;

BEGIN TRY
    -- Insert into Product table
    INSERT INTO Production.Product (Name, ProductNumber, ListPrice)
    VALUES ('Road Bike', 'FB-1234', 1200.00);

    -- Insert into ProductInventory table
    INSERT INTO Production.ProductInventory (ProductID, LocationID, Quantity)
    VALUES (@@IDENTITY, 1, 100);

    -- Commit transaction
    COMMIT TRANSACTION;
END TRY
BEGIN CATCH
    -- Rollback transaction
    ROLLBACK TRANSACTION;

    -- Capture error details
    SELECT
        ERROR\_NUMBER() AS ErrorNumber,
        ERROR\_MESSAGE() AS ErrorMessage;
END CATCH;
```

This ensures that if any statement within the transaction fails, the entire transaction is rolled back, preserving data integrity. Any errors encountered are captured and can be logged or handled appropriately.

RAISEERROR Statement

The RAISEERROR statement allows you to generate custom error messages. This is useful for raising specific errors when certain database constraints are violated:

```
IF (SELECT COUNT(*) FROM Production.Product WHERE ListPrice < 0) > 0
BEGIN
    RAISERROR('Product list price cannot be negative.', 16, 1);
END
```

The RAISEERROR statement specifies the message text, severity level (16 indicates a user-defined error), and the state (a value from 0 to 255 used to identify the location in the code where the error occurred).

THROW Statement

SQL Server 2012 introduced the THROW statement, which provides a simpler syntax for raising errors. Unlike RAISEERROR, THROW allows re-throwing the original error details with its syntax:

```
BEGIN TRY
    -- Some code that can cause an error
    SELECT 1 / 0;
END TRY
BEGIN CATCH
    THROW;
END CATCH;
```

If THROW is issued without parameters within a CATCH block, it re-throws the original error information, simplifying error handling logic.

Implementing Error Logging

In practice, error details should be logged for further analysis. A dedicated error logging table can store error information:

```
CREATE TABLE ErrorLog
(
    ErrorLogID INT IDENTITY(1,1) PRIMARY KEY,
    ErrorDateTime DATETIME DEFAULT(GETDATE()),
    UserName NVARCHAR(128),
    ErrorMessage NVARCHAR(4000),
    ErrorSeverity INT,
    ErrorState INT,
    ErrorLine INT,
    ErrorProcedure NVARCHAR(128)
);
```

Then, within the CATCH block, insert the captured error details into this table:

```
BEGIN CATCH
    INSERT INTO ErrorLog (UserName, ErrorMessage, ErrorSeverity, ErrorState,
          ErrorLine, ErrorProcedure)
    VALUES (SUSER\_NAME(), ERROR\_MESSAGE(), ERROR\_SEVERITY(),
          ERROR\_STATE(), ERROR\_LINE(), ERROR\_PROCEDURE());

    -- Re-throw the error
    THROW;
```

```
END CATCH;
```

Logging errors in this manner provides a persistent record of issues, facilitating diagnostic processes and improving the overall reliability of the system.

Maintaining well-structured, efficient error handling routines in your SQL Server applications helps prevent unexpected failures, enhances the user experience, and simplifies debugging processes. Implementing a combination of TRY...CATCH blocks, meaningful error messages via RAISEERROR or THROW, and comprehensive error logging ensures that your database application can handle and recover from unexpected scenarios effectively.

Chapter 6

Understanding and Using Indexes

This chapter provides a comprehensive overview of indexes in SQL Server, explaining their types and how to create them. It distinguishes between clustered and non-clustered indexes, and covers composite, unique, filtered, and columnstore indexes. The chapter also discusses index maintenance and rebuilding, performance considerations, and best practices for indexing to optimize database performance.

6.1 Introduction to Indexes

Indexes in SQL Server are special data structures that improve the speed of data retrieval operations on a database table, at the cost of additional writes and storage space to maintain them. Just as an index in a book helps you quickly locate the information you seek, an index in a database allows SQL Server to find data more efficiently. Understanding how indexes work and how they can be used effectively is crucial for optimizing database performance.

At its core, an index is a copy of selected columns of data from a table, designed to enable rapid search and random lookups. This copy is sorted in a specific order to allow for quick location of data. Hence, the presence of an index can significantly reduce the need for a full table scan. For example, without an index, searching for a particular record in a table requires scanning all rows in the table, which is inefficient, especially for large tables. An index allows SQL Server to quickly locate the necessary rows.

Indexes are implemented through a system of B-trees in SQL Server, where B-tree stands for Balanced Tree. In this data structure, there is a root node, intermediate nodes, and leaf nodes. The root node is the top level of the hierarchy, followed by intermediate nodes that connect the root to the leaf nodes, which contain the actual pointer to the data rows in the table. This hierarchical structure ensures that the database engine can traverse the tree from the root to the leaf in a relatively short number of steps, typically logging the number of entries.

Let's consider a simple example to illustrate the concept of an index. Suppose you have the following table Employees with the columns EmployeeID, FirstName, and LastName.

```
CREATE TABLE Employees (
    EmployeeID INT PRIMARY KEY,
    FirstName NVARCHAR(50),
    LastName NVARCHAR(50)
);
```

If you frequently query this table to find employees by their LastName, you might create an index on that column to speed up the lookup process.

```
CREATE INDEX idx_LastName ON Employees (LastName);
```

With the index idx_LastName, when you execute a query to find an employee by last name, SQL Server can use the index to locate the position of relevant rows much faster than scanning each row of the table.

```
SELECT * FROM Employees WHERE LastName = 'Doe';
```

Internally, SQL Server uses the index idx_LastName to quickly identify all rows where LastName is 'Doe'.

In addition to facilitating rapid searches, indexes also support efficient sorting and grouping operations. For example, the clause ORDER BY in your SQL queries can take advantage of indexes to sort query results swiftly. Similarly, the GROUP BY clause can perform grouping operations more rapidly if an appropriate index exists.

Indexing is not without its drawbacks. It is important to understand the trade-offs involved in using indexes. Creating and maintaining indexes incurs overhead. Every time a table is modified with INSERT, UPDATE, or DELETE operations, the indexes on that table must be kept in sync with the underlying data. This maintenance can introduce performance penalties, especially for write-heavy workloads. Additionally, indexes consume disk space. For large tables with many indexes, the storage requirement can become significant.

Here are some key points to consider:

- **Selectivity**: High selectivity means that the indexed column has many unique values. High selectivity indexes are typically more efficient because they allow SQL Server to narrow down the number of rows quickly. Columns with low selectivity (many repeated values) may not benefit as much from indexing.
- **Index Density**: This refers to how densely the index pages are packed with data. Less dense pages can mean quicker access but require more storage.
- **Covered Queries**: A covered query is a query where all requested columns are included in the index itself, allowing SQL Server to retrieve the queried data from the index pages without accessing the table data pages.

Understanding the workload and query patterns is crucial in deciding which indexes to create for a specific database. The balance between read and write performance must be carefully managed. Indexes that benefit read-intensive scenarios may negatively impact write-heavy operations due to the additional maintenance overhead.

By judiciously creating and maintaining indexes, the overall performance of SQL Server databases can be significantly enhanced. Proper index design is a fundamental aspect of database optimization and requires careful consideration of the specific needs and characteristics of the applications and workloads involved.

6.2 Types of Indexes

Indexes in SQL Server are essential for improving the speed and efficiency of query execution. An index can be thought of as a data structure that improves the retrieval speed of rows from a table. Different types of indexes cater to various use cases and data query patterns.

Understanding the various types of indexes offered by SQL Server is crucial for implementing effective database optimization strategies.

Clustered Indexes: A clustered index sorts and stores the data rows in the table or view based on the index key. There can be only one clustered index per table because the data rows themselves are stored in this sorted order. When a clustered index is created on a table, the data rows are rearranged to match the index order. The leaf level of a clustered index consists of the actual data pages of the table.

```
-- Creating a clustered index on the \texttt{CustomerID} column in the \texttt{
    Customers} table
CREATE CLUSTERED INDEX IDX\_Customers\_CustomerID
ON Customers (CustomerID);
```

Non-Clustered Indexes: In contrast, a non-clustered index creates a separate structure from the data rows, providing a logical ordering based on the index key. The leaf level of a non-clustered index contains pointers to the data rows that contain the index key. These pointers can be row locators or cluster keys, depending on whether the underlying table has a clustered index.

```
-- Creating a non-clustered index on the \texttt{LastName} column in the \texttt{
    Employees} table
CREATE NONCLUSTERED INDEX IDX\_Employees\_LastName
ON Employees (LastName);
```

Unique Indexes: Unique indexes ensure the uniqueness of the values in one or more columns. Unlike primary keys, which automatically create a unique clustered index, unique indexes can be applied to any column or combination of columns. This is crucial for maintaining data integrity by preventing duplicate values.

```
-- Creating a unique index on the \texttt{EmailAddress} column in the \texttt{Users}
    table
CREATE UNIQUE INDEX IDX\_Users\_EmailAddress
ON Users (EmailAddress);
```

Composite Indexes: Composite indexes contain multiple columns used as the index key. These indexes are particularly useful when queries filter or sort by multiple columns. Proper ordering of columns in a composite index can significantly impact query performance.

```
-- Creating a composite index on the \texttt{FirstName} and \texttt{LastName}
    columns in the \texttt{Contacts} table
CREATE INDEX IDX\_Contacts\_FullName
ON Contacts (FirstName, LastName);
```

Filtered Indexes: A filtered index is an optimized non-clustered index, especially useful for queries that operate on a well-defined subset of data. By indexing only a portion of the data, filtered indexes provide improved performance and reduced storage costs.

```
-- Creating a filtered index for active users in the \texttt{Users} table
CREATE NONCLUSTERED INDEX IDX\_Users\_Filtered\_Active
ON Users (LastName)
WHERE IsActive = 1;
```

Columnstore Indexes: Columnstore indexes are designed for high-performance analysis of large data sets, leveraging column-based storage and query processing. These indexes enable efficient query execution and data compression, making them suitable for OLAP (Online Analytical Processing) workloads. Columnstore indexes can be both clustered and non-clustered.

```
-- Creating a clustered columnstore index on the \texttt{Sales} table
CREATE CLUSTERED COLUMNSTORE INDEX IDX\_Sales\_Columnstore
ON Sales;
```

Understanding the specific use cases and characteristics of these varied types of indexes allows for the effective design and optimization of SQL Server databases. Each type of index provides unique benefits that can be leveraged according to the specific requirements of the queries and applications accessing the database. The careful selection and management of indexes thus play a critical role in enhancing the overall performance and efficiency of SQL Server environments.

6.3 Creating Indexes

Indexes are essential for optimizing the performance of SQL Server queries by allowing faster data retrieval. In this section, we will discuss how to create indexes using Transact-SQL (T-SQL) and SQL Server Management Studio (SSMS). We will also explore various options that can be specified during index creation to fine-tune their performance.

Creating an index using T-SQL involves the CREATE INDEX statement. The basic syntax for creating a non-clustered index is as follows:

```
CREATE INDEX index_name
ON table_name (column1 [ASC|DESC], column2 [ASC|DESC], ...);
```

To understand this better, let's create a sample table and then add an index to it.

```
CREATE TABLE Employees (
```

```
    EmployeeID INT PRIMARY KEY,
    FirstName NVARCHAR(50),
    LastName NVARCHAR(50),
    DepartmentID INT,
    HireDate DATE
);
```

Suppose we frequently query the Employees table based on the LastName. To speed up these queries, we can create an index on the LastName column:

```
CREATE INDEX idx_lastname
ON Employees (LastName);
```

The above command creates a non-clustered index named idx_lastname on the LastName column. By default, the index is created in ascending order.

In scenarios where the query involves multiple columns, a composite index can be more effective. A composite index includes multiple columns from the same table, which can significantly speed up queries that filter or sort on these columns. For instance, if our queries often involve both LastName and FirstName, we can create an index on both columns:

```
CREATE INDEX idx_name
ON Employees (LastName, FirstName);
```

This composite index will be particularly useful for queries filtering or sorting on both LastName and FirstName.

We can further customize the index by specifying additional options. For example, you can control the sort order of the index:

```
CREATE INDEX idx_name_desc
ON Employees (LastName DESC, FirstName ASC);
```

This command creates an index where LastName is sorted in descending order and FirstName in ascending order.

Indexes can also be created with the INCLUDE option, which allows you to add columns to the leaf-level of the index. These columns are not part of the index key but are included in the structure to improve the performance of certain queries. Consider the following example:

```
CREATE INDEX idx_hiredate
ON Employees (HireDate)
INCLUDE (FirstName, LastName);
```

Here, the index is on the HireDate column, but FirstName and Last-

Name are included in the index without being indexed themselves. This is beneficial for queries that retrieve FirstName and LastName columns along with filtering or sorting by HireDate.

SQL Server Management Studio (SSMS) provides a graphical interface to create indexes, which can be helpful for those who prefer not to write T-SQL code manually. To create an index using SSMS:

- Right-click on the table in Object Explorer.
- Select Indexes and then New Index.
- Choose the type of index you want to create.
- Fill in the necessary details such as the index name and the columns to be included in the index.
- Configure additional options such as included columns or sort order.
- Click OK to create the index.

Finally, to view the index information, you can query the sys.indexes catalog view:

```
SELECT
    name AS IndexName,
    type_desc AS IndexType,
    is_unique,
    fill_factor
FROM sys.indexes
WHERE object_id = OBJECT_ID('Employees');
```

The result provides details about the indexes on the Employees table, including the index name, type, uniqueness, and fill factor.

```
IndexName     | IndexType            | is_unique | fill_factor
--------------------------------------------------------------
PK_Employees | CLUSTERED INDEX      | 1         | 0
idx_lastname | NONCLUSTERED INDEX  | 0         | 0
idx_name      | NONCLUSTERED INDEX  | 0         | 0
idx_hiredate | NONCLUSTERED INDEX  | 0         | 0
```

Creating indexes proficiently is crucial for enhancing SQL Server's performance. Understanding the syntax and options available allows you to fine-tune indexes to meet specific application requirements, paving the way for optimized query performance and efficient data management.

6.4 Clustered vs. Non-Clustered Indexes

In SQL Server, indexes are critical for efficient query performance. The two primary types of indexes are clustered and non-clustered indexes. Understanding their differences and appropriate usage is essential for optimizing database performance.

A **clustered index** determines the physical order of the data in a table. When a clustered index is created on a column, SQL Server rearranges the rows in the table to match the index order. Each table can have only one clustered index because the data rows themselves can be sorted in only one way. The clustered index key is stored with the data, meaning the leaf nodes of a clustered index contain the actual data pages.

The following code demonstrates how to create a clustered index:

```
CREATE CLUSTERED INDEX idx\_Employee\_ID
ON Employees(EmployeeID);
```

In this example, we create a clustered index named idx_Employee_ID on the EmployeeID column of the Employees table.

A **non-clustered index**, on the other hand, does not alter the physical order of the data within the table. Instead, it creates a separate object within the table that points to the data rows. Each table can have multiple non-clustered indexes, and they are used to improve the performance of queries that do not require the physical ordering of rows.

The following code demonstrates how to create a non-clustered index:

```
CREATE NONCLUSTERED INDEX idx\_Employee\_LastName
ON Employees(LastName);
```

In this example, we create a non-clustered index named idx_Employee_LastName on the LastName column of the Employees table.

A key difference between clustered and non-clustered indexes is how they handle lookups. Since a clustered index contains the actual data rows in its leaf nodes, it provides faster retrieval for queries that benefit from ordering based on the indexed column. Non-clustered indexes, however, contain pointers to the data rows, which means additional steps are required to retrieve the actual data. This can introduce slight overhead, particularly with large datasets or complex queries.

For example, consider a query to fetch an employee's details by their EmployeeID:

```
SELECT * FROM Employees
```

```
WHERE EmployeeID = 102;
```

If EmployeeID has a clustered index, the query optimizer will directly access the required rows due to their physical arrangement. Conversely, if using a non-clustered index, an intermediate step retrieves row pointers, followed by fetching the actual data rows.

Additionally, non-clustered indexes can include one or more **included columns**, which store copies of these columns in the leaf nodes of the index to enhance query performance. This can reduce the need for additional lookups.

An example of a non-clustered index with included columns is shown below:

```
CREATE NONCLUSTERED INDEX idx\_Employee\_LastName
ON Employees(LastName)
INCLUDE (FirstName, HireDate);
```

Here, the LastName field is used for the primary index key, and FirstName and HireDate are included in the index to optimize specific query operations.

When deciding between clustered and non-clustered indexes, consider the following performance implications:

- **Selectivity**: Clustered indexes are best suited for high-selective queries where the indexed column returns a small percentage of rows.
- **Insert/Update Operations**: Clustered indexes can introduce overhead for INSERT and UPDATE operations as the physical order of data may need rearranging. Non-clustered indexes, however, typically result in less intensive maintenance.
- **Sorting Requirements**: Queries that require sorted results can benefit significantly from clustered indexes as no additional sorting step is required.
- **Index Key Size**: Since non-clustered indexes store pointers, key size has less impact compared to clustered indexes, where key size can influence the data structure's organization and efficiency.

Understanding these factors and effectively leveraging both clustered and non-clustered indexes enables efficient database design and improved query performance.

6.5 Composite Indexes

Composite indexes, also referred to as multi-column indexes, are a fundamental feature in SQL Server that allow database administrators and developers to create indexes on multiple columns within a table. This capability can significantly enhance query performance, especially for queries that filter or sort by multiple columns concurrently.

A composite index consists of a unique identifier that is derived from the values of more than one column. When SQL Server processes queries, it uses these combined values to quickly locate rows, thus allowing for faster retrieval times compared to single-column indexes in certain scenarios. The effectiveness of composite indexes largely depends on how well they match the patterns of queries executed against the database.

Creating Composite Indexes

Creating a composite index in SQL Server is straightforward. The CREATE INDEX statement is used, specifying the columns to be included in the index. An example syntax to create a composite index on columns FirstName and LastName in a Customers table is shown below:

```
CREATE INDEX IX_Customers_FirstName_LastName
ON Customers (FirstName, LastName);
```

In this query, the notation IX_Customers_FirstName_LastName designates the index name, and the FirstName and LastName columns are the fields upon which the index is built. The order of columns listed in the composite index definition holds significance; SQL Server prioritizes the leading column first during query optimization.

Index Usage and Query Performance

Composite indexes are beneficial for queries that use the specified columns in their search conditions, join conditions, or ordering criteria. Consider the following query:

```
SELECT *
FROM Customers
WHERE FirstName = 'John' AND LastName = 'Doe';
```

SQL Server can efficiently use the IX_Customers_FirstName_LastName composite index to locate rows where FirstName = 'John' and LastName = 'Doe', thereby minimizing the number of row accesses needed.

Furthermore, if a query only references the leading column of the composite index, the index remains partially useful:

```
SELECT *
FROM Customers
WHERE FirstName = 'John';
```

In this scenario, the composite index is still beneficial as it narrows the search candidates based on FirstName, though it won't yield the same level of efficiency as querying both indexed columns.

Best Practices for Composite Indexes

Several best practices should be considered when working with composite indexes to maximize their utility and minimize potential drawbacks:

- **Column Order:** Always place the most selective column first if possible, followed by lesser selective columns. Selectivity refers to the uniqueness of the column's data; a highly selective column is one with high cardinality (many unique values).
- **Index Usage:** Ensure that queries frequently access the leading column of the composite index to leverage optimum performance benefits.
- **Index Consolidation:** Avoid creating multiple indexes with overlapping columns, which can lead to unnecessary duplication and increased maintenance overhead.
- **Included Columns:** Use included columns to cover more queries without expanding the composite key size. This approach can sometimes mitigate the need for additional composite indexes.

Consider the performance impact of composite indexes on data modification operations such as inserts, updates, and deletes. Each modification affecting indexed columns requires maintaining the index structure. For example:

```
INSERT INTO Customers (FirstName, LastName, Age)
VALUES ('John', 'Doe', 30);
```

In this case, the new row insertion necessitates adjustments to the IX_Customers_FirstName_LastName composite index, which can introduce additional computational overhead and potentially reduce the throughput of insert operations.

Query Execution Plans

Analyzing the execution plan of queries is essential for understanding the utilization of composite indexes. Execution plans provide insights into the index's contribution to query performance. SQL Server Management Studio (SSMS) can present an execution plan using the graphical interface or by running the following command:

```
SET SHOWPLAN_TEXT ON;
GO
SELECT *
FROM Customers
WHERE FirstName = 'John' AND LastName = 'Doe';
GO
SET SHOWPLAN_TEXT OFF;
```

This command generates a text representation of the execution plan, highlighting the index seek operations carried out by the composite index. Observing whether the index is being effectively used can guide further tuning decisions or adjustments to the index definition.

Composite indexes are a powerful tool in SQL Server for optimizing query performance, particularly in complex querying scenarios involving multiple columns. Properly defined and judiciously applied, composite indexes can greatly reduce query response times and contribute to overall database efficiency.

6.6 Unique Indexes

A unique index enforces the uniqueness of the values in one or more columns. This type of index ensures that any two rows in the indexed table cannot have the same value for the specified columns. Unique indexes are particularly useful for columns that must contain distinct values, such as primary keys (although primary keys themselves implicitly create unique indexes) and other fields that require distinct entries.

In SQL Server, creating a unique index involves specifying the UNIQUE keyword. Below is an example of how to create a unique index using Transact-SQL:

```
CREATE UNIQUE INDEX idx_Unique_Email
ON Users(Email);
```

In this example, we created a unique index idx_Unique_Email on the Email column of the Users table. This ensures that no two users can have the same email address in the table. If an insert or update operation attempts to insert a duplicate value into the Email column, SQL Server will reject the operation and return an error.

Additionally, unique indexes can be created on multiple columns, making them composite unique indexes. Below is an example illustrating this concept:

```
CREATE UNIQUE INDEX idx_Unique_FullName
ON Employees(FirstName, LastName);
```

In this example, the unique index idx_Unique_FullName on the Employees table ensures that no two employees can have the same combination of first and last names. As with single-column unique indexes, attempts to insert duplicate combinations will result in an error.

Unique indexes play a key role in data integrity by enforcing constraints at the database level. The maintenance of such indexes is internally handled by SQL Server, ensuring that the database remains in a consistent state.

To manage unique indexes effectively, consider the following best practices:

- **Minimal Columns:** Only include the columns necessary to enforce uniqueness. Including redundant columns can lead to unnecessary complexity and performance overhead.
- **Balanced Usage:** Ensure that unique indexes are used judiciously. Overuse can lead to performance degradation during insert and update operations due to increased index maintenance.
- **Proper Naming Conventions:** Use clear and descriptive names for unique indexes to make database schema easier to understand and maintain.

Overhead consideration is important while implementing unique indexes. Although they ensure data integrity, they can introduce performance impacts, including slower insert and update operations. This is due to the need to maintain the unique constraint, performing checks against existing index values before allowing data modifications.

Here is a typical workflow demonstrating the impact of a unique index during an insert operation:

```
-- Assuming a table with a unique index on \texttt{Email}
INSERT INTO Users (UserID, Email, Name)
VALUES (1, 'john.doe@example.com', 'John Doe');
```

If the above operation is executed with a Users table having a unique index on the Email column, SQL Server will first check the idx_Unique_Email index for any occurrence of 'john.doe@example.com'. If a match is found, the operation will fail with an error message:

```
Msg 2627, Level 14, State 1, Line 1
Violation of UNIQUE KEY constraint 'idx_Unique_Email'.
Cannot insert duplicate key in object 'dbo.Users'.
The duplicate key value is (john.doe@example.com).
```

Thus, unique indexes ensure data integrity by preventing duplicate values but at the cost of additional computational checks.

Understanding the mechanics and implications of unique indexes allows database administrators and developers to design more robust and reliable database schemas while managing performance and integrity constraints appropriately.

6.7 Filtered Indexes

Filtered indexes provide a mechanism to improve query performance and reduce index maintenance by indexing a subset of rows in a table. A filtered index uses a filter predicate to index only the rows that meet a specified condition, as opposed to a full-table index that includes all rows. This type of index is particularly useful in scenarios where a large table contains subsets of data that are frequently queried.

Consider the scenario where a table contains a column with many NULL values, but often queries exclude these NULLs. By creating a filtered index on the non-NULL rows, SQL Server can improve query performance because the index is smaller and more efficient to navigate.

Filtered indexes are defined using the WHERE clause to specify the filter condition. The syntax for creating a filtered index is as follows:

```
CREATE INDEX index_name
ON table_name (column_name1, column_name2, ...)
WHERE <filter\_condition>;
```

For example, assume there is a table named Orders with columns OrderID, CustomerID, OrderDate, and IsShipped. To create a filtered index that only includes orders that have been shipped, you could use the following SQL command:

```
CREATE INDEX IX\_Orders\_IsShipped
ON Orders (OrderID, OrderDate)
```

```
WHERE IsShipped = 1;
```

In this example, the filtered index IX_Orders_IsShipped is created on the OrderID and OrderDate columns for rows where IsShipped equals 1. This index facilitates faster query performance for retrieving shipped orders without scanning the entire Orders table.

Filtered indexes have several benefits:

- **Improved Performance**: By indexing only a subset of the rows, filtered indexes reduce the size of the index and the amount of I/O required to access the desired rows. This is particularly effective for queries that frequently target a small percentage of rows.
- **Reduced Storage Costs**: Since the index only includes a subset of the table's rows, the storage space required is less than that of a full-table index. This can lead to significant storage savings, especially for large tables.
- **Faster Index Maintenance**: Smaller indexes require less time and resources to maintain. Operations such as rebuilding or reorganizing indexes will be faster for filtered indexes compared to full-table indexes.

To illustrate the practical use of a filtered index, consider the following query, which seeks all orders placed by a particular customer that have been shipped:

```
SELECT OrderID, OrderDate
FROM Orders
WHERE CustomerID = 12345 AND IsShipped = 1;
```

With the filtered index IX_Orders_IsShipped, SQL Server can efficiently retrieve the relevant rows without scanning the entire table. The query optimizer can use the filtered index to quickly locate orders where IsShipped equals 1, and further filter by CustomerID.

Filtered indexes can also be combined with other types of indexes, such as unique or composite indexes. For instance:

```
CREATE UNIQUE INDEX IX\_Unique\_Orders
ON Orders (OrderID)
WHERE IsShipped = 1;
```

This example creates a unique filtered index on the OrderID column for shipped orders, ensuring that each OrderID is unique within the subset of shipped orders.

It is important to consider the appropriate use cases for filtered indexes. Scenarios where filtered indexes show significant performance gains include:

- Tables with large numbers of NULL values where queries frequently exclude these NULLs.
- Columns with highly selective predicates (e.g., a Status column with a value indicating a specific state).
- Filtering on frequently queried date ranges or numerical ranges.
- Indexing active versus inactive records (e.g., active orders, active users).

When creating filtered indexes, be mindful of their limitations and behaviors:

- **Statistics and Optimization**: Filtered indexes are built with statistics based only on the rows included in the index. This can sometimes influence how the query optimizer chooses to utilize the index.
- **Maintenance Considerations**: While filtered indexes reduce maintenance overhead, they still need to be maintained and aligned with data modification patterns.
- **Predicate Preciseness**: The filter predicate must precisely match the query conditions for the query optimizer to effectively use the filtered index.

Properly leveraging filtered indexes can bring substantial performance improvements and efficiencies, enhancing the overall effectiveness of SQL Server indexing strategies.

6.8 Columnstore Indexes

Columnstore indexes are a powerful feature introduced in SQL Server to optimize the performance of data warehousing queries. Unlike traditional rowstore indexes that store data row-by-row, columnstore indexes store data column-by-column. This storage mechanism enables significant data compression and increased query performance, especially for analytical queries that often involve large scans of the same columns.

Columnstore indexes are particularly effective for read-heavy workloads where the primary objective is to quickly retrieve and analyze large datasets. They are designed to work well with SQL Server's batch processing modes, which further enhance query performance by processing entire batches of rows at once.

Storage Format and Mechanism

Columnstore indexes leverage a columnar storage format that offers several advantages. Each column is stored independently of other columns, and data within each column is stored in a highly compressed format. This columnar storage approach aligns well with the needs of analytical queries, allowing for reduced I/O and improved cache efficiency.

The internal storage is divided into segments, each of which contains a large number of column values. Each segment is further divided into smaller units called rows groups, typically containing around one million rows. This organization allows SQL Server to perform optimal compression and efficient execution of queries.

Benefits of Columnstore Indexes

- **Compression:** Due to the high level of redundancy within columns, columnstore indexes achieve compression rates significantly higher than rowstore indexes. This compression reduces the storage footprint and improves query performance by reducing the amount of data that needs to be read from disk.

- **Query Performance:** Analytical queries often involve aggregations and scans across several columns. By storing each column separately, columnstore indexes allow queries to read only the relevant columns, reducing the amount of data transferred and processed. Batch processing mode further enhances performance by allowing SQL Server to process data in larger, more efficient chunks.

- **Storage Savings:** The high compression ratios offered by columnstore indexes translate to storage savings. This reduction in storage also means lower costs for storage infrastructure and less physical I/O.

Creating and Managing Columnstore Indexes

Columnstore indexes can be created as either clustered or non-clustered. A clustered columnstore index physically reorganizes the data in the table into the columnar format. This is particularly useful for large fact tables in a data warehousing context. A non-clustered columnstore index, on the other hand, leaves the underlying table organization intact and stores a separate columnar index.

To create a clustered columnstore index, you can use the following SQL command:

```
CREATE CLUSTERED COLUMNSTORE INDEX CCI\_Sales
ON SalesTable;
```

Non-clustered columnstore indexes can be created using:

```
CREATE NONCLUSTERED COLUMNSTORE INDEX NCCI\_Sales
ON SalesTable (Column1, Column2, Column3);
```

Updating Data in Columnstore Indexes

While columnstore indexes offer numerous benefits for read-heavy analytical workloads, it is important to consider their impact on write operations. Columnstore indexes are optimized for bulk insert and update operations, but individual row insertions or updates can be less efficient due to the need to reorganize data within the columnar format.

SQL Server uses a mechanism called the delta store to handle small, frequent updates efficiently. The delta store is a rowstore-based structure that temporarily holds new and updated rows before they are eventually migrated to the main columnstore format during an operation known as a tuple mover. This approach ensures that columnstore indexes can handle both heavy read and moderate write workloads effectively.

Hybrid Transactional and Analytical Processing (HTAP)

Columnstore indexes enable Hybrid Transactional and Analytical Processing (HTAP) by allowing transactional (OLTP) and analytical (OLAP) queries to coexist efficiently within the same database environment. With the introduction of updateable non-clustered columnstore indexes, SQL Server allows tables to support fast transactional processing while also providing efficient analytical query performance.

Performance Tuning and Best Practices

- **Batch Mode Processing:** Ensure that queries are optimized to leverage batch mode processing by avoiding functions and operators that force query execution to revert to row mode.

- **Appropriate Data Types:** Use appropriate data types for columns to maximize compression and performance. Smaller and fixed-length data types typically compress better and lead to more efficient queries.
- **Minimizing Updates:** Given the high cost of updates in columnar storage, design the database schema and application logic to minimize the frequency of individual row updates. Batch updates or inserts are more efficient.
- **Index Maintenance:** Regularly monitor and maintain columnstore indexes by reorganizing or rebuilding them as necessary to ensure that they continue to perform optimally.

Columnstore indexes are a transformative feature in SQL Server that provide substantial benefits for analytical workloads. They enable high compression rates, efficient data processing, and support for HTAP scenarios, making them an essential tool for modern data warehousing and analytics.

6.9 Index Maintenance and Rebuilding

The ongoing performance of a SQL Server database significantly depends on meticulous maintenance and periodic rebuilding of indexes. As data within a database is constantly inserted, updated, and deleted, indexes can become fragmented and inefficient over time. This section delves into the methods and strategies for maintaining and rebuilding indexes, ensuring sustained database performance and optimized query execution.

Index fragmentation occurs when the logical order of pages in an index does not match the physical order in the data files. Fragmentation is generally of two types: internal fragmentation and external fragmentation. Internal fragmentation refers to wasted space within pages, whereas external fragmentation is the mismatch between the logical and physical order of the pages. Both types require attention to maintain efficient index performance.

SQL Server provides several tools and commands to detect, analyze, and rectify index fragmentation. The primary tools for index maintenance are the sys.dm_db_index_physical_stats system function and the ALTER INDEX statement. The sys.dm_db_index_physical_stats function can be used to obtain fragmentation information for indexes across the database, while the ALTER INDEX statement facilitates the reorganization or rebuilding of indexes to address fragmentation.

To detect index fragmentation, the following SQL script can be utilized to query the sys.dm_db_index_physical_stats function:

```
SELECT
    dbschemas.[name] as 'Schema',
    dbtables.[name] as 'Table',
    dbindexes.[name] as 'Index',
    indexstats.alloc_unit_type_desc,
    indexstats.avg_fragmentation_in_percent,
    indexstats.page_count
FROM
    sys.dm_db_index_physical_stats(DB_ID(), NULL, NULL, NULL, 'DETAILED')
        AS indexstats
    INNER JOIN sys.tables AS dbtables
        ON indexstats.object_id = dbtables.object_id
    INNER JOIN sys.schemas AS dbschemas
        ON dbtables.schema_id = dbschemas.schema_id
    INNER JOIN sys.indexes AS dbindexes
        ON indexstats.object_id = dbindexes.object_id
        AND indexstats.index_id = dbindexes.index_id
WHERE
    indexstats.database_id = DB_ID()
ORDER BY
    dbschemas.[name], dbtables.[name], dbindexes.[name];
```

The results of this query provide valuable insights into the extent of fragmentation for each index. The avg_fragmentation_in_percent column is particularly critical, highlighting the average fragmentation percentage. It is generally recommended to reorganize an index if the fragmentation is between 5% and 30%, and to rebuild it if the fragmentation exceeds 30%.

The ALTER INDEX statement supports both REORGANIZE and REBUILD operations. The REORGANIZE operation is less intensive and suitable for moderate fragmentation. It defragments the leaf level of the index by physically reordering the pages. The command for reorganizing an index is shown below:

```
ALTER INDEX [IndexName] ON [TableName]
REORGANIZE;
```

For severe fragmentation, a complete rebuild of the index is recommended. The REBUILD operation creates a new index from scratch, removing all fragmentation. This process is more resource-intensive but yields a highly optimized index. The command for rebuilding an index is as follows:

```
ALTER INDEX [IndexName] ON [TableName]
REBUILD;
```

It is often beneficial to automate index maintenance through scheduled tasks. SQL Server Agent can be leveraged to create jobs that periodically execute scripts to check for fragmentation and perform necessary reorganizations or rebuilds. A sample script for automated index maintenance might include logic to decide whether to reorganize or rebuild based on fragmentation thresholds. An example follows:

```
DECLARE @objectid INT;
DECLARE @indexid INT;
DECLARE @partitioncount BIGINT;
DECLARE @schemaname NVARCHAR(128);
DECLARE @tablename NVARCHAR(128);
DECLARE @indexname NVARCHAR(128);
DECLARE @avg_fragmentation_in_percent FLOAT;

DECLARE @sql NVARCHAR(MAX);

-- Cursor to loop through each index
DECLARE index_cursor CURSOR FOR
SELECT
    stats.database_id, object_id, index_id,
    partition_number, avg_fragmentation_in_percent
FROM sys.dm_db_index_physical_stats (DB_ID(), NULL, NULL , NULL, '
      SAMPLED') stats
 WHERE avg_fragmentation_in_percent > 5;

OPEN index_cursor;
FETCH NEXT FROM index_cursor INTO @objectid, @indexid, @partitioncount,
   @avg_fragmentation_in_percent;

WHILE @@FETCH_STATUS = 0
BEGIN
    SELECT @schemaname = OBJECT_SCHEMA_NAME(@objectid),
           @tablename = OBJECT_NAME(@objectid),
           @indexname = i.name
    FROM sys.indexes AS i WHERE i.object_id = @objectid AND i.index_id =
          @indexid;

    IF @avg_fragmentation_in_percent > 30
        SET @sql = 'ALTER INDEX [' + @indexname + '] ON [' + @schemaname + '
              ].[' + @tablename + '] REBUILD;';
    ELSE
        SET @sql = 'ALTER INDEX [' + @indexname + '] ON [' + @schemaname + '
              ].[' + @tablename + '] REORGANIZE;';

    EXEC sp_executesql @sql;

    FETCH NEXT FROM index_cursor INTO @objectid, @indexid, @partitioncount,
          @avg_fragmentation_in_percent;
END;
CLOSE index_cursor;
DEALLOCATE index_cursor;
```

In addition to organizing and rebuilding indexes, it is crucial to update statistics regularly to ensure that the query optimizer has accurate information. Statistics provide a histogram of column values, helping the optimizer determine the most efficient execution plan. Statistics can be updated using the following command:

```
UPDATE STATISTICS [TableName] [IndexName] WITH FULLSCAN;
```

Combining index maintenance with regular updates to statistics helps in preserving optimal query performance. Best practices also dictate that index maintenance operations be scheduled during maintenance windows or periods of low activity to minimize the impact on regular database operations.

Effective index maintenance and rebuilding form a cornerstone of database performance optimization, ensuring indexes continue to function efficiently as the underlying data evolves. Properly maintained indexes contribute significantly to faster query execution times and overall system responsiveness.

6.10 Performance Considerations with Indexes

Performance optimization in SQL Server using indexes is not simply a matter of creating as many indexes as possible. A deep understanding of how indexes affect query performance and system resources is crucial. Here, we explore the various factors and considerations that should shape indexing strategies to enhance database performance effectively.

Index Impact on Read vs. Write Performance

Indexes can significantly improve read performance because they allow the database engine to quickly locate and retrieve the data without scanning the entire table. Conversely, indexes have an adverse impact on write performance. Each insert, update, or delete operation requires additional work to maintain the index structures.

For instance, consider a scenario where we have a table named Orders with the columns OrderID, CustomerID, OrderDate, and TotalAmount. An index on the OrderDate column would allow the database engine to rapidly satisfy queries that filter or sort by OrderDate.

```
CREATE INDEX idx_OrderDate ON Orders(OrderDate);
```

However, adding this index means every new order inserted into the Orders table must update the index, as shown below:

```
INSERT INTO Orders (OrderID, CustomerID, OrderDate, TotalAmount)
VALUES (1, 100, '2023-04-01', 250.75);
```

Thus, the presence of the idx_OrderDate index introduces overhead during insertion, which can be detrimental to performance during high-volume write operations.

Selectivity and Cardinality

To achieve optimal performance, an index should have high selectivity, meaning it should filter out a large portion of the rows. Selectivity is expressed as the fraction of rows returned by the index compared to the total number of rows in the table. High selectivity can result in a lower number of I/O operations.

Cardinality, the uniqueness of values in a column, also plays a critical role in choosing columns to index. A high cardinality column, such as a primary key, is a good candidate for indexing, while a low cardinality column, such as a boolean flag, may not benefit much from indexing.

Index Fragmentation and Maintenance

Indexes can become fragmented over time due to updates, deletes, and inserts. Fragmentation affects the efficiency of index lookups, leading to degraded performance. Monitoring and addressing fragmentation is essential to maintaining the desired performance levels.

To check index fragmentation, one can use the sys.dm_db_index_physical_stats dynamic management function:

```
SELECT
    dbschemas.[name] AS 'Schema',
    dbtables.[name] AS 'Table',
    dbindexes.[name] AS 'Index',
    indexstats.avg_fragmentation_in_percent
FROM
    sys.dm_db_index_physical_stats (DB_ID(), NULL, NULL, NULL, NULL) AS
        indexstats
    INNER JOIN sys.tables dbtables ON dbtables.[object_id] = indexstats.[object_id]
    INNER JOIN sys.schemas dbschemas ON dbtables.[schema_id] = dbschemas.[
        schema_id]
    INNER JOIN sys.indexes AS dbindexes ON dbindexes.[object_id] = indexstats.[
        object_id]
    AND indexstats.index_id = dbindexes.index_id
ORDER BY
    indexstats.avg_fragmentation_in_percent DESC;
```

Based on the fragmentation levels, one can decide whether to reorganize or rebuild indexes:

```
-- To reorganize an index (less than 30\% fragmentation)
ALTER INDEX idx_OrderDate ON Orders REORGANIZE;

-- To rebuild an index (greater than 30\% fragmentation)
ALTER INDEX idx_OrderDate ON Orders REBUILD;
```

Clustered vs. Non-Clustered Index Choice

The decision between using a clustered or non-clustered index has significant performance implications. A table can have only one clustered index, which determines the physical order of rows. Non-clustered indexes store a separate copy of column data and reference the clustered index.

Clustered indexes are generally better for range queries because the rows are stored in order, reducing the number of page reads required. Non-clustered indexes are useful for lookups and when covering indexes include all the columns needed by a query.

Covering Indexes

A covering index is a non-clustered index that includes all the columns a query needs; thus, the query can be satisfied entirely by the index without touching the base table. This can significantly enhance performance by reducing I/O operations.

```
CREATE INDEX idx_Covering ON Orders(OrderDate) INCLUDE (CustomerID,
      TotalAmount);
```

This index can cover queries like:

```
SELECT CustomerID, TotalAmount
FROM Orders
WHERE OrderDate = '2023-04-01';
```

Indexing Strategy for OLTP vs. OLAP Systems

Online Transaction Processing (OLTP) and Online Analytical Processing (OLAP) systems have different indexing needs. OLTP systems benefit from indexes that support fast inserts, updates, and short queries, usually requiring narrow and highly selective indexes. OLAP systems, focusing on read-heavy operations, can benefit from wider indexes, including covering indexes and those supporting complex analytical queries.

In summary, careful consideration of read-write balance, selectivity, fragmentation, appropriate use of clustered and non-clustered indexes, and tailoring index strategies to system-specific requirements are paramount for achieving optimal performance in SQL Server databases.

6.11 Indexing Best Practices

Proper indexing is crucial for the performance and efficiency of SQL Server databases. Adopting best practices for indexing is essential to ensure databases perform optimally under varying workloads. Effective index design balances improved read performance with the overhead introduced during write operations such as inserts, updates, and deletes. Below are detailed best practices to consider when working with indexes in SQL Server.

1. Understand the Workload

Before creating indexes, thoroughly analyze the query patterns and database workload. Identify the most frequently executed queries and the columns involved in joins, WHERE clauses, and ORDER BY clauses. Use performance monitoring tools such as SQL Server Profiler, Extended Events, and Dynamic Management Views (DMVs) to gather detailed workload information.

2. Use Appropriate Index Types

Different types of indexes serve different purposes. Determine the appropriate index type for your workload:

- **Clustered Indexes:** Use for columns with unique or nearly unique values and frequently used in range queries.
- **Non-Clustered Indexes:** Use for columns frequently involved in search conditions and to cover queries.
- **Composite Indexes:** Use for queries involving multiple columns in the WHERE clause, JOIN conditions, or ORDER BY clauses.
- **Unique Indexes:** Ensure data integrity by enforcing uniqueness on one or more columns.
- **Filtered Indexes:** Optimize queries accessing a specific subset of data, reducing index size and maintenance overhead.

- **Columnstore Indexes:** Suitable for analytical queries that involve large datasets, providing significant performance improvements in data warehousing scenarios.

3. Optimize Index Key Selection

Choose index keys wisely to maximize index efficiency:

- Select columns with high selectivity (unique or nearly unique values).
- Place columns with high cardinality at the beginning of composite indexes.
- Avoid indexing columns with low cardinality (few distinct values), such as boolean flags.

4. Covering Indexes

A covering index includes all the columns needed by a query, so the query can be answered entirely from the index without accessing the base table. This reduces I/O operations and improves performance. Use the INCLUDE clause to add non-key columns to non-clustered indexes to create covering indexes where appropriate.

5. Limit the Number of Indexes

While indexes improve read performance, they introduce overhead on write operations. Limit the number of indexes to avoid excessive maintenance costs. Regularly review and analyze index usage with tools such as the sys.dm_db_index_usage_stats DMV to identify and remove unused or redundant indexes.

6. Monitor and Maintain Indexes

Regularly monitor index fragmentation and perform necessary maintenance tasks such as rebuilding or reorganizing indexes. Use the following commands to manage index fragmentation:

```
-- Reorganizing an index (lower overhead, can be done online)
ALTER INDEX index\_name ON table\_name REORGANIZE;

-- Rebuilding an index (higher overhead, but more effective, can be done online with
     some limitations)
ALTER INDEX index\_name ON table\_name REBUILD;
```

Analyze index fragmentation using the sys.dm_db_index_physical_stats DMV and decide the appropriate action based on fragmentation levels:

- **< 10%:** No action required.
- **10% - 30%:** Reorganize the index.
- **> 30%:** Rebuild the index.

7. Use Data Compression

SQL Server supports row and page-level compression, which can reduce the storage space required by indexes and improve query performance. Evaluate the use of compression based on your data access patterns and storage needs. Enable compression with the following command:

```
-- Enabling row-level compression
ALTER INDEX index\_name ON table\_name
REBUILD WITH (DATA\_COMPRESSION = ROW);

-- Enabling page-level compression
ALTER INDEX index\_name ON table\_name
REBUILD WITH (DATA\_COMPRESSION = PAGE);
```

8. Leverage Automated Index Tuning

SQL Server provides features like the Database Engine Tuning Advisor and the Automatic Tuning feature in Azure SQL Database, which can recommend and apply index changes based on observed query patterns. Use these tools to assist in index management but review and validate recommendations before implementation.

9. Avoid Over-Indexing on High-Write Tables

Tables that experience high volumes of write operations should be carefully indexed to avoid significant write performance degradation. Prioritize essential indexes for these tables and remove indexes that provide minimal performance benefits.

10. Review Indexes Regularly

Indexing is not a one-time task but requires continual monitoring and adjustment. Regularly review index effectiveness, usage patterns, and database performance to make necessary adjustments.

Employing these best practices helps in achieving an optimal balance between read and write performance, ensuring that the database remains responsive and efficient under different workloads.

Chapter 7

Database Design and Normalization

This chapter focuses on the principles of database design and the importance of data modeling. It explains entity-relationship diagrams (ERD) and discusses the process of normalization, including First, Second, and Third Normal Forms (1NF, 2NF, 3NF), as well as Boyce-Codd Normal Form (BCNF). The chapter also covers denormalization techniques, designing tables and relationships, and best practices in database design to ensure efficiency and scalability.

7.1 Principles of Database Design

Database design is a meticulous process involving the organization and structuring of data within a database. Proper design ensures the database meets both the operational and performance requirements of the system. The principles of database design encompass several key aspects, such as data integrity, redundancy control, data independence, and scalability. These principles are pivotal for the development of a robust, efficient, and scalable database.

Data Integrity is fundamental to database design. It ensures the accuracy, consistency, and reliability of data over its lifecycle. There are several types of data integrity constraints:

- **Entity Integrity**: Ensures that each table has a primary key and that the value of this key is unique and not null. This is critical for uniquely identifying each record in a table.
- **Referential Integrity**: Maintains the consistency between tables through foreign keys. A foreign key in one table points to a primary key in another table, ensuring that relationships between tables remain valid.
- **Domain Integrity**: Involves restricting the data type, format, and range of possible values for each attribute. This ensures that the data entered into a column must adhere to predefined rules.
- **User-Defined Integrity**: Encompasses any additional rules specified by the user that do not fall under the other integrity types. These could include business rules specific to the operational constraints of the organization.

Redundancy Control refers to minimizing duplicate data within the database, which is a common goal to prevent data inconsistencies and reduce storage costs. One key method for controlling redundancy is through the process of normalization, which is discussed in subsequent sections of this chapter. By organizing data into tables where each piece of data is stored only once, normalization helps reduce repetition and prevent anomalies during data operations (insertion, deletion, and update).

Data Independence is another crucial principle. It refers to the separation of data from the applications that use the data. This ensures that changes in the database schema do not affect the application programs or the way data is accessed and vice versa. Data independence is achieved through a three-level architecture:

- **Physical Level**: The lowest level of abstraction describes how the data is physically stored. It deals with physical storage devices and data organization.
- **Logical Level**: The middle level of abstraction describes what data is stored in the database and the relationships among those data. It provides a higher-level view of the data without considering the physical structures.
- **View Level**: The highest level of abstraction deals with the end-user interaction with the database. It provides a convenient user

interface and allows different user groups to have different perspectives of the database.

Scalability is a principle that involves designing the database to handle an increase in load gracefully. This includes both an increase in the amount of data and the number of transactions. Scalability can be achieved through:

- **Partitioning**: Dividing a database into smaller, more manageable pieces. Horizontal partitioning (sharding) spreads rows of a table across multiple tables, while vertical partitioning divides a table by columns.

- **Indexing**: Creating indexes on columns that are frequently searched or sorted, which can vastly improve performance.

- **Replication**: Maintaining copies of the database in different locations to improve query performance and provide availability during failures.

- **Load Balancing**: Distributing workloads across multiple database servers to prevent any one server from becoming a bottleneck.

Usability involves designing the database in a way that makes it easy to use by end-users and applications. This includes:

- **Consistency and Uniformity**: Ensuring consistent naming conventions, data types, and coding practices across the database.

- **Robust Documentation**: Providing detailed descriptions and usage examples for the database schema, tables, relationships, and constraints.

- **Efficient Query Design**: Structuring data and indexes to optimize common queries, which enhances performance and user experience.

Applying these fundamental principles during the database design phase is crucial for developing a system that is not only functional and efficient but also easily maintainable and scalable.

7.2 Understanding Data Modeling

Data modeling is a critical aspect of database design which involves creating a data model for the data to be stored in the database. It is a conceptual representation of the data structures that are required by a database. Through data modeling, we strive to organize data correctly, thereby facilitating efficient retrieval, storage, update, and integrity of the data.

At the core of data modeling, we have entities, attributes, and relationships:

- Entities: These are objects or concepts about which data is collected. They represent real-world objects, such as customers, products, or orders.
- Attributes: These are properties or details of an entity. For example, a customer entity might have attributes such as name, address, and phone number.
- Relationships: These define how entities interact with one another. For instance, a customer places an order, which establishes a relationship between the customer entity and the order entity.

When engaging in data modeling, we differentiate between three types of models:

- Conceptual Data Model: This high-level model defines what the system contains. It is typically created during the initial project phase to accurately capture the data requirements.
- Logical Data Model: This model provides more detail than the conceptual model. It defines the structure of the data elements and the relationships between them, independent of physical considerations.
- Physical Data Model: This model translates the logical description into the technical specifications necessary to create and implement the database. It includes table structures, column names, data types, and constraints among other details.

Considerations during data modeling:

- Scalability: The model should accommodate future growth in data volume and complexity without significant redesign.
- Performance: Proper indexing, normalization, and structure can drastically influence query performance. The designed model should facilitate efficient data retrieval and update operations.
- Integrity and Accuracy: Leverage constraints such as primary keys, foreign keys, and unique constraints to maintain data integrity and accuracy.
- Security: Implement access controls and permissions to protect sensitive data from unauthorized access.
- Consistency: Ensure that data remains consistent across the database, applying transactions and ACID (Atomicity, Consistency, Isolation, Durability) properties to bolster this consistency.

```
CREATE TABLE Customer (
    customerID INT PRIMARY KEY,
    name VARCHAR(100) NOT NULL,
    address VARCHAR(255),
    phone VARCHAR(15),
    email VARCHAR(50) UNIQUE
);
```

```
Output:
Table "Customer" created with columns:
- customerID, INT, Primary Key
- name, VARCHAR(100), Not Null
- address, VARCHAR(255), Nullable
- phone, VARCHAR(15), Nullable
- email, VARCHAR(50), Unique
```

The process of creating a data model typically encompasses several steps, including requirements analysis, conceptual modeling, logical modeling, and physical modeling.

During requirements analysis, stakeholders gather and document the necessary data and functions that the system must support. This involves detailed discussions with end-users, analyzing existing documentation, and understanding the business needs.

In conceptual modeling, the focus is on constructing a model that captures the essentials, using tools like entity-relationship diagrams (ERDs). These diagrams facilitate communication between stakeholders and database designers, ensuring clarity and shared understanding of the data requirements.

Moving to logical modeling, the conceptual models are further refined. Here, entities and relationships are elaborated upon with more specifics, typically free from any physical considerations. Logical models are often represented using normalized table structures ensuring that redundancy is minimized and data integrity is maximized.

Finally, in physical modeling, the logical model is translated into a schema that can be implemented in the database management system (DBMS). This includes selecting appropriate data types for each attribute, indexing strategies for optimization, and defining constraints to enforce the required business rules.

The following SQL code exemplifies the logical to physical transition for an entity relationship:

```
CREATE TABLE Orders (
    orderID INT PRIMARY KEY,
    orderDate DATE NOT NULL,
    customerID INT,
    FOREIGN KEY (customerID) REFERENCES Customer(customerID)
);
```

```
Output:
Table "Orders" created with columns:
- orderID, INT, Primary Key
- orderDate, DATE, Not Null
- customerID, INT, Foreign Key referencing Customer(customerID)
```

In this example, the Orders table includes a foreign key constraint on customerID that references the customerID in the Customer table, establishing a direct relationship between customers and their orders.

Sound data modeling ensures that the database will be well-structured, efficient, and able to evolve with changing requirements, all while maintaining data integrity and security. Adequately addressing aspects like scalability, performance, integrity, security, and consistency is a fundamental step towards building robust and reliable database systems.

7.3 Entity-Relationship Diagrams (ERD)

Entity-Relationship Diagrams (ERDs) serve as a pivotal tool in the database design process, providing a graphical representation of the data and relationships within an information system. This facilitates clear, precise communication of the database schema to stakeholders, developers, and analytical teams. ERDs are integral during the initial design phase and continue to offer value throughout the database lifecycle.

ERDs comprise several key components: entities, attributes, and relationships.

Entities represent objects or concepts within the system, such as Customer, Order, or Product. Entities are typically denoted by rectangles in an ER diagram. Each entity should encapsulate a distinct and identifiable concept relevant to the system. For instance, in a retail database, potential entities could be Customer, Order, Product, and Supplier.

Attributes describe the properties or characteristics of an entity. These are illustrated as ovals connected to their respective entities. Key attributes include primary keys (unique identifiers for an entity) and foreign keys (which reference primary keys in another entity to denote relationships). Below is an example of entity and attribute representation:

```
+-------------+
| Product |
+-------------+
| ProductID | <-- Primary Key
| Name |
| Description |
| Price |
| SupplierID | <-- Foreign Key
+-------------+
```

Relationships illustrate how entities interact with one another. These are shown as diamonds or labeled lines connecting entities and are usually annotated with cardinality (e.g., one-to-one, one-to-many, many-to-many). Cardinality defines the numerical mapping between instances of the entities involved. For example, a Customer places Orders, which implies a one-to-many relationship: one Customer can place multiple Orders, but each Order is placed by a single Customer.

Consider the following ERD elements:

```
+---------------+  places  +-------------+
|   Customer    | o---------<|   Order     |
+---------------+           +-------------+
| CustomerID    |  Itemizes  | OrderID     |
| Name          | >---------o | OrderDate  |
| Email         |            | TotalAmount |
+---------------+            +-------------+

                    has
  +--------------+ o-------------< +---------------+
  |   Product    |                 | Supplier      |
  +--------------+                 +---------------+
  | ProductID    |                 | SupplierID    |
  | Name         |                 | Name          |
  | Description  |                 | ContactInfo   |
  | Price        |                 +---------------+
  | SupplierID   |
  +--------------+
```

In this diagram:

- The Customer entity is connected to the Order entity through a one-to-many relationship, symbolized by an "o" (zero or one) near Customer and "<" (many) near Order.
- The Order entity contains attributes such as OrderID, OrderDate, and TotalAmount.
- The Product entity has an implied foreign key relationship with Supplier through SupplierID.
- The relationship between Product and Supplier is one-to-many, i.e., one Supplier can provide multiple Products.

Entities must be carefully identified to avoid ambiguity. This entails precise naming conventions and delimiting each entity's scope. Attributes must be chosen to ensure they encapsulate all necessary details without redundancy. Relationships should be annotated clearly, providing appropriate cardinality constraints to reflect the business rules accurately.

To illustrate this concept, consider the SQL script to create tables based on the ERD:

```
CREATE TABLE Customer (
    CustomerID INT PRIMARY KEY,
    Name VARCHAR(100),
    Email VARCHAR(100)
);

CREATE TABLE Order (
    OrderID INT PRIMARY KEY,
    OrderDate DATE,
    TotalAmount DECIMAL(10, 2),
    CustomerID INT,
    FOREIGN KEY (CustomerID) REFERENCES Customer(CustomerID)
);

CREATE TABLE Supplier (
    SupplierID INT PRIMARY KEY,
    Name VARCHAR(100),
    ContactInfo VARCHAR(100)
);

CREATE TABLE Product (
    ProductID INT PRIMARY KEY,
    Name VARCHAR(100),
    Description VARCHAR(255),
    Price DECIMAL(10, 2),
    SupplierID INT,
    FOREIGN KEY (SupplierID) REFERENCES Supplier(SupplierID)
);
```

The SQL script enforces the relationships defined in the ER diagram. The CustomerID in the Order table establishes the link between orders and customers, ensuring referential integrity through foreign keys. Similarly, the SupplierID in the Product table links products to suppliers.

Using ERDs during the design phase not only fosters a clear understanding of system requirements but also ensures a robust framework for efficient database development and future maintenance. Proper implementation of ERDs translates to optimized data retrieval paths and organized schema management, pivotal for scalable, consistent database solutions.

7.4 Normalization and Its Importance

Normalization is a fundamental concept in database design, aimed at improving data consistency and reducing redundancy. It involves organizing the fields and tables of a database to minimize dependency and data anomalies. The motivation behind normalization is to ensure the database is structured in a way that optimally supports the management of data integrity and query performance.

A properly normalized database prohibits certain undesirable characteristics, such as unnecessary repetition of data, known as redundancy, and inadvertent production of anomalies during data operations like insertions, updates, and deletions. Normalization also ensures that the relationships between entities are accurately represented. The process is carried out through a series of steps called normal forms, which progressively enforce stricter rules to govern database structure.

The normal forms, specifically the First Normal Form (1NF), Second Normal Form (2NF), Third Normal Form (3NF), and Boyce-Codd Normal Form (BCNF), offer different levels of normalization. Each subsequent normal form addresses specific problems that might not be resolved in the previous ones. Below, we delve into the importance and implications of each normal form within the context of normalization.

The First Normal Form (1NF) ensures that the database table is two-dimensional, with rows and columns, and that each column contains atomic (indivisible) values only. Composite and multi-valued attributes must be eliminated. Thus, by adhering to 1NF, we remove repeating groups and ensure each attribute contains only one type of value.

The Second Normal Form (2NF) builds on the principles of 1NF by addressing issues related to partial dependency. A table is considered to be in 2NF if it is in 1NF and every non-key attribute is fully functionally dependent on the primary key. This eliminates redundancy caused by partial dependencies and ensures that all attributes are functionally dependent on the entire primary key.

The Third Normal Form (3NF) advances further by eliminating transitive dependencies. A table is in 3NF if it is in 2NF and no non-key attribute is transitively dependent on the primary key. Transitive dependencies occur when a non-key attribute depends on another non-key attribute, leading to potential anomalies during database operations.

Boyce-Codd Normal Form (BCNF) is a refinement of 3NF, addressing certain types of anomalies that 3NF may not fully resolve. A table is in BCNF if it is in 3NF and for every functional dependency, $X -> Y$, X is a super key. BCNF ensures the elimination of any anomalies that could still exist despite 3NF.

Recognizing the importance of normalization, we illustrate through a practical example. Consider the following table $\mathrm{Student\_Courses}$ before normalization:

```
StudentID | StudentName | CourseID | CourseName | InstructorName
--------- | ----------- | -------- | ---------- | ---------------
001 | Alice | C001 | Math | Dr. Smith
002 | Bob | C002 | English | Dr. Brown
002 | Bob | C001 | Math | Dr. Smith
```

This table contains several anomalies: redundancy of $\mathrm{CourseName}$ and $\mathrm{InstructorName}$ for repeated courses, and potential update anomalies where a course instructor change requires multiple row updates.

Applying 1NF, we ensure atomicity of values:

```
StudentID | StudentName | CourseID
--------- | ----------- | --------
001 | Alice | C001
002 | Bob | C002
002 | Bob | C001

CourseID | CourseName | InstructorName
-------- | ---------- | ---------------
C001 | Math | Dr. Smith
C002 | English | Dr. Brown
```

This separation removes repeating groups. Each attribute now contains a single value per tuple.

Proceeding to 2NF, we eliminate partial dependencies by ensuring that non-key attributes are fully dependent on the primary key:

```
StudentID | StudentName
--------- | -----------
001 | Alice
002 | Bob

StudentID | CourseID
--------- | --------
001 | C001
002 | C002
002 | C001

CourseID | CourseName | InstructorName
-------- | ---------- | --------------
C001 | Math | Dr. Smith
C002 | English | Dr. Brown
```

After normalization to 2NF, each non-key attribute is entirely dependent on the cumulative primary key.

Next, we address transitive dependencies for 3NF. Here, InstructorName is dependent on CourseID, so we separate it:

```
StudentID | StudentName
--------- | -----------
001 | Alice
002 | Bob

StudentID | CourseID
--------- | --------
001 | C001
002 | C002
002 | C001

CourseID | CourseName
-------- | ----------
C001 | Math
C002 | English

CourseID | InstructorName
-------- | --------------
C001 | Dr. Smith
C002 | Dr. Brown
```

Now, our tables fit the criteria for 3NF since each non-key attribute is directly dependent on the primary key, and we removed transitive dependencies, ensuring more robust data integrity and reducing anomalies.

BCNF makes sure that every determinant is a candidate key. For this case, since the current 3NF structure satisfies BCNF rules, no further alterations are necessary.

In a normalized database, the structuring supports more efficient data manipulation while significantly reducing redundancy and the risk of data anomalies. Properly normalized databases enhance query performance, data integrity, and ease of maintenance. The normalization process, while occasionally perceived as complex, is critical in the pursuit of an efficient and reliable database design.

7.5 First Normal Form (1NF)

The First Normal Form (1NF) is a fundamental property of a relational database. A table is said to be in 1NF if it satisfies the following conditions: all the attributes in that relation (table) contain only atomic (indivisible) values, and each record must be unique.

To better understand what it means for a table to be in 1NF, let's consider the following aspects in detail:

- Each column in the table should contain only atomic, indivisible values. This means that each column must hold single values only, and there should not be any composite or multi-valued attributes.
- Each row in the table must be unique. This requires that there is at least one key in the table (known as the primary key) that uniquely identifies each row.
- The order in which data is stored must not matter, and the relational model should not depend on the physical storage order of the rows or columns.

Atomicity of Values

Ensuring atomicity means that each cell within a table contains a single value. For instance, consider a table representing employees' contact information.

```
CREATE TABLE Employees (
    EmployeeID INT,
    FullName VARCHAR(100),
    Contacts VARCHAR(100)
);

INSERT INTO Employees (EmployeeID, FullName, Contacts)
VALUES
(1, 'John Doe', 'john.doe@example.com, +123456789'),
(2, 'Jane Smith', 'jane.smith@example.com, +987654321');
```

In the example above, the Contacts column contains multiple values (both email and phone number), violating the principle of atomicity. To transform the table into the 1NF, we need to separate the composite values into distinct columns:

```
CREATE TABLE Employees\_1NF (
    EmployeeID INT,
    FullName VARCHAR(100),
    Email VARCHAR(100),
    PhoneNumber VARCHAR(20)
);

INSERT INTO Employees\_1NF (EmployeeID, FullName, Email, PhoneNumber)
VALUES
(1, 'John Doe', 'john.doe@example.com', '+123456789'),
(2, 'Jane Smith', 'jane.smith@example.com', '+987654321');
```

Uniqueness of Records

Each record within a table should be unique, which mandates the presence of a primary key. A primary key is an attribute (or a set of attributes) that uniquely identifies a record. Consider the following example:

```
CREATE TABLE Employees\_No\_PK (
    FullName VARCHAR(100),
    Email VARCHAR(100)
);

INSERT INTO Employees\_No\_PK (FullName, Email)
VALUES
('John Doe', 'john.doe@example.com'),
('Jane Smith', 'jane.smith@example.com'),
('John Doe', 'john.doe@anotherexample.com');
```

In this case, we can see there are duplicate entries for "John Doe". To ensure 1NF, we establish a primary key for the table:

```
CREATE TABLE Employees\_PK (
    EmployeeID INT PRIMARY KEY,
    FullName VARCHAR(100),
    Email VARCHAR(100)
);

INSERT INTO Employees\_PK (EmployeeID, FullName, Email)
VALUES
(1, 'John Doe', 'john.doe@example.com'),
(2, 'Jane Smith', 'jane.smith@example.com'),
(3, 'John Doe', 'john.doe@anotherexample.com');
```

With the introduction of the EmployeeID as a primary key, each record can now be uniquely identified.

No Ordering Dependency

A table in 1NF should adhere to the principle that data retrieval should not depend on the ordering of rows and columns. This inherently means that operations involve relational algebra, such as selection and projection, which ensure data are handled in a manner insensitive to order.

Consider the scenario of retrieving employee names stored in an ordered list:

```
SELECT FullName
FROM Employees
WHERE EmployeeID = 1;
```

The above query retrieves the name based on the EmployeeID rather than the position of the record within the table. This ensures that changes in the physical storage order of the data do not affect the outcome.

Examples and Practical Understanding

To further solidify the concept of 1NF, let's observe a non-1NF table representing products and their multiple suppliers, and then convert it into 1NF.

Non-1NF Table example:

```
CREATE TABLE Products (
    ProductID INT,
    ProductName VARCHAR(100),
    Suppliers VARCHAR(255)
);

INSERT INTO Products (ProductID, ProductName, Suppliers)
VALUES
(1, 'Widget', 'SupplierA, SupplierB'),
(2, 'Gadget', 'SupplierC, SupplierD, SupplierE');
```

Converted to 1NF:

```
CREATE TABLE Products\_1NF (
    ProductID INT,
    ProductName VARCHAR(100),
    SupplierID INT,
    SupplierName VARCHAR(100)
);

INSERT INTO Products\_1NF (ProductID, ProductName, SupplierID, SupplierName)
VALUES
(1, 'Widget', 101, 'SupplierA'),
(1, 'Widget', 102, 'SupplierB'),
```

```
(2, 'Gadget', 103, 'SupplierC'),
(2, 'Gadget', 104, 'SupplierD'),
(2, 'Gadget', 105, 'SupplierE');
```

This transformation splits the composite value in the Suppliers column into separate records, each containing atomic data in a properly normalized form, satisfying 1NF.

Ensuring adherence to the First Normal Form is the first step towards a well-structured and efficient database design, providing a foundation for subsequent normalization efforts.

The application of 1NF ensures that data redundancy is minimized, data integrity is maintained, and anomalies related to insertion, update, and deletion are reduced by ensuring each attribute contains atomic values and each record is uniquely identifiable.

7.6 Second Normal Form (2NF)

Second Normal Form (2NF) builds upon the principles of First Normal Form (1NF) and is a crucial step in reducing data redundancy and enhancing data integrity. A table is said to be in 2NF if it meets the following conditions:

- It is already in First Normal Form (1NF).
- It has no partial dependency, meaning no non-prime attribute is functionally dependent on any proper subset of a candidate key.

To elaborate, a partial dependency occurs when a non-key attribute is dependent on a part of a composite key rather than on the whole key. Transitioning from a state of 1NF to 2NF primarily involves ensuring that all non-key attributes depend on the entire primary key.

Consider an example of a table where partial dependencies exist:

```
CREATE TABLE Orders (
    OrderID INT,
    ProductID INT,
    Quantity INT,
    ProductName VARCHAR(255),
    PRIMARY KEY (OrderID, ProductID)
);
```

In the Orders table, OrderID and ProductID form a composite key. The table is already in 1NF since it does not have repeating groups. However, it is not yet in 2NF because the ProductName attribute depends solely on ProductID, not on the entire composite key (OrderID, ProductID).

To transform this table into 2NF, we must eliminate such partial dependencies. We can achieve this by decomposing the original table into two separate tables:

```
CREATE TABLE Orders (
    OrderID INT,
    ProductID INT,
    Quantity INT,
    PRIMARY KEY (OrderID, ProductID)
);

CREATE TABLE Products (
    ProductID INT PRIMARY KEY,
    ProductName VARCHAR(255)
);
```

The Orders table now contains only the attributes dependent on the composite key (OrderID, ProductID). The Products table retains the ProductName, which is now dependent solely on the primary key ProductID. This normalization removes the partial dependency and promotes the Orders table to 2NF.

This decomposition achieves:

- Elimination of redundancy: The ProductName is stored only once in the Products table.
- Consistency: Any change to the ProductName attribute needs to be updated only once.
- Referential integrity: The ProductID in the Orders table can be linked to the Products table, enforcing integrity and preventing orphaned records.

Another example can help illustrate the concept further. Suppose we have the following StudentClasses table:

```
CREATE TABLE StudentClasses (
    StudentID INT,
    ClassID INT,
    ClassName VARCHAR(255),
    PRIMARY KEY (StudentID, ClassID)
);
```

In this table, StudentID and ClassID together serve as the primary key. Just like the previous example, the ClassName depends only on ClassID, which represents a partial dependency. To promote this table to 2NF, we decompose it into:

```
CREATE TABLE StudentClasses (
    StudentID INT,
    ClassID INT,
    PRIMARY KEY (StudentID, ClassID)
);

CREATE TABLE Classes (
    ClassID INT PRIMARY KEY,
    ClassName VARCHAR(255)
);
```

This ensures that ClassName depends solely on ClassID, removing the partial dependency from the StudentClasses table, thus normalizing it to 2NF.

The transition from 1NF to 2NF is pivotal in constructing a relational database that is free from anomalous dependencies, which can lead to update, deletion, and insertion anomalies. With the database structured to 2NF, we move closer to achieving a more logical and efficient design, facilitating easier maintenance and reduced redundancy.

Tables normalized to 2NF should be reviewed periodically as part of ongoing database maintenance and optimization to ensure that as new data requirements emerge, the structure remains optimal and the principles of normalization continue to be applied correctly.

7.7 Third Normal Form (3NF)

The Third Normal Form (3NF) is one of the pivotal concepts in database normalization that aims to eliminate redundancy and enhance data integrity. A database relation is in 3NF if it is already in the Second Normal Form (2NF), and every non-prime attribute is non-transitively dependent on every key of the relation. In other words, a relation is in 3NF if it is in 2NF and no non-prime attribute depends on another non-prime attribute.

To understand the rationale behind 3NF, it is crucial to revisit the concept of transitive dependency. Transitive dependency occurs when a non-prime attribute depends on another non-prime attribute rather than depending solely on the primary key. This indirect dependency introduces redundancy and potential anomalies during data manipulation operations such as insertion, update, or deletion.

Definition: Third Normal Form (3NF)

A relation R is in Third Normal Form if and only if it satisfies the following conditions:

- R is in Second Normal Form (2NF).
- Every non-prime attribute of R is non-transitively dependent on every key of R.

To put it mathematically, let A, B, and C be attributes of a relation R. If $A \to B$ and $B \to C$, then there is a transitive dependency $A \to C$ if A is a candidate key and C is not part of any key. For R to be in 3NF, C must be directly dependent on A, not via B.

Example and Transformation

Consider the following relation that contains Student records along with details of Courses and Instructors:

```
StudentCourse(
    StudentID,
    StudentName,
    CourseID,
    CourseName,
    InstructorName
)
```

This relation might exhibit anomalies due to transitive dependency. Here, StudentID is a primary key, and CourseID, CourseName, and InstructorName have dependencies that can lead to redundancy. Specifically, CourseName and InstructorName are both dependent on CourseID rather than solely on StudentID.

To convert this into Third Normal Form, we must eliminate transitive dependencies by decomposing the relation into smaller relations that fulfill the 3NF requirements. The decomposition process results in the following:

```
Student(
    StudentID,
    StudentName
)

Course(
    CourseID,
    CourseName,
    InstructorName
)

Enrollment(
    StudentID,
```

```
    CourseID
)
```

With this decomposition:

- The Student relation stores individual student records.
- The Course relation stores individual course details, including the instructor's name.
- The Enrollment relation maps students to courses.

This restructuring ensures that attributes such as CourseName and InstructorName are directly dependent on CourseID rather than being dependent through other non-key attributes. By isolating these dependencies into distinct relations, we have effectively brought the database schema into 3NF, mitigating redundancy and improving consistency.

Technical Verification of 3NF

Verification that a database schema adheres to 3NF involves examining each relation to ensure that non-prime attributes are directly dependent solely on candidate keys. Consider the relations from our previous example:

```
Student(
    StudentID (PK),
    StudentName
)
```

No transitive dependency exists; hence, this is in 3NF.

```
Course(
    CourseID (PK),
    CourseName,
    InstructorName
)
```

Both CourseName and InstructorName are directly dependent on CourseID without intermediary attributes, ensuring 3NF compliance.

```
Enrollment(
    StudentID (FK),
    CourseID (FK)
)
```

This relation is a straightforward mapping without any attributes beyond foreign keys, inherently satisfying 3NF.

Adhering to 3NF provides significant advantages, including reduced data duplication and enhanced data integrity. However, a strict 3NF design must be balanced against performance considerations, particularly in high-read environments where join operations may introduce performance overheads. Advanced database design sometimes uses partial denormalization to strike an optimal balance between normalization benefits and system performance metrics. Nevertheless, the foundational understanding and application of 3NF remain indispensable for robust database design, ensuring architectural clarity and operational efficiency.

7.8 Boyce-Codd Normal Form (BCNF)

Boyce-Codd Normal Form (BCNF) represents a stricter version of the Third Normal Form (3NF) for relational database normalization. It addresses certain types of anomalies that are not handled by 3NF. To fully appreciate BCNF, one must comprehend the underlying principles of functional dependencies and candidate keys, which are pivotal in the analysis and design of relational schemas.

A relational schema is considered in BCNF if, and only if, every determinant is a candidate key. A determinant is an attribute on which some other attribute is fully functionally dependent. Formally, consider a relation R with a set of attributes $\{A_1, A_2, \ldots, A_n\}$ and a set of functional dependencies F. The relation R is in BCNF if, for every non-trivial functional dependency $X \rightarrow Y$ in F, X is a candidate key. This stringent requirement means that any anomalies in database operations, such as insertions, deletions, and updates, are further minimized compared to 3NF.

To illustrate these concepts, consider the following example relation R.

Course_ID	Instructor	Time	Room
CS101	Prof. Smith	09:00	Room 101
CS101	Prof. Smith	10:00	Room 102
CS102	Prof. Brown	10:00	Room 101
CS103	Prof. Miller	11:00	Room 103

Assuming the following functional dependencies:

$$\{\text{Course\_ID} \rightarrow \text{Instructor}, \text{Time}, \text{Room}\}.$$

In this case, Course_ID is the determinant and given the above functional dependencies, it is clear that any non-trivial dependency violation of BCNF does not exist.

Next, we consider an alternative relation R:

Student_ID	Course_ID	Instructor	Grade
S01	CS101	Prof. Smith	A
S02	CS102	Prof. Brown	B
S01	CS103	Prof. Miller	A
S03	CS101	Prof. Smith	B

And the dependencies are:

$$\{\text{Student\_ID}, \text{Course\_ID} \to \text{Grade}, \text{Course\_ID} \to \text{Instructor}\}.$$

Here, $\{\text{Student\_ID}, \text{Course\_ID}\}$ is a candidate key, but Course_ID determines Instructor, violating BCNF since Course_ID is not a candidate key. To convert this schema into BCNF, one must decompose it into two schemas:

```
R1(Student_ID, Course_ID, Grade)
R2(Course_ID, Instructor)
```

This decomposition results in two relations:

- $R1(\text{Student\_ID}, \text{Course\_ID}, \text{Grade})$
- $R2(\text{Course\_ID}, \text{Instructor})$

In these decomposed relations, every determinant is a candidate key, thus satisfying the criteria for BCNF.

To elaborate, consider the properties of functional dependencies in these relations. In $R2$, Course_ID is the sole key and it determines Instructor. In $R1$, the candidate key is $\{\text{Student\_ID}, \text{Course\_ID}\}$, and this pair determines Grade. There is no partial dependency or transitive dependency issue, confirming the adherence to BCNF.

Employing BCNF can significantly minimize redundancy. By ensuring that every non-trivial dependency results in keys that uniquely identify records, the integrity and efficiency of the database systems are greatly enhanced. Through careful decomposition of relations exhibiting violations, one can construct a well-normalized database schema that is both robust and efficient in its operation.

7.9 Denormalization Techniques

Denormalization is the process of intentionally introducing redundancy into a database design to improve performance. While normalization aims to eliminate redundancy and ensure data integrity, denormalization can help optimize read queries at the cost of potentially increased complexity in write operations and data consistency management. Understanding when and how to apply denormalization techniques is critical for designing databases that efficiently handle specific workloads and access patterns.

One common denormalization technique involves combining multiple related tables into a single table. This approach reduces the number of join operations required to retrieve data, thereby improving read performance. For instance, consider two tables: Customers and Orders. In a normalized schema, these tables might be designed as follows:

```
CREATE TABLE Customers (
    CustomerID INT PRIMARY KEY,
    CustomerName VARCHAR(100),
    ContactInfo VARCHAR(100)
);

CREATE TABLE Orders (
    OrderID INT PRIMARY KEY,
    CustomerID INT,
    OrderDate DATE,
    FOREIGN KEY (CustomerID) REFERENCES Customers(CustomerID)
);
```

In this normalization, every query to retrieve customer orders would require a join between the Customers and Orders tables. In a denormalized schema, the Customers and Orders tables might be combined into a single table:

```
CREATE TABLE CustomerOrders (
    OrderID INT PRIMARY KEY,
    CustomerID INT,
    CustomerName VARCHAR(100),
    ContactInfo VARCHAR(100),
    OrderDate DATE
);
```

This denormalization technique reduces the need for join operations, allowing for faster query performance at the expense of data redundancy and potential update anomalies. Any changes to customer information must now be propagated to multiple rows in the CustomerOrders table.

Another denormalization technique involves adding redundant columns to store aggregated values. For example, calculating the total number of orders for a customer might involve a costly aggregation query. By storing the total number of orders directly in the Customers table, we can avoid repeated calculations:

```
CREATE TABLE Customers (
    CustomerID INT PRIMARY KEY,
    CustomerName VARCHAR(100),
    ContactInfo VARCHAR(100),
```

```
    TotalOrders INT
);
```

However, this approach requires additional logic to update the TotalOrders column whenever relevant orders are added, modified, or deleted. This can increase the complexity of the application code and the risk of data inconsistencies.

Materialized views represent another denormalization technique. They are precomputed views that cache the results of a query, which can include joins and aggregations. Unlike standard views, which recompute results on every access, materialized views improve performance by maintaining a snapshot of the query result. For instance:

```
CREATE MATERIALIZED VIEW CustomerOrderSummary AS
SELECT
    Customers.CustomerID,
    Customers.CustomerName,
    COUNT(Orders.OrderID) AS TotalOrders,
    MAX(Orders.OrderDate) AS LastOrderDate
FROM
    Customers
LEFT JOIN
    Orders ON Customers.CustomerID = Orders.CustomerID
GROUP BY
    Customers.CustomerID, Customers.CustomerName;
```

Materialized views must be refreshed periodically to ensure that they reflect the current state of the underlying base tables. This can be achieved through scheduled refreshes or triggers that update the view upon data changes.

Index denormalization is another technique involving the creation of redundant indexes to speed up query performance. This is particularly beneficial for read-heavy workloads. For instance, if a table has frequent queries filtering by multiple columns, composite indexes combining those columns can significantly improve performance. Creating such indexes involves:

```
CREATE INDEX idx\_customer\_order ON Orders (CustomerID, OrderDate);
```

While composite indexes speed up query retrievals, they also require additional storage and can slow down write operations such as insert, update, and delete due to the maintenance of the indexed structures.

Data partitioning is a scalable denormalization strategy where a large table is divided into smaller, more manageable pieces, or "partitions." Each partition can be optimized individually, and queries can target specific partitions for improved performance. Partitioning strategies include range partitioning, list partitioning, and hash partitioning. For example, range partitioning might involve:

```
CREATE TABLE Orders (
    OrderID INT,
    CustomerID INT,
    OrderDate DATE
)
PARTITION BY RANGE (OrderDate) (
    PARTITION p0 VALUES LESS THAN ('2021-01-01'),
    PARTITION p1 VALUES LESS THAN ('2022-01-01'),
    PARTITION p2 VALUES LESS THAN ('2023-01-01')
);
```

Finally, rollups and cubes in SQL provide mechanisms for aggregating data across multiple dimensions, which can be precomputed and stored to facilitate rapid querying. These techniques are often employed in OLAP (Online Analytical Processing) systems:

```
SELECT
    CustomerID,
    YEAR(OrderDate) AS OrderYear,
    MONTH(OrderDate) AS OrderMonth,
    COUNT(OrderID) AS TotalOrders
FROM
    Orders
GROUP BY
    ROLLUP (CustomerID, YEAR(OrderDate), MONTH(OrderDate));
```

Applying denormalization techniques requires careful consideration of the trade-offs between read performance, write performance, data consistency, and maintenance complexity. By judiciously implementing these strategies, database designers can tailor their schemas to meet the specific demands of their applications and workloads.

```
+------------+-----------+------------+-------------+
| CustomerID | OrderYear | OrderMonth | TotalOrders |
+------------+-----------+------------+-------------+
|     1      |   2021    |     12     |      5      |
|     1      |   2021    |    NULL    |      5      |
|     1      |   NULL    |    NULL    |      5      |
|     2      |   2022    |     1      |      3      |
|     2      |   2022    |     2      |      2      |
|     2      |   2022    |    NULL    |      5      |
|     2      |   NULL    |    NULL    |      5      |
|   NULL     |   NULL    |    NULL    |     10      |
+------------+-----------+------------+-------------+
```

The denormalization process must be approached with a clear understanding of the application requirements and anticipated query patterns to ensure that the benefits outweigh the challenges.

7.10 Designing Tables and Relationships

Designing tables and relationships is a critical step in the database design process. Properly structured tables and well-defined relationships ensure the efficiency, scalability, and maintainability of a database system. This section explores the methodology of designing tables, defining appropriate data types, setting primary and foreign keys, and establishing relationships between tables.

Designing Tables:

When designing tables, it's essential to identify the entities that need to be represented and the attributes of each entity. Each table in a database represents an entity, while the columns in the table represent the attributes of that entity.

Steps for Designing Tables:

- **Identify Entities:** Determine the main objects or entities in your database model. For example, in a university database, entities might include Student, Course, Instructor, and Department.
- **Define Attributes:** Specify the attributes for each entity. Attributes hold the data related to each entity. For instance, attributes for the Student entity might include StudentID, FirstName, LastName, DateOfBirth, and Major.
- **Choose Data Types:** Select appropriate data types for each attribute based on the nature of the data. For example, StudentID might be an integer, FirstName and LastName might be VARCHAR types, and DateOfBirth could be a DATE type.
- **Set Constraints:** Implement constraints such as NOT NULL, UNIQUE, and CHECK to enforce data integrity. For instance, to ensure every student has a unique ID and that no student can have a NULL ID, both the PRIMARY KEY and NOT NULL constraints can be applied to StudentID.

```
CREATE TABLE Student (
    StudentID INT PRIMARY KEY,
    FirstName VARCHAR(50) NOT NULL,
    LastName VARCHAR(50) NOT NULL,
    DateOfBirth DATE NOT NULL,
    Major VARCHAR(50) NOT NULL
);
```

Defining Primary and Foreign Keys

Defining primary and foreign keys is fundamental to establishing relationships between tables. Primary keys uniquely identify each record within a table, while foreign keys create a link between related tables.

Primary Key:

- Must contain unique values.
- Cannot contain NULL values.
- Each table should primarily have one primary key, although composite keys are possible.

Foreign Key:

- Attributes in one table that refer to the primary key in another table.
- Establishes referential integrity between the related tables.
- Can contain duplicate values and NULL, unless specified otherwise.

Establishing Relationships

Relationships among tables are classified into three types: one-to-one, one-to-many, and many-to-many.

One-to-One (1:1) Relationship: In this relationship, each record in Table A is linked to one unique record in Table B, and vice versa. This is often established when splitting data with many attributes into multiple tables to avoid excessive NULL values.

```
CREATE TABLE StudentDetails (
    StudentID INT PRIMARY KEY,
    Phone VARCHAR(15),
    Address VARCHAR(100),
    CONSTRAINT fk_Student FOREIGN KEY (StudentID)
    REFERENCES Student(StudentID)
);
```

One-to-Many (1:N) Relationship: One record in Table A can be associated with zero or more records in Table B, but each record in Table B can be associated with only one record in Table A. This is a common relationship type, for example, an instructor teaching multiple courses.

```
CREATE TABLE Course (
    CourseID INT PRIMARY KEY,
    CourseName VARCHAR(100) NOT NULL,
    InstructorID INT,
    CONSTRAINT fk_Instructor FOREIGN KEY (InstructorID)
    REFERENCES Instructor(InstructorID)
);
```

Many-to-Many (M:N) Relationship: In this relationship, one or more records in Table A can be associated with one or more records in Table B. This requires a junction table (also known as a join table or associative entity) to link the primary keys of both tables.

```
CREATE TABLE StudentCourse (
    StudentID INT,
    CourseID INT,
    PRIMARY KEY (StudentID, CourseID),
    FOREIGN KEY (StudentID) REFERENCES Student(StudentID),
    FOREIGN KEY (CourseID) REFERENCES Course(CourseID)
);
```

Foreign Key Constraints:

- ON DELETE CASCADE ensures that if a record in the parent table is deleted, all corresponding records in the child table are also deleted.

- ON UPDATE CASCADE ensures that changes to the primary key in the parent table are propagated to the foreign key in the child table.

```
ALTER TABLE Course
ADD CONSTRAINT fk_Instructor
FOREIGN KEY (InstructorID)
REFERENCES Instructor(InstructorID)
ON DELETE CASCADE
ON UPDATE CASCADE;
```

Designing tables and relationships with careful consideration ensures that the database schema is logical and supports efficient data retrieval and manipulation operations. Properly defined relationships and constraints safeguard data integrity and enhance the overall performance of the database system.

7.11 Best Practices in Database Design

Database design is a critical aspect of ensuring the performance, integrity, and scalability of a database system. Best practices in database design guide the creation of efficient, robust, and maintainable databases. This section elucidates key principles and practices that experienced database designers adhere to, ensuring their databases serve well across different scenarios and workloads.

Understand Business Requirements

Proper database design begins with a thorough understanding of the business requirements. This includes comprehending the various data elements that need to be stored and their relationships. Engage with stakeholders to gather detailed requirements and document all the necessary functionalities. Translating business needs into a coherent data model is the foundation of effective database design.

Prioritize Normalization

Normalization is fundamental to eliminating data redundancy and ensuring data integrity. While this chapter extensively covers different normal forms, remember that applying these forms can dramatically improve how data is stored and accessed. Typically, databases should be normalized up to the Third Normal Form (3NF). However, specific cases may require higher normalization forms such as Boyce-Codd Normal Form (BCNF).

Design for Scalability

Anticipate future growth and plan the database to handle increasing data volumes and user loads. Use partitioning strategies where necessary to manage large datasets and consider the use of replication for distributed environments. For instance, horizontal partitioning can split a table into multiple tables that can be stored across different databases.

Optimize Indexing Strategies

Indexes are powerful tools for improving query performance but can impact write operations negatively due to additional overhead. Carefully analyze query patterns and create indexes to optimize read operations. It is often beneficial to use a combination of clustered and non-clustered indexes. Regularly review and tune indexes based on the changing nature of queries.

Consider Denormalization Judiciously

While normalization aims to reduce redundancy, in some cases, denormalization can be useful. Situations where read performance is critical, and the cost of joins is high, may benefit from denormalization. However, this should be approached cautiously, as it can introduce redundancy and inconsistent data updates.

Enforce Data Integrity

Utilize constraints such as primary keys, foreign keys, unique constraints, and check constraints to enforce data integrity. These constraints ensure that only valid data is entered into the database. For instance, a foreign key constraint ensures that a record in one table corresponds to a valid record in another table.

Use Descriptive Naming Conventions

Maintain clear, consistent, and descriptive naming conventions for database objects. Table names, column names, indexes, and constraints should reflect their purpose and use. This practice enhances readability and maintainability. For example, name tables using singular nouns like Customer or Order and their columns in a manner that clearly indicates the data they store, like CustomerID or OrderDate.

Document the Schema

Documenting the database schema and its entities is crucial. This includes ER diagrams, table definitions, relationships, constraints, and indexes. Documentation serves as a reference for developers and database administrators and aids in onboarding new team members. Use tools that generate documentation directly from the database to ensure it is always up-to-date.

Plan for Security

Security should be an integral part of the database design process. Implement least privilege principles by granting users the minimum level of access required to perform their jobs. Use views, stored procedures, and roles to control data access. Encrypt sensitive data, both at rest and in transit, to protect against unauthorized access and data breaches.

Implement Regular Backups

Plan and implement a robust backup and recovery strategy. Regular backups safeguard against data loss due to hardware failures, human errors, or other unforeseen events. Test backups periodically to ensure data can be restored successfully. Use tools and scripts to automate backup processes.

Monitor and Maintain

Ongoing monitoring and maintenance are crucial to the health of a database. Regularly check for slow-performing queries, outdated statistics, and fragmentation of indexes. Use database monitoring tools to track performance metrics and set up alerts for anomalies.

Use Transactions and Locking Appropriately

Transactions ensure that a series of database operations are executed in an all-or-nothing manner, maintaining the consistency of the database. Use transactions to group related operations. However, be mindful of the isolation levels and locking mechanisms, as they can impact concurrency and performance. Proper understanding and implementation of ACID properties (Atomicity, Consistency, Isolation, Durability) are vital.

Leverage Database Management Tools

Utilize database management systems (DBMS) and associated tools to streamline development and maintenance processes. Tools for database design, query optimization, backup management, and performance monitoring can significantly enhance productivity and ensure best practices are followed consistently.

Attention to these best practices ensures that a database not only meets current requirements but is also resilient, scalable, and easier to manage in the long term.

Chapter 8

Stored Procedures and Functions

This chapter explains the creation and execution of stored procedures and user-defined functions in SQL Server. It covers passing parameters to stored procedures, differentiating between scalar and table-valued functions, and using system-stored procedures and functions. The chapter also addresses error handling, nesting, and recursion in stored procedures, as well as best practices and performance considerations for writing and securing stored procedures and functions.

8.1 Introduction to Stored Procedures and Functions

Stored procedures and functions are essential components of SQL Server, providing a modular approach to programming within the database environment. They encapsulate a set of SQL statements and control-of-flow language into a single logical unit, which can then be executed repeatedly, thereby improving code reusability, maintainability, and performance.

Stored procedures are pre-compiled collections of Transact-SQL (T-SQL) statements and optional control-of-flow statements stored under a name and processed as a unit. Users can invoke these procedures to execute the encapsulated group of statements as often as needed, optimizing performance by reducing parsing and compilation overhead. Stored procedures support input and output parameters, allowing dynamic operations and enhanced interaction with data. They are frequently used for data validation, access control, complex queries, and transaction management.

The basic syntax for creating a stored procedure in SQL Server is as follows:

```
CREATE PROCEDURE procedure\_name
AS
BEGIN
    -- SQL statements go here
END
```

Functions in SQL Server, on the other hand, are routines that encapsulate a series of T-SQL statements, similar to stored procedures. However, unlike stored procedures, functions return a single value or a table and can be used in SQL expressions, making them highly versatile for incorporating complex calculations and data transformations within queries.

Functions are categorized into scalar functions and table-valued functions. Scalar functions return a single data value of a specific data type, whereas table-valued functions return a table data type, which can be utilized in the FROM clause of a SELECT statement, just like a regular table.

The syntax for creating a scalar function is:

```
CREATE FUNCTION function\_name
(
    @parameter\_name data\_type,
    ...
)
RETURNS data\_type
AS
BEGIN
    -- Function body goes here
    RETURN scalar\_value
END
```

And for a table-valued function:

```
CREATE FUNCTION function\_name
(
    @parameter\_name data\_type,
    ...
)
RETURNS TABLE
AS
RETURN
```

```
(
    -- Query to return a table
    SELECT ...
)
```

These stored procedures and functions significantly contribute to the modularization of database code, enabling more organized, readable, and manageable SQL scripts. They facilitate encapsulation of business logic within the database, enhancing data processing efficiency.

In terms of procedural logic, stored procedures are well-suited for a wide range of operations from simple queries to complex transaction management, while functions are ideal for scenarios requiring reusable logic that can be embedded directly within SQL statements. Both stored procedures and functions support error handling, which will be discussed in subsequent sections.

The execution context of stored procedures and functions also preserves transactional integrity, allowing developers to manage transactions explicitly within the procedures or functions. This ensures that complex operations can either be committed entirely or rolled back, maintaining data consistency.

As we delve deeper into stored procedures and functions in the coming sections, we will explore various ways to optimize their usage, ensure security, and understand their role in robust database application development.

8.2 Creating and Executing Stored Procedures

Stored procedures in SQL Server serve as a way to encapsulate one or more SQL statements for reuse and better management. A stored procedure is a precompiled collection of Transact-SQL (T-SQL) statements that perform a specific task, allowing for increased performance and ease of maintenance.

To create a stored procedure, the CREATE PROCEDURE or CREATE PROC statement is used, followed by the procedure name and the T-SQL statements that define the procedure's behavior. Here is a basic example of a stored procedure creation:

```
CREATE PROCEDURE GetEmployeeDetails
AS
BEGIN
```

```
    SELECT EmployeeID, FirstName, LastName, JobTitle
    FROM Employees;
END;
```

In this example, the stored procedure GetEmployeeDetails is created, which retrieves a list of employees along with specific fields such as EmployeeID, FirstName, LastName, and JobTitle from the Employees table.

Executing a stored procedure is straightforward. The EXEC or EXECUTE statement is used followed by the procedure name. To execute the GetEmployeeDetails procedure, you could write:

```
EXEC GetEmployeeDetails;
```

Stored procedures can also accept parameters, allowing them to be more dynamic and versatile. Parameters are defined within the procedure definition. Here's an example where a procedure takes one input parameter:

```
CREATE PROCEDURE GetEmployeeByID
    @EmployeeID INT
AS
BEGIN
    SELECT EmployeeID, FirstName, LastName, JobTitle
    FROM Employees
    WHERE EmployeeID = @EmployeeID;
END;
```

To execute this stored procedure, you pass a value for the @EmployeeID parameter:

```
EXEC GetEmployeeByID @EmployeeID = 5;
```

Stored procedures can include multiple parameters, both input and output. Output parameters allow the procedure to return values back to the calling program. Here is an example that includes both input and output parameters:

```
CREATE PROCEDURE GetEmployeeNameByID
    @EmployeeID INT,
    @FirstName NVARCHAR(50) OUTPUT,
    @LastName NVARCHAR(50) OUTPUT
AS
BEGIN
    SELECT @FirstName = FirstName, @LastName = LastName
    FROM Employees
    WHERE EmployeeID = @EmployeeID;
END;
```

To execute a stored procedure with output parameters, the following syntax is used:

```
DECLARE @FirstName NVARCHAR(50), @LastName NVARCHAR(50);

EXEC GetEmployeeNameByID
    @EmployeeID = 5,
    @FirstName = @FirstName OUTPUT,
    @LastName = @LastName OUTPUT;

PRINT @FirstName;
PRINT @LastName;
```

Stored procedures in SQL Server also support default values for parameters, allowing for optional arguments. Here is an example where the default value is set for a parameter:

```
CREATE PROCEDURE GetEmployeeByJobTitle
    @JobTitle NVARCHAR(50) = 'Sales Representative'
AS
BEGIN
    SELECT EmployeeID, FirstName, LastName, JobTitle
    FROM Employees
    WHERE JobTitle = @JobTitle;
END;
```

Executing this stored procedure without providing a parameter will use the default value:

```
EXEC GetEmployeeByJobTitle;
```

or, to provide a specific value:

```
EXEC GetEmployeeByJobTitle @JobTitle = 'Engineer';
```

To modify an existing stored procedure, the ALTER PROCEDURE statement is used, which follows the same syntax as creating a new procedure. For instance, to alter the GetEmployeeDetails procedure to include an additional column, the syntax would be:

```
ALTER PROCEDURE GetEmployeeDetails
AS
BEGIN
    SELECT EmployeeID, FirstName, LastName, JobTitle, Department
    FROM Employees;
END;
```

Dropping or deleting a stored procedure is achieved via the DROP PROCEDURE statement. Caution should be taken when dropping procedures to ensure they are not being referenced by other database objects:

```
DROP PROCEDURE GetEmployeeDetails;
```

With these fundamental operations—creating, executing, altering, and dropping procedures—SQL Server supports robust database management practices that ensure consistency, performance optimization, and ease of deployment.

8.3 Parameters in Stored Procedures

Parameters in stored procedures enable the customization of the procedure's execution by passing values or references. This feature enhances the reusability and flexibility of stored procedures. Parameters can be classified into input parameters, output parameters, and input-output parameters. Understanding how to define and utilize these types of parameters is essential for writing efficient and dynamic stored procedures in SQL Server.

To define a parameter in a stored procedure, you specify its name and data type within the procedure's definition. Parameters are declared within the parentheses following the procedure's name. Here is a basic example illustrating the declaration of input parameters:

```
CREATE PROCEDURE GetEmployeeDetails
    @EmployeeID INT,
    @DepartmentID INT
AS
BEGIN
    SELECT EmployeeName, JobTitle
    FROM Employees
    WHERE EmployeeID = @EmployeeID
        AND DepartmentID = @DepartmentID;
END;
```

In this example, the stored procedure GetEmployeeDetails accepts two input parameters: @EmployeeID and @DepartmentID, both of which are integers. These parameters enable the procedure to fetch details specific to an employee and their department.

To execute the above stored procedure with specific parameter values, you use the EXEC command as shown:

```
EXEC GetEmployeeDetails @EmployeeID = 123, @DepartmentID = 456;
```

- **Output Parameters**

  Output parameters are used to return values from a stored procedure to the caller. They are declared using the OUTPUT keyword. Below is an example demonstrating the use of an output parameter:

```
CREATE PROCEDURE CalculateEmployeeBonus
    @EmployeeID INT,
    @BonusAmount DECIMAL(10, 2) OUTPUT
AS
BEGIN
    SELECT @BonusAmount = Salary * 0.1
    FROM Employees
    WHERE EmployeeID = @EmployeeID;
END;
```

In this example, the stored procedure CalculateEmployeeBonus calculates a bonus amount for an employee based on their salary and returns this amount through the @BonusAmount output parameter. To utilize this stored procedure with an output parameter, the invocation would look like this:

```
DECLARE @EmployeeBonus DECIMAL(10, 2);
EXEC CalculateEmployeeBonus @EmployeeID = 123, @BonusAmount =
      @EmployeeBonus OUTPUT;
PRINT @EmployeeBonus;
```

The DECLARE statement initializes a variable to store the output, which is then passed to the procedure and printed after execution.

- **Input-Output Parameters**

  Input-output parameters can serve both as inputs to a stored procedure and outputs from it. They are also declared using the OUTPUT keyword. The following example illustrates the use of an input-output parameter:

```
CREATE PROCEDURE AdjustEmployeeSalary
    @EmployeeID INT,
    @SalaryAdjustment DECIMAL(10, 2) OUTPUT
AS
BEGIN
    UPDATE Employees
    SET Salary = Salary + @SalaryAdjustment
    WHERE EmployeeID = @EmployeeID;

    SELECT @SalaryAdjustment = Salary
    FROM Employees
    WHERE EmployeeID = @EmployeeID;
END;
```

This stored procedure AdjustEmployeeSalary receives an input amount to adjust the salary and subsequently returns the new salary using the same parameter. The invocation would be as follows:

```
DECLARE @AdjustmentAmount DECIMAL(10, 2) = 1000.00;
EXEC AdjustEmployeeSalary @EmployeeID = 123, @SalaryAdjustment =
      @AdjustmentAmount OUTPUT;
```

```
PRINT @AdjustmentAmount;
```

The above script adjusts the employee's salary by the specified amount and then outputs the updated salary.

- **Default Parameter Values**

  A stored procedure can also have parameters with default values. This feature allows the procedure to be executed without explicitly providing values for such parameters. Default values are specified in the parameter declaration:

```
CREATE PROCEDURE GetDepartmentReport
    @DepartmentID INT = 1
AS
BEGIN
    SELECT EmployeeName, JobTitle
    FROM Employees
    WHERE DepartmentID = @DepartmentID;
END;
```

  Here, @DepartmentID has a default value of 1. As a result, calling the procedure without specifying this parameter will default to retrieving data for the department with ID 1:

```
EXEC GetDepartmentReport;
```

  Specifying the parameter explicitly overrides the default:

```
EXEC GetDepartmentReport @DepartmentID = 2;
```

- **Named and Positional Parameter Passing**

  Parameters can be passed either positionally or by their names. Positional passing requires providing the parameters in the order of their declaration, while named passing allows specifying parameters in any order:

  Positional Passing:

```
EXEC GetEmployeeDetails 123, 456;
```

  Named Passing:

```
EXEC GetEmployeeDetails @DepartmentID = 456, @EmployeeID = 123;
```

  Named passing is particularly useful when dealing with procedures having numerous parameters or when only a subset of optional parameters is specified.

Using parameters effectively enhances the modularity and adaptability of stored procedures, allowing for more sophisticated and dynamic SQL operations tailored to diverse requirements. Understanding the various types and methods of parameter utilization is crucial for efficient database management and application development.

8.4 Creating and Using User-Defined Functions

User-defined functions (UDFs) in SQL Server allow developers to encapsulate reusable logic. By creating functions, processes become modular, and code becomes easier to maintain, troubleshoot, and optimize. UDFs can return either a single scalar value or a table, and can be classified as scalar functions or table-valued functions (TVFs).

A scalar function returns a single value, such as an integer or a string, whereas a table-valued function returns a table, which can be treated similarly to a regular table in SQL queries. We will delve into the creation, syntax, and usage of both types of functions.

To create a scalar function, use the following syntax:

```
CREATE FUNCTION [schema_name.] function_name
(
    @parameter_name data_type [ = default_value ] [ ,...n ]
)
RETURNS return_data_type
AS
BEGIN
    -- Function body
    RETURN scalar_expression
END
```

Example: Creating a Scalar Function

Consider a scenario where you need a function to calculate the total cost after applying tax to the initial cost. The following scalar function calculates this based on a specified tax rate:

```
CREATE FUNCTION dbo.CalculateTotalCost
(
    @InitialCost DECIMAL(10, 2),
    @TaxRate FLOAT
)
RETURNS DECIMAL(10, 2)
AS
BEGIN
    RETURN @InitialCost + (@InitialCost * @TaxRate)
END
```

To use this function, include it in a query as shown below:

```
SELECT dbo.CalculateTotalCost(100.00, 0.05) AS TotalCost;
```

```
TotalCost
---------
105.00
```

Table-Valued Functions

A table-valued function (TVF) returns a table and can be used much like a view or another table in SQL queries. TVFs can be further categorized into Inline Table-Valued Functions (ITVF) and Multi-statement Table-Valued Functions (MTVF).

Example: Creating an Inline Table-Valued Function

An inline TVF is essentially a parameterized view. The creation syntax is:

```
CREATE FUNCTION [schema_name.] function_name
(
    @parameter_name data_type [ ,...n ]
)
RETURNS TABLE
AS
RETURN
(
    --Single SELECT statement
)
```

Consider a function that returns all orders for a specific customer:

```
CREATE FUNCTION dbo.GetCustomerOrders
(
    @CustomerID INT
)
RETURNS TABLE
AS
RETURN
(
    SELECT OrderID, OrderDate, TotalAmount
    FROM Orders
    WHERE CustomerID = @CustomerID
)
```

This function can then be used in a query like so:

```
SELECT * FROM dbo.GetCustomerOrders(1);
```

```
OrderID  OrderDate   TotalAmount
-------  ----------  ------------
101      2023-01-01      299.99
102      2023-02-14      159.50
```

Multi-Statement Table-Valued Functions

In contrast, a Multi-Statement TVF allows for more complex logic, including the use of multiple statements. The syntax is as follows:

```
CREATE FUNCTION [schema_name.] function_name
(
    @parameter_name data_type [ ,...n ]
)
RETURNS @return_variable TABLE
(
    column_name data_type [ ,...n ]
)
AS
BEGIN
    -- Multiple SQL statements that populate @return_variable
    RETURN;
END
```

Example: Creating a Multi-Statement TVF

Suppose we need a function to return the top N customers by total purchase amount. We can define such a function as below:

```
CREATE FUNCTION dbo.GetTopCustomers
(
    @TopN INT
)
RETURNS @TopCustomers TABLE
(
    CustomerID INT,
    TotalPurchased DECIMAL(10, 2)
)
AS
BEGIN
    INSERT INTO @TopCustomers
    SELECT TOP (@TopN) CustomerID, SUM(TotalAmount) AS TotalPurchased
    FROM Orders
    GROUP BY CustomerID
    ORDER BY TotalPurchased DESC;

    RETURN;
END
```

To call this function, use the following query:

```
SELECT * FROM dbo.GetTopCustomers(5);
```

```
CustomerID  TotalPurchased
----------  ---------------
5                 12345.67
3                  9876.54
2                  8765.43
8                  7654.32
6                  6543.21
```

The function's body includes an `@TopCustomers` statement that populates the table variable `@TopCustomers`. The table structure and column types must match the data being inserted.

User-defined functions in SQL Server offer flexibility and code reusability. Scalar functions simplify computations that need a single value result while table-valued functions, both inline and multi-statement, provide powerful ways to return and manipulate table data. Correctly leveraging these functions enhances the efficiency and maintainability of database-driven applications.

8.5 Scalar vs. Table-Valued Functions

In SQL Server, functions can be categorized into scalar functions and table-valued functions (TVFs). Understanding the differences and appropriate use cases for each is crucial for efficient database management and query optimization.

A scalar function returns a single value of a specific data type, such as an integer, varchar, or datetime. It is commonly used for calculations and simple transformations that are applied to each row in the result set. For instance, a function that calculates the square of a given number is a scalar function.

A table-valued function, on the other hand, returns a table data type. It is used when the operation requires the output to be in a set of rows and columns, similar to a regular table. TVFs can be further divided into inline table-valued functions (ITVFs) and multi-statement table-valued functions (MTVFs). Detailed below are the characteristics and usage of scalar functions and the two types of TVFs.

Scalar Functions

Scalar functions are invoked for each row processed by a query. An example is shown in the following SQL script:

```
CREATE FUNCTION dbo.CalculateSquare (@Number INT)
RETURNS INT
AS
BEGIN
    RETURN @Number * @Number
END
```

In the above example, the CalculateSquare function takes an integer as input and returns its square. This function can be used anywhere in SQL Server where you can use an integer expression. Below is an example of how to use it in a query:

```
SELECT dbo.CalculateSquare(4) AS SquareResult
```

The result of executing the above query will be:

```
SquareResult
-------------
16
```

Since scalar functions are called once per row in a query, their performance impact can be significant if the function is complex or the data set is large.

Inline Table-Valued Functions (ITVFs)

Inline table-valued functions are similar to views but with parameters. The function body contains a single SELECT statement. The table returned inherits the column names and data types from the result set of the SELECT statement.

Creating an ITVF involves defining the function with the RETURNS TABLE clause. Here is an example:

```
CREATE FUNCTION dbo.GetEmployeeDetails (@DepartmentID INT)
RETURNS TABLE
AS
RETURN
(
    SELECT EmployeeID, FirstName, LastName, JobTitle
    FROM Employees
    WHERE DepartmentID = @DepartmentID
)
```

The GetEmployeeDetails function returns a table of employees filtered by the specified DepartmentID. This function can be used in SELECT statements as if it were a table:

```
SELECT * FROM dbo.GetEmployeeDetails(3)
```

The output will be a table containing EmployeeID, FirstName, LastName, and JobTitle of employees in department 3.

Multi-Statement Table-Valued Functions (MTVFs)

Multi-statement TVFs allow for multiple SQL statements to be executed within the function body. This provides the flexibility to perform complex operations before populating the table variable that will be returned.

The syntax includes the RETURNS @TableVariable clause and a BEGIN...END block. Here is an example:

```
CREATE FUNCTION dbo.GetEmployeeSummary(@DepartmentID INT)
RETURNS @EmployeeSummary TABLE
(
    EmployeeID INT,
    FullName VARCHAR(100),
    JobTitle VARCHAR(50)
```

```
)
AS
BEGIN
    INSERT INTO @EmployeeSummary
    SELECT EmployeeID, FirstName + ' ' + LastName AS FullName, JobTitle
    FROM Employees
    WHERE DepartmentID = @DepartmentID

    RETURN
END
```

This function constructs a table by concatenating first and last names of employees. It can be queried as follows:

```
SELECT * FROM dbo.GetEmployeeSummary(3)
```

Executing this will result in a table containing EmployeeID, FullName, and JobTitle for employees in department 3.

Comparing Scalar and Table-Valued Functions

Scalar and table-valued functions serve different purposes in SQL Server:

- Scalability: Scalar functions are simpler and faster for single-value computations. TVFs provide scalability for operations requiring set-based logic and returning multiple rows.
- Usability: Use scalar functions for straightforward computations applied to single rows. Utilize ITVFs for inline queries with parameters and MTVFs for complex multi-step processes returning tabular data.
- Performance: Scalar functions may introduce performance bottlenecks, especially in large datasets, due to repeated execution per row. TVFs are optimized for set-based operations, particularly ITVFs.
- Maintenance: Scalar functions are easier to write and maintain for simple operations. TVFs, while more complex, encapsulate multi-step logic and improve code reuse.

Efficient database design leverages both types of functions appropriately. Understanding when to use each enhances performance and maintainability in SQL Server.

8.6 Error Handling in Stored Procedures

Error handling in stored procedures is a fundamental aspect of ensuring robust and reliable database operations. SQL Server provides mechanisms to detect, handle, and troubleshoot errors that occur during the execution of stored procedures. This section discusses how to implement error handling in stored procedures and the different strategies and tools available for effective error management.

TRY...CATCH Blocks

SQL Server's primary method for handling errors in T-SQL code is the use of TRY...CATCH blocks. These blocks enable developers to define a set of statements for which errors will be monitored, and a separate set of statements to execute in case an error is detected. The structure of a TRY...CATCH block is straightforward.

```
BEGIN TRY
    -- Statements that may cause an error
END TRY
BEGIN CATCH
    -- Error handling statements
END CATCH
```

Within the CATCH block, several system functions are available to obtain detailed information about the error, including:

- ERROR_NUMBER(): Returns the error number.
- ERROR_MESSAGE(): Returns the complete error message.
- ERROR_SEVERITY(): Returns the severity level of the error.
- ERROR_STATE(): Returns the state number of the error.
- ERROR_PROCEDURE(): Returns the name of the stored procedure or trigger where the error occurred.
- ERROR_LINE(): Returns the line number where the error occurred.

An example utilizing these functions within a TRY...CATCH block is shown below:

```
BEGIN TRY
    -- Intentionally cause a divide by zero error
    DECLARE @result INT;
    SET @result = 5 / 0;
```

```
END TRY
BEGIN CATCH
    PRINT 'Error Number: ' + CAST(ERROR_NUMBER() AS NVARCHAR(10));
    PRINT 'Error Message: ' + ERROR_MESSAGE();
    PRINT 'Error Severity: ' + CAST(ERROR_SEVERITY() AS NVARCHAR(10));
    PRINT 'Error State: ' + CAST(ERROR_STATE() AS NVARCHAR(10));
    PRINT 'Error Procedure: ' + ISNULL(ERROR_PROCEDURE(), '-');
    PRINT 'Error Line: ' + CAST(ERROR_LINE() AS NVARCHAR(10));
END CATCH;
```

This example demonstrates the capture and logging of error details when an attempt to divide by zero occurs.

Transaction Management with Error Handling

In transactional operations, it is crucial to ensure that an error does not leave the database in an inconsistent state. TRY...CATCH blocks play a significant role in managing transactions. Within these blocks, it is common practice to include BEGIN TRANSACTION at the start of the TRY block and to either COMMIT or ROLLBACK the transaction within the CATCH block, depending on the presence of errors.

```
BEGIN TRY
    BEGIN TRANSACTION;

    -- Perform transactional operations
    INSERT INTO TableA (Column1) VALUES ('Value1');
    INSERT INTO TableB (Column2) VALUES ('Value2');

    -- Commit the transaction if no errors occur
    COMMIT TRANSACTION;
END TRY
BEGIN CATCH
    -- Roll back the transaction if an error occurs
    IF XACT\_STATE() <> 0
    BEGIN
        ROLLBACK TRANSACTION;
    END;

    PRINT 'Error Number: ' + CAST(ERROR_NUMBER() AS NVARCHAR(10));
    PRINT 'Error Message: ' + ERROR_MESSAGE();
END CATCH;
```

In this example, if an error occurs during any of the insert operations, the transaction is rolled back, ensuring the database remains consistent by discarding all operations within the transaction.

XACT_STATE() Function

The XACT_STATE() function is particularly useful in a CATCH block to determine the current state of a transaction:

- 1: Indicates an active user-defined transaction exists, and it can be safely committed.

- 0: Indicates no active transaction exists.
- -1: Indicates an uncommittable transaction, which must be rolled back.

Incorporating XACT_STATE() helps avoid nested transaction issues. The transaction can only be rolled back if the state is 1 or -1.

RAISERROR

The RAISERROR statement allows developers to generate their own errors. This can be useful for handling application-specific logic and for debugging purposes. RAISERROR can be used to return a custom error number, message, and severity level:

```
RAISERROR ('Custom error message', 16, 1);
```

The above code will generate an error with a severity of 16, which indicates an error that can be corrected by the user, such as a data integrity violation.

More complex usage involves including arguments and defining user message IDs from the sys.messages catalog view:

```
RAISERROR (50001, 16, 1, 'Custom argument');
```

Here, 50001 is a user-defined message ID, which must be defined in the sys.messages table prior to usage.

```
EXEC sp\_addmessage @msgnum = 50001,
                    @severity = 16,
                    @msgtext = N'Custom error occurred: %s';
```

THROW Statement

SQL Server 2012 introduced the THROW statement, which provides a simpler and more modern way to raise errors compared to RAISERROR. THROW can be used without specifying parameters or can re-raise the original error caught in a CATCH block:

```
THROW 50001, 'Custom error message', 1;
```

Unlike RAISERROR, THROW does not require a message to be defined in sys.messages.

In cases where an error has been caught, re-throwing the error can be done using:

```
BEGIN TRY
    -- Statements that may cause an error
```

```
END TRY
BEGIN CATCH
    THROW;
END CATCH;
```

This rethrows the original error with its original error number and message, and is especially useful when simply logging the error details in the CATCH block.

Best Practices for Error Handling

When implementing error handling in stored procedures, several best practices can enhance reliability and maintainability:

- Always use TRY...CATCH blocks to handle known and unexpected errors.
- Log errors to a designated error log table for post-mortem analysis.
- Use transactions to maintain data integrity and ensure all operations either complete successfully or rollback in case of failure.
- Utilize the XACT_STATE() function within the CATCH block to validate the transaction state before issuing a ROLLBACK.
- Prefer THROW over RAISERROR for newer implementations for simplicity and readability.
- Where possible, encapsulate error handling logic within utility procedures to avoid redundancy and enhance modularity.

Proper error handling not only improves the resilience of stored procedures but also simplifies debugging and maintenance, fostering a more stable database environment.

8.7 Using System Stored Procedures and Functions

System stored procedures and functions are pre-defined stored procedures and functions available in SQL Server. They provide a broad range of functionalities for database administration, configuration management, and information retrieval about server instance properties.

Utilizing these system-provided utilities can significantly enhance productivity and minimize the need for custom scripts for common tasks. This section elaborates on some of the essential system stored procedures and functions, including their syntax and applications.

Common System Stored Procedures

Several system stored procedures are commonly used in SQL Server for routine administrative tasks. Below are key examples:

- **sp_help**: Provides detailed information about database objects.

  ```
  EXEC sp_help 'Employees';
  ```

  This command returns metadata about the Employees table, including column definitions, constraints, and indexes.

- **sp_rename**: Changes the name of a user-created object in the current database.

  ```
  EXEC sp_rename 'OldTableName', 'NewTableName';
  ```

  This command renames the table OldTableName to NewTableName.

- **sp_configure**: Displays or changes global configuration settings for the SQL Server instance.

  ```
  EXEC sp_configure 'show advanced options', 1;
  RECONFIGURE;
  EXEC sp_configure;
  ```

  These commands enable advanced options and then display all configuration options available in the server instance.

- **sp_who2**: Provides information about current users, sessions, and processes.

  ```
  EXEC sp_who2;
  ```

  This command returns a result set summarizing active processes and their states, which is useful for identifying performance bottlenecks or blocking sessions.

Common System Functions

System functions in SQL Server are built-in functions that perform system-related operations. Here are a few examples:

- **@@SERVERNAME**: Returns the name of the local server running SQL Server.

  ```
  SELECT @@SERVERNAME;
  ```

  This query retrieves the name of the server instance.

- **@@VERSION**: Provides the version, processor architecture, build date, and operating system for the current installation.

  ```
  SELECT @@VERSION;
  ```

  Executing this query gives a detailed string containing the SQL Server version and other deployment details.

- **DB_ID**: Returns the database ID of a specified database.

  ```
  SELECT DB_ID('AdventureWorks');
  ```

  This code snippet obtains the database ID of the AdventureWorks database.

- **DB_NAME**: Returns the database name based on the specified database ID.

  ```
  SELECT DB_NAME(5);
  ```

  This query fetches the name of the database with the ID 5.

Practical Examples

Combining system stored procedures and functions can provide powerful insights and administrative control. Consider the following practical examples:

```
-- Retrieve server name and version
SELECT @@SERVERNAME AS 'Server Name', @@VERSION AS 'SQL Server Version'
    ;

-- Obtain information about all tables in the current database
EXEC sp_MSforeachtable @command1="EXEC sp_help '?'";
```

In this example, the first query concurrently retrieves the server name and SQL Server version, encapsulating the information in a single result set. The second line uses sp_MSforeachtable to execute the sp_help command on every table within the current database, providing a comprehensive metadata overview for all tables.

```
-- Enable advanced options and configure 'max degree of parallelism'
EXEC sp_configure 'show advanced options', 1;
```

```
RECONFIGURE;
EXEC sp_configure 'max degree of parallelism', 4;
RECONFIGURE;
```

This query sequence first enables advanced server configuration options, then sets the max degree of parallelism to 4, effectively controlling how the server handles parallel processes during query execution.

```
Name
------------------------------------
MainServer
Microsoft SQL Server 2019 - 15.0.2070
```

Effective use of system stored procedures and functions can immensely simplify tasks for database administrators, providing quick access to critical information and control over server configurations. Understanding their syntax and applications ensures efficient management and robust performance tuning.

```
Table Name          Column Name          Data Type        Length
-----------------   -----------------    -------------    ------
Employees           EmployeeID           INT              4
Employees           FirstName            NVARCHAR           50
...
```

8.8 Nesting and Recursion in Stored Procedures

Nesting and recursion in stored procedures are pivotal concepts in SQL Server that allow for robust and modular code development. These strategies enable developers to break down complex problems into simpler, manageable pieces, often resulting in more readable and maintainable code.

Nesting refers to the process of calling one stored procedure from within another. This technique encourages code reuse and cleaner modularization. By encapsulating specific logic in standalone stored procedures, other procedures can invoke this logic without redundancy. Recursion, on the other hand, involves a stored procedure calling itself, either directly or indirectly. Recursion is particularly useful for operations on hierarchical data structures, such as organizational charts or family trees.

A crucial consideration in both nesting and recursion is the depth of calls. SQL Server limits the nesting level to 32. Attempting to exceed this threshold results in an error. Adequate error handling and control mechanisms are necessary to manage deep nesting and recursion effectively.

Nesting Stored Procedures

To illustrate nesting, consider two stored procedures: usp_ParentProcedure and usp_ChildProcedure. The usp_ParentProcedure calls usp_ChildProcedure to execute its encapsulated logic.

```
CREATE PROCEDURE usp_ChildProcedure
AS
BEGIN
    PRINT 'This is the child procedure.'
    -- Additional logic can be placed here.
END
```

```
CREATE PROCEDURE usp_ParentProcedure
AS
BEGIN
    PRINT 'This is the parent procedure.'
    EXEC usp_ChildProcedure
END
```

In the above example, executing usp_ParentProcedure results in the invocation of usp_ChildProcedure. The output demonstrates the sequence of calls.

```
This is the parent procedure.
This is the child procedure.
```

Recursion in Stored Procedures

For recursion, consider a stored procedure designed to calculate the factorial of a number. Factorial calculation is a classic example that naturally lends itself to a recursive approach.

```
CREATE PROCEDURE usp_Factorial
    @Number INT,
    @Result BIGINT OUTPUT
AS
BEGIN
    IF @Number = 1
    BEGIN
        SET @Result = 1
    END
    ELSE
    BEGIN
        DECLARE @TempResult BIGINT
        EXEC usp_Factorial @Number - 1, @TempResult OUTPUT
        SET @Result = @Number * @TempResult
    END
END
```

In this example, usp_Factorial calls itself with a decremented value of Number until it reaches the base case where Number is 1. The termination condition (@Number = 1) ensures the recursion ceases, avoiding an infinite loop.

Executing the factorial procedure involves the following:

```
DECLARE @Result BIGINT
EXEC usp_Factorial 5, @Result OUTPUT
SELECT @Result AS FactorialResult
```

```
FactorialResult
---------------
120
```

The output confirms the correct calculation of 5!, demonstrating the effective application of recursion.

Error Handling in Nested and Recursive Procedures

Handling errors is critical to prevent stack overflow and infinite recursion. SQL Server provides the TRY...CATCH construct to manage exceptions within stored procedures. Integrating error handling ensures that any anomalies are caught and managed gracefully.

```
CREATE PROCEDURE usp_SafeFactorial
    @Number INT,
    @Result BIGINT OUTPUT
AS
BEGIN
    BEGIN TRY
        IF @Number <= 0
            THROW 50001, 'Number must be positive', 1

        IF @Number = 1
        BEGIN
            SET @Result = 1
        END
        ELSE
        BEGIN
            DECLARE @TempResult BIGINT
            EXEC usp_SafeFactorial @Number - 1, @TempResult OUTPUT
            SET @Result = @Number * @TempResult
        END
    END TRY
    BEGIN CATCH
        PRINT ERROR_MESSAGE()
        SET @Result = NULL
    END CATCH
END
```

The inclusion of the TRY...CATCH block captures any exceptional conditions—like non-positive inputs—and handles them appropriately, setting the @Result to NULL and printing the error message.

Considerations for Performance

Nesting and recursion, while powerful, can influence performance.

Deeply nested or highly recursive procedures can lead to excessive CPU and memory usage, affecting overall server performance. Monitoring and optimizing these procedures is essential.

To mitigate potential performance issues, consider the following strategies:

- Use iteration wherever possible to replace recursion, particularly for large datasets.
- Optimize each nested procedure for efficiency to reduce cumulative overhead.
- Leverage SQL Server's performance monitoring tools to track and analyze execution metrics.

Properly managed, nesting and recursion enhance the modularity and clarity of SQL Server stored procedures, facilitating more effective and maintainable database operations.

8.9 Best Practices for Writing Stored Procedures

Adhering to best practices when writing stored procedures is critical for ensuring efficiency, maintainability, and performance of your SQL Server databases. By following well-established principles, you can avoid common pitfalls and streamline the development process. Key best practices for writing stored procedures include:

1. Use Meaningful and Consistent Naming Conventions: Names of stored procedures should clearly describe their purpose and functionality. Consistent naming conventions enhance readability and maintainability. A commonly adopted convention is using a verb-noun format, such as usp_GetCustomerOrders or usp_UpdateProductInventory.

2. Include Comments and Documentation: Thorough comments and documentation within stored procedures are essential for future maintenance and for other developers who may work on the code. Comments should explain the procedure's purpose, the parameters, and any complex logic. For example:

```
-- usp_GetCustomerOrders: Retrieves orders for a specified customer
-- Params:
-- @CustomerID (INT) - The ID of the customer
```

```
CREATE PROCEDURE usp_GetCustomerOrders
    @CustomerID INT
AS
BEGIN
    ...
END
```

3. Maintain Modular Code: Decompose complex procedures into smaller, reusable units. Modular code is easier to debug, test, and maintain. Use user-defined functions or other stored procedures to break down tasks logically.

4. Avoid Using SELECT *: Explicitly specify the required columns in the SELECT statement rather than using the wildcard *. This practice reduces the amount of data transferred and makes the code more robust to schema changes.

```
-- Instead of
SELECT * FROM Orders;

-- Use
SELECT OrderID, OrderDate, CustomerID FROM Orders;
```

5. Implement Error Handling: Implement robust error handling using TRY...CATCH blocks to capture and handle exceptions. This practice improves error diagnostics and ensures that resources are released and transactions are properly managed.

```
BEGIN TRY
    -- Code that may cause an error
    ...
END TRY
BEGIN CATCH
    -- Error handling code
    DECLARE @ErrorMessage NVARCHAR(4000);
    SET @ErrorMessage = ERROR_MESSAGE();
    RAISERROR(@ErrorMessage, 16, 1);
END CATCH;
```

6. Avoid Cursors When Possible: Cursors can be inefficient and slow, especially when processing large datasets. Whenever possible, use set-based operations, which are generally more efficient. If a cursor is necessary, ensure it is optimized for performance.

7. Use Transactions Appropriately: Properly manage transactions to ensure data integrity. Use BEGIN TRANSACTION, COMMIT, and ROLLBACK statements appropriately to handle multi-step operations atomically.

```
BEGIN TRANSACTION;
BEGIN TRY
    -- Perform multiple operations
```

```
    ...
    COMMIT TRANSACTION;
END TRY
BEGIN CATCH
    ROLLBACK TRANSACTION;
    -- Error handling
    ...
END CATCH;
```

8. Optimize for Performance: Use indexing wisely, consider the execution plan, and avoid unnecessary computations within the stored procedure. Evaluate the procedure's performance regularly and refine queries to adhere to best performance practices.

9. Secure Access to Stored Procedures: Limit permissions to stored procedures based on the principle of least privilege. Grant execute permissions only to necessary users, and avoid granting direct access to the underlying tables.

```
-- Grant execute permission to a role
GRANT EXECUTE ON usp_GetCustomerOrders TO SalesRole;
```

10. Utilize Version Control: Maintain version control on your stored procedure definitions. Track changes, manage versions, and ensure you can revert to previous versions if needed. This practice aids in debugging and auditing.

11. Validate Input Parameters: Ensure that input parameters are validated to prevent SQL injection and other forms of malicious input. Use input validation techniques to check the data type, range, and expected format.

```
-- Example of parameter validation
IF (@OrderID IS NULL OR @OrderID <= 0)
BEGIN
    RAISERROR('Invalid Order ID', 16, 1);
    RETURN;
END;
```

12. Normalize Data Access: Centralize data access logic within stored procedures to promote consistency and reuse. Avoid embedding query logic directly within application code.

Following these best practices will contribute significantly to the stability, security, and performance of your SQL Server stored procedures. These guidelines also support better collaboration among team members and future-proof your database applications against changes and growth.

8.10 Performance Considerations with Stored Procedures

Optimizing the performance of stored procedures is crucial in managing large datasets and ensuring efficient application responsiveness. Several strategies and best practices can be employed to achieve optimal performance.

Index Optimization: Efficient indexing is the cornerstone of database performance. Properly indexed columns can significantly reduce the time taken to search and retrieve data. The execution plan can be examined using SQL Server Management Studio (SSMS) to identify whether the used indexes are appropriate. Consider the following SQL script to create an index:

```
CREATE INDEX idx\_customer\_name ON Customers (LastName, FirstName);
```

This multi-column index on LastName and FirstName enables quicker retrieval of customers by their full names.

Avoiding Cursors: Cursors can be detrimental to performance as they process each row individually. Instead, set-based operations are preferred. The following example demonstrates converting a cursor-based operation into a set-based operation:

```
-- Using a cursor
DECLARE @CustomerId INT
DECLARE CustomerCursor CURSOR FOR
SELECT CustomerId FROM Customers

OPEN CustomerCursor
FETCH NEXT FROM CustomerCursor INTO @CustomerId

WHILE @@FETCH_STATUS = 0
BEGIN
   -- Processing logic here
   FETCH NEXT FROM CustomerCursor INTO @CustomerId
END

CLOSE CustomerCursor
DEALLOCATE CustomerCursor

-- Set-based equivalent
UPDATE Customers
SET Processed = 1
WHERE Processed = 0
```

Minimizing Blocking and Deadlocks: Locking can cause significant performance issues. Using appropriate isolation levels can reduce contention. The use of NOLOCK hint can be effective in some scenarios where dirty reads are acceptable:

```
SELECT CustomerId, LastName
FROM Customers WITH (NOLOCK)
```

However, caution must be exercised as NOLOCK can result in reading uncommitted data.

Efficient Query Writing: Writing efficient queries involves several aspects, such as avoiding unnecessary columns in SELECT statements, reducing the use of subqueries or nested queries, and preferring JOIN operations over subqueries where applicable:

```
-- Avoiding unnecessary columns
SELECT CustomerId, LastName, FirstName
FROM Customers;

-- Reducing the use of subqueries
SELECT Orders.OrderId, Customers.LastName
FROM Orders
JOIN Customers ON Orders.CustomerId = Customers.CustomerId;
```

Parameter Sniffing: Parameter sniffing can lead to suboptimal execution plans if not managed properly. One way to manage this is by using option recompile:

```
CREATE PROCEDURE GetCustomerOrders @CustomerId INT
AS
BEGIN
    SELECT OrderId, OrderDate
    FROM Orders
    WHERE CustomerId = @CustomerId
    OPTION (RECOMPILE)
END;
```

This forces SQL Server to recompile the query and consider the current parameter value.

Batch Processing: Large operations can be more efficient if processed in smaller batches. This avoids long locks and makes resource usage more manageable:

```
DECLARE @BatchSize INT = 1000;

WHILE EXISTS (SELECT 1 FROM Customers WHERE Processed = 0)
BEGIN
    UPDATE TOP (@BatchSize) Customers
    SET Processed = 1
    WHERE Processed = 0;

    -- Other processing logic here
END;
```

Execution Plans: Analyzing and understanding the execution plan generated by SQL Server for stored procedures can reveal inefficiencies. Use the following command to display the execution plan:

```
SET SHOWPLAN\_XML ON;
GO
EXEC GetCustomerOrders @CustomerId = 1;
GO
SET SHOWPLAN\_XML OFF;
```

Scalability: Designing stored procedures with scalability in mind ensures that performance remains efficient even as data volume grows. This includes writing modular and reusable code, careful consideration of resource allocation, and regular maintenance tasks like index rebuilding and statistics updating:

```
-- Rebuilding indexes
ALTER INDEX ALL ON Orders
REBUILD;

-- Updating statistics
UPDATE STATISTICS Customers;
```

8.11 Securing Stored Procedures and Functions

Securing stored procedures and functions in SQL Server is crucial for maintaining the integrity and confidentiality of the database. This section explores various methods and best practices for securing these database objects. It covers permissions, encryption, signing, and schema binding, providing a comprehensive guide to ensuring that only authorized users have access to modify or execute these database elements.

Permissions Management: The first layer of security involves managing who has access to the stored procedures and functions. SQL Server employs a robust permission model allowing granular control over database objects. The relevant commands are GRANT, REVOKE, and DENY.

To grant execution rights on a stored procedure to a specific user or role, use the following syntax:

```
GRANT EXECUTE ON [ProcedureName] TO [UserOrRoleName];
```

Similarly, to revoke previously granted permissions:

```
REVOKE EXECUTE ON [ProcedureName] FROM [UserOrRoleName];
```

To explicitly deny permissions, thus preventing a user from executing a procedure regardless of other granted permissions:

```
DENY EXECUTE ON [ProcedureName] TO [UserOrRoleName];
```

Encryption: SQL Server allows encryption of stored procedures, which hides the definition of the procedure from unauthorized users. This feature protects intellectual property and business logic from being viewed or altered. Here's how to create an encrypted stored procedure:

```
CREATE PROCEDURE [ProcedureName]
WITH ENCRYPTION
AS
BEGIN
    -- Procedure logic here
END;
```

However, it is important to note that once a stored procedure or function is encrypted, there is no straightforward way to decrypt it within SQL Server, thus making it vital to keep an unencrypted version of the code in source control.

Code Signing: Another method for securing stored procedures and functions involves signing the code with a certificate. This process involves creating a certificate, signing the stored procedure with it, and then managing permissions on the certificate. First, create a certificate:

```
CREATE CERTIFICATE [CertificateName]
WITH SUBJECT = 'Certificate for signing procedures';
```

Next, sign the stored procedure with this certificate:

```
ADD SIGNATURE TO [ProcedureName] BY CERTIFICATE [CertificateName];
```

Finally, grant execution permissions to the certificate and associate it with a database user. This allows for execution of the procedure without directly granting user permissions, thereby providing an additional security layer.

```
GRANT EXECUTE ON [ProcedureName] TO [UserOrRoleName];
CREATE USER [SigningUser] FOR CERTIFICATE [CertificateName];
```

Schema Binding: Binding stored procedures and functions to a schema enhances security and manages dependencies effectively. When a stored procedure or function is created with schema binding, it means that the referenced objects cannot be modified without modifying the procedure or function first. This prevents inadvertent or unauthorized changes to critical database objects.

Here's an example of creating a function with schema binding:

```
CREATE FUNCTION [dbo].[FuncName]
(@Param INT)
RETURNS INT
WITH SCHEMABINDING
AS
BEGIN
    RETURN (SELECT COUNT(*) FROM dbo.TableName WHERE ColumnName =
        @Param);
END;
```

In the above example, the function [dbo].[FuncName] is bound to the schema, ensuring that no changes can be made to the referenced table dbo.TableName or its ColumnName without first altering the function.

Audit and Monitoring: Regular auditing and monitoring of stored procedures and functions are essential to detect and prevent unauthorized access or modifications. SQL Server Audit provides a way to log events and track activities. To set up an audit, follow these steps:

```
CREATE SERVER AUDIT [AuditName]
TO FILE (FILEPATH = 'C:\AuditLogs\Audit.log')
WITH (ON_FAILURE = CONTINUE);
```

Next, create the audit specification to log specific actions on the stored procedures:

```
CREATE DATABASE AUDIT SPECIFICATION [AuditSpecName]
FOR SERVER AUDIT [AuditName]
ADD (EXECUTE ON DATABASE::[DatabaseName] BY [Public]);
```

Enable the audit to start logging events:

```
ALTER SERVER AUDIT [AuditName] WITH (STATE = ON);
ALTER DATABASE AUDIT SPECIFICATION [AuditSpecName] WITH (STATE =
    ON);
```

Distribution of responsibilities, consistent monitoring, and applying least privilege principles are essential strategies in safeguarding stored procedures and functions in SQL Server.

Security maintenance requires continuous attention, regular updates to the security policies, and adherence to best practices in database management. Employing these techniques effectively secures intellectual property and ensures data integrity.

Chapter 9

Transactions and Concurrency

This chapter explores the fundamentals of transactions, including the ACID properties, and explains how to create explicit and implicit transactions. It discusses nested transactions, transaction isolation levels, and concurrency control techniques. The chapter also covers handling deadlocks, using savepoints, and the differences between optimistic and pessimistic concurrency. Best practices for managing transactions are highlighted to ensure data integrity and consistency in multi-user environments.

9.1 Introduction to Transactions

A transaction in the context of SQL Server is a sequence of operations performed as a single logical unit of work. This logical unit must exhibit four key properties, abbreviated as ACID properties, which will be detailed in subsequent sections. Transactions ensure that database modifications are executed in a reliable manner, maintaining the integrity of data even in the presence of hardware failures, system crashes, or real-time concurrent processing anomalies.

When creating or manipulating data in a relational database management system (RDBMS), it is crucial to ensure that the actions are performed completely or not at all. This all-or-nothing principle guarantees that the system will transition from one consistent state to another, leaving no room for partial or inconsistent states. Let's delve into the core concepts that form the basis of transactions in SQL Server.

Atomicity: Atomicity ensures that all the operations within a transaction are treated as a single unit, which either entirely succeeds or fails. SQL Server employs mechanisms to maintain atomicity by generating logs that track each individual operation within the transaction. If any operation fails, the entire transaction can be rolled back to leave the system unaltered.

Consistency: Consistency ensures that a transaction takes the database from one valid state to another, maintaining the predefined rules and constraints. SQL Server checks these constraints before and after the transaction to verify that integrity rules such as primary keys, foreign keys, and other business rules are satisfied.

Isolation: Isolation ensures that concurrent execution of transactions leaves the database in the same state as if the transactions were executed sequentially. SQL Server uses various isolation levels to control the visibility of changes made by one transaction to another, which prevents phenomena like dirty reads, non-repeatable reads, and phantom reads.

Durability: Durability guarantees that once a transaction has been committed, it will remain so, even in the event of a system crash. SQL Server achieves durability by writing transaction logs to disk. In the event of a failure, the logs can be used to reconstruct the committed transactions, ensuring that no data is permanently lost.

Transactions in SQL Server can be implemented in two primary forms: explicit transactions and implicit transactions. Explicit transactions are manually started by users with the BEGIN TRANSACTION statement and can involve multiple operations between the BEGIN and the COMMIT or ROLLBACK points. Implicit transactions, on the other hand, are automatically initiated by SQL Server as an inherent part of the DML operations.

By using explicit transactions, developers and database administrators gain fine-grained control over the start and end points of the transaction. Here is an example of an explicit transaction in SQL Server:

```
BEGIN TRANSACTION;

INSERT INTO Employees (EmployeeID, FirstName, LastName)
VALUES (1, 'John', 'Doe');

UPDATE Employees
```

```
SET LastName = 'Smith'
WHERE EmployeeID = 1;

COMMIT TRANSACTION;
```

In this example, all operations between BEGIN TRANSACTION and COMMIT TRANSACTION form a single logical unit of work. If any statement within this block fails, the entire transaction can be rolled back to its initial state before executing the BEGIN TRANSACTION statement.

Implicit transactions operate under a different paradigm. In SQL Server, implicit transactions are initiated automatically by the server when certain DML operations like INSERT, UPDATE, DELETE, or SELECT statements are issued. The transaction remains active until an explicit COMMIT or ROLLBACK statement is executed. This mode can be particularly useful in environments where batch processing or dynamic T-SQL execution is frequent.

Understanding transactions is essential for ensuring data integrity, consistency, and performance in a multi-user SQL Server environment. By mastering both explicit and implicit transactions, database professionals can effectively manage how changes to the data are synchronized, isolated, and made durable in the face of concurrent access and potential system failures. Proper implementation and management of transactions underpin the reliability and robustness of any database application.

9.2 ACID Properties

ACID is an acronym that stands for Atomicity, Consistency, Isolation, and Durability. These properties are essential to ensure that database transactions are processed reliably and ensure data integrity. Understanding each of these properties is crucial for proficient database management and optimization. Below we explore each property in detail.

Atomicity dictates that a transaction must be all-or-nothing: either the entire transaction is committed, or none of it is. This ensures that the database is not left in an inconsistent state. Atomicity is primarily handled by the database management system (DBMS) using a mechanism known as a transaction log. This log makes it possible to track changes and roll back the transaction if any part fails.

Consistency ensures that a transaction brings the database from one valid state to another, maintaining database invariants. Role-based constraints, cascades, triggers, and validations are mechanisms used to enforce consistency. For example, if a transaction includes a violation of referential integrity, the DBMS will roll back the transaction to maintain a consistent state.

Isolation means that concurrently executing transactions do not affect each other. SQL Server uses isolation levels to manage concurrent transactions. The four primary isolation levels are Read Uncommitted, Read Committed, Repeatable Read, and Serializable. Each level provides a balance between data accuracy and performance, as shown below:

- **Read Uncommitted**: Allows dirty reads, where transactions can read uncommitted changes from other transactions. It offers the highest concurrency but the lowest data integrity.
- **Read Committed**: Ensures that any data read is committed at the moment it is read. It prevents dirty reads but allows non-repeatable reads and phantom reads.
- **Repeatable Read**: Prevents non-repeatable reads by ensuring that if a transaction reads a data item, no other transaction can modify that data item until the first transaction completes.
- **Serializable**: Ensures complete isolation from other transactions, preventing dirty reads, non-repeatable reads, and phantom reads. This is the strictest isolation level and maintains the highest level of data integrity but reduces concurrency.

Durability guarantees that once a transaction has been committed, it will remain so, even in the event of a system failure. SQL Server achieves durability through its write-ahead logging (WAL) protocol, which ensures that transaction log records are written to disk before any changes. This approach means that in the event of a crash, transactions can be reconstructed from the log files.

Below is an example of a SQL transaction that demonstrates the ACID properties:

```
BEGIN TRANSACTION;

-- Atomicity: The whole transaction will fail if any part fails
UPDATE accounts SET balance = balance - 100 WHERE account_id = 123;
UPDATE accounts SET balance = balance + 100 WHERE account_id = 456;

-- Consistency: Consistency checks ensure constraints are met
```

```
IF (SELECT balance FROM accounts WHERE account_id = 123) < 0
BEGIN
    ROLLBACK TRANSACTION;
    PRINT 'Transaction rolled back due to insufficient balance';
END
ELSE
BEGIN
    COMMIT TRANSACTION;
    PRINT 'Transaction committed successfully';
END
```

In the above SQL transaction:

- **Atomicity** is ensured as both balance updates form a single transaction. If one update fails, the entire transaction is rolled back.
- **Consistency** is maintained by checking if the balance goes negative, ensuring business rules are enforced.
- **Isolation** is provided through the implicit transaction isolation level settings of SQL Server, ensuring concurrent transactions do not interfere.
- **Durability** is guaranteed by the DBMS, as the changes in a committed transaction are stored in the transaction log even if a system failure occurs.

Example output if the transaction commits:

```
Transaction committed successfully
```

Example output if the transaction rolls back:

```
Transaction rolled back due to insufficient balance
```

This section detailed the constituent properties of ACID, which collectively provide a robust framework ensuring transactional reliability, consistency, and fault tolerance in SQL Server. Each property plays an integral role in managing and securing the transactions effectively.

9.3 Creating Explicit Transactions

Creating explicit transactions is a fundamental aspect of managing database operations in SQL Server. Explicit transactions provide developers with fine-grained control over the execution of multiple SQL statements, ensuring that a sequence of operations either completes successfully as a unit or is completely rolled back to maintain data integrity.

A transaction is explicitly initiated using the BEGIN TRANSACTION command and concludes with either a COMMIT TRANSACTION to save the changes or a ROLLBACK TRANSACTION to undo the changes. Explicit transactions are particularly useful in scenarios where multiple operations must be executed atomically, preserving the ACID (Atomicity, Consistency, Isolation, Durability) properties.

Consider the following example:

```
BEGIN TRANSACTION;

UPDATE Account
SET Balance = Balance - 100
WHERE AccountID = 1;

UPDATE Account
SET Balance = Balance + 100
WHERE AccountID = 2;

IF @@ERROR = 0
BEGIN
   COMMIT TRANSACTION;
END
ELSE
BEGIN
   ROLLBACK TRANSACTION;
END;
```

In this example, the transaction starts with BEGIN TRANSACTION. Two UPDATE statements are executed to transfer 100 units from AccountID 1 to AccountID 2. The IF @@ERROR = 0 construct checks if any error occurred during the execution of the updates. If no error is detected (@@ERROR = 0), the transaction is committed with COMMIT TRANSACTION, making all changes permanent. If an error occurs (@@ERROR is not 0), ROLLBACK TRANSACTION is issued to undo all changes.

The following steps elaborate on key components and considerations for creating explicit transactions:

- **Begin the Transaction:** Every explicit transaction starts with the BEGIN TRANSACTION command. This action signals the start of a series of operations that form a single logical unit of work.

```
BEGIN TRANSACTION;
```

- **Execute SQL Statements:** Within the transaction block, multiple SQL statements are executed. These can include INSERT,

UPDATE, DELETE, or any other data modification operations.

```
UPDATE Product
SET Stock = Stock - 5
WHERE ProductID = 101;

INSERT INTO Sales (ProductID, Quantity)
VALUES (101, 5);
```

- **Check for Errors:** Insert error-checking mechanisms to ensure all operations within the transaction are successful. @@ERROR is a system function in SQL Server that returns the error number for the last Transact-SQL statement executed.

```
IF @@ERROR <> 0
BEGIN
    ROLLBACK TRANSACTION;
END;
```

- **Commit the Transaction:** If all operations are executed successfully without any errors, the changes can be made permanent using COMMIT TRANSACTION.

```
COMMIT TRANSACTION;
```

- **Rollback the Transaction:** If any of the operations fail or an error is detected, the entire set of operations can be undone using ROLLBACK TRANSACTION.

```
ROLLBACK TRANSACTION;
```

Ensuring Atomicity: By enclosing the critical operations within BEGIN TRANSACTION and COMMIT TRANSACTION or ROLLBACK TRANSACTION, explicit transactions ensure that either all operations within the transaction are performed, or none are. This approach eliminates partial updates that can lead to data inconsistencies.

Design Considerations: It is imperative to design explicit transactions to be as short and efficient as possible. Long-running transactions can lead to increased lock contention and reduced performance. Furthermore, while within a transaction, resources are held, impacting overall system concurrency.

In multi-user database environments, explicit transactions play a crucial role in maintaining data integrity and consistency. By appropriately using BEGIN TRANSACTION, COMMIT TRANSACTION, and ROLLBACK TRANSACTION, developers can handle complex sequences of dependent SQL operations reliably and safely.

9.4 Implicit Transactions

Implicit transactions are a crucial concept in SQL Server that significantly impact how transactions are managed and executed. Unlike explicit transactions, where the transaction boundaries are explicitly defined by BEGIN TRANSACTION and COMMIT or ROLLBACK, implicit transactions are automatically managed by the SQL Server, with the transaction boundaries being implicitly determined by the system based on specific user actions.

Implicit transactions are useful in scenarios where the user prefers the database system to handle transactional control to ensure data consistency without explicitly managing the transaction states.

To enable implicit transactions, the SET IMPLICIT_TRANSACTIONS command is employed. This command can be turned on or off, essentially controlling whether SQL Server should begin a transaction implicitly after each statement that modifies the database.

```
-- Turning on implicit transactions
SET IMPLICIT_TRANSACTIONS ON;

-- Example DML operation within an implicit transaction
INSERT INTO Employees (EmployeeID, Name, Position, Salary)
VALUES (1, 'John Doe', 'Software Engineer', 70000);

-- The implicit transaction is still open, and must be manually committed
COMMIT;

-- Turning off implicit transactions
SET IMPLICIT_TRANSACTIONS OFF;
```

When implicit transactions are enabled, after each of the following statements, SQL Server implicitly begins a new transaction:

- ALTER TABLE
- INSERT
- DELETE
- UPDATE
- SELECT (when used within a transaction)
- TRUNCATE TABLE
- CREATE
- DROP

Upon executing one of these statements, the transaction remains open until it is explicitly committed or rolled back using the COMMIT or ROLLBACK commands, respectively.

```
-- Setting implicit transactions on
SET IMPLICIT_TRANSACTIONS ON;

-- Insert operation starts an implicit transaction
INSERT INTO Employees (EmployeeID, Name, Position, Salary)
VALUES (2, 'Jane Smith', 'Data Analyst', 60000);

-- Rolling back the implicit transaction
ROLLBACK;
```

In the example above, the INSERT operation initiates a new implicit transaction automatically when SET IMPLICIT_TRANSACTIONS is enabled. However, this transaction is not committed immediately after the INSERT statement. Instead, the transaction remains open until a COMMIT or ROLLBACK statement is explicitly issued. In this case, since we issued a ROLLBACK command, the insert operation is undone, and the changes are not persisted in the database.

Using implicit transactions can be beneficial in ensuring that unintended data modifications are minimal, as each transaction requires explicit acknowledgment to be committed. However, it is vital to remember that failing to commit or rollback open transactions could lead to unintended locks on the affected resources, potentially causing blocking issues or deadlocks in multi-user environments. Therefore, it is essential to follow best practices and ensure all transactions are appropriately managed and concluded.

Implicit transactions also play a role in transaction scopes when working with nested procedures. Consider a stored procedure that performs several modifications:

```
-- Enabling implicit transactions
SET IMPLICIT_TRANSACTIONS ON;

-- Creating a stored procedure to insert an employee record
CREATE PROCEDURE AddEmployee
    @EmployeeID INT,
    @Name NVARCHAR(100),
    @Position NVARCHAR(50),
    @Salary DECIMAL(10, 2)
AS
BEGIN
    -- Insert operation starts an implicit transaction
    INSERT INTO Employees (EmployeeID, Name, Position, Salary)
    VALUES (@EmployeeID, @Name, @Position, @Salary);
    -- Explicitly committing the implicit transaction
    COMMIT;
END;
```

In this stored procedure, each time it is called, the INSERT statement will begin an implicit transaction if they have been enabled with SET IMPLICIT_TRANSACTIONS ON. The transaction remains open until the COMMIT statement is reached.

However, it is generally recommended to manage transactions explicitly within stored procedures to have better control over the transaction boundaries and ensure that resources are properly released.

An essential aspect to note is the behavior of implicit transactions in error scenarios. If an error occurs within an implicit transaction, the transaction will remain open until it is explicitly rolled back. Therefore, proper error handling routines must be implemented to manage such scenarios effectively.

```
-- Enabling implicit transactions
SET IMPLICIT_TRANSACTIONS ON;

-- Error handling in implicit transaction
BEGIN TRY
    -- Insert operation starts an implicit transaction
    INSERT INTO Employees (EmployeeID, Name, Position, Salary)
    VALUES (3, 'Alice Johnson', 'Project Manager', 80000);
    -- Explicitly committing the implicit transaction
    COMMIT;
END TRY
BEGIN CATCH
    -- Rolling back the implicit transaction in case of error
    ROLLBACK;
    -- Optional: Log the error or take corrective actions
    PRINT('An error occurred: ' + ERROR_MESSAGE());
END CATCH;
```

In the example, the BEGIN TRY and BEGIN CATCH blocks provide a robust mechanism to handle any errors that may occur during the transaction. If an error occurs, the CATCH block ensures that the transaction is explicitly rolled back, thus preventing any partial changes to the database.

Understanding implicit transactions and their proper management is essential for maintaining data consistency and ensuring that database operations are executed as intended without inadvertently leaving open transactions that could lead to resource locking issues.

9.5 Nested Transactions

In complex database operations, it is often necessary to manage multiple levels of transactions to preserve data integrity and consistency.

Nested transactions provide a mechanism to allow transactions within transactions, which can be particularly useful in modular application designs and scenarios where a series of operations might need to be rolled back independently of others.

A nested transaction begins within the context of an outer transaction. SQL Server allows you to create nested transactions procedurally within a single database session. Each nested transaction has a parent transaction, and the completion of a nested transaction is dependent on the success or failure of the outermost transaction.

To illustrate the concept, consider the following sequence of SQL commands where inner transactions are nested inside an outer transaction:

```
BEGIN TRAN OuterTransaction;
    -- Perform some operations
    INSERT INTO Accounts (AccountID, Balance) VALUES (1, 100);
    SAVEPOINT SavePoint1;

    BEGIN TRAN InnerTransaction1;
        -- Perform some operations within the first inner transaction
        UPDATE Accounts SET Balance = Balance + 50 WHERE AccountID = 1;
        SAVEPOINT SavePoint2;

        BEGIN TRAN InnerTransaction2;
            -- Perform some operations within the second inner transaction
            UPDATE Accounts SET Balance = Balance - 25 WHERE AccountID = 1;
        COMMIT TRAN InnerTransaction2;

    ROLLBACK TRAN InnerTransaction1 TO SavePoint2;
    -- Only the changes after SavePoint2 are rolled back

    COMMIT TRAN OuterTransaction;
```

In this example, the OuterTransaction contains two nested transactions, InnerTransaction1 and InnerTransaction2. The usage of savepoints allows partial rollbacks within nested transactions, which provides a granular level of control over data modifications.

Upon execution:

- The initial balance insertion creates an account with a balance of 100.
- The first inner transaction increases the balance by 50.
- The second inner transaction, nested within the first, decreases the balance by 25.
- When ROLLBACK is called on InnerTransaction1 to the savepoint SavePoint2, only modifications made after this savepoint

within the scope of InnerTransaction1 are reverted. Thus, the balance adjusted in InnerTransaction2 remains intact.

- Finally, committing the outer transaction finalizes all changes.

SQL Server manages the commit or rollback of nested transactions hierarchically. If the outermost transaction is committed (COMMIT TRAN OuterTransaction), all inner transactions' changes are committed. However, if the outermost transaction is rolled back, any modifications made during the inner transactions are also rolled back, regardless of their committed states.

The following example demonstrates the rollback effect on nested transactions:

```
BEGIN TRAN OuterTransaction;
   SAVEPOINT OuterSavePoint;
   -- Perform some operations
   INSERT INTO Orders (OrderID, Status) VALUES (1, 'Pending');

   BEGIN TRAN InnerTransaction1;
      -- Perform some operations within the first inner transaction
      UPDATE Orders SET Status = 'Processed' WHERE OrderID = 1;
      SAVEPOINT InnerSavePoint;

      BEGIN TRAN InnerTransaction2;
         -- Perform some operations within the second inner transaction
         INSERT INTO OrderItems (OrderID, ItemID, Quantity) VALUES (1, 101,
             2);
      COMMIT TRAN InnerTransaction2;

   -- Intentional rollback to OuterSavePoint
   ROLLBACK TRAN OuterTransaction TO OuterSavePoint;
   -- All changes after the outer savepoint are rolled back

COMMIT TRAN OuterTransaction;
```

Here, the OuterTransaction involves an operation on the Orders table and contains inner transactions that further modify the Orders table and add entries to the OrderItems table. When the rollback occurs to OuterSavePoint, all changes made by the nested transactions initiated after this savepoint are reverted. Consequently, the insertion into the OrderItems table and the update to the Orders table are undone, demonstrating the orthogonal rollback capabilities provided by nested transactions.

This behavior underscores the importance of understanding savepoints and transaction control as they allow fine-grained error handling and ensure that intermediate operations can be safely rolled back without affecting the stability of other operations. By appropriately using nested transactions and savepoints, database practitioners can design resilient and robust transaction management systems that provide consistent and reliable outcomes even in the presence of errors or unexpected behaviors.

9.6 Transaction Isolation Levels

Transaction isolation levels are crucial in managing how concurrent transactions interact with each other in a relational database management system (RDBMS) such as SQL Server. Isolation levels determine the visibility of one transaction's changes to other transactions, ensuring data consistency and preventing phenomena that can compromise data integrity. The SQL standard defines four isolation levels: Read Uncommitted, Read Committed, Repeatable Read, and Serializable. SQL Server also includes an additional isolation level called Snapshot. Each level offers a different balance between consistency and concurrency.

The SQL standard phenomena that transaction isolation levels aim to control are:

- Dirty Reads
- Non-Repeatable Reads
- Phantom Reads

Read Uncommitted is the least restrictive isolation level. In this level, transactions are allowed to read uncommitted changes made by other transactions. This can lead to dirty reads, where a transaction reads data that might be rolled back. While this level offers the highest degree of concurrency, it provides the lowest level of data consistency.

```
SET TRANSACTION ISOLATION LEVEL READ UNCOMMITTED;
BEGIN TRANSACTION;
-- Example query
SELECT * FROM Orders;
COMMIT;
```

Output of such a query may vary if another concurrent transaction modifies the Orders table and rolls back the transaction.

```
OrderID | CustomerID | OrderDate
--------+------------+----------
101     | 1          | 2023-01-01
102     | 2          | 2023-01-02
103     | 1          | 2023-01-03
```

Read Committed is the default isolation level in SQL Server. Transactions can only read data that has been committed by other transactions. This isolation level prevents dirty reads but allows non-repeatable reads and phantom reads. The read consistency is higher compared to Read Uncommitted, providing a safer execution context.

```
SET TRANSACTION ISOLATION LEVEL READ COMMITTED;
BEGIN TRANSACTION;
-- Example query
SELECT * FROM Orders WHERE CustomerID = 1;
COMMIT;
```

Repeatable Read isolation level ensures that if a transaction reads a row, any other concurrent transaction cannot modify that row until the initial transaction completes. This level prevents both dirty reads and non-repeatable reads but does not prevent phantom reads.

```
SET TRANSACTION ISOLATION LEVEL REPEATABLE READ;
BEGIN TRANSACTION;
-- Example query
SELECT * FROM Orders WHERE CustomerID = 1;
-- Performing some operations
COMMIT;
```

During the execution of a query under Repeatable Read, if a second transaction attempts to update a row that has already been read, it will be blocked until the first transaction completes.

Serializable is the most restrictive isolation level. It ensures complete isolation from other transactions, effectively serializing access to the data. This level prevents dirty reads, non-repeatable reads, and phantom reads, but at the cost of reduced concurrency and potential for higher contention.

```
SET TRANSACTION ISOLATION LEVEL SERIALIZABLE;
BEGIN TRANSACTION;
-- Example query
SELECT * FROM Orders WHERE CustomerID BETWEEN 1 AND 10;
-- Performing some operations
COMMIT;
```

Serializable isolation level guarantees that no other transactions can insert, update or delete any rows that would impact the rows being read by the current transaction. This can significantly reduce concurrency but ensures the highest level of consistency.

Snapshot isolation level introduces a mechanism to provide a view of the data as it was at the start of the transaction, isolating it from changes made by other transactions. Snapshot isolation prevents dirty reads, non-repeatable reads, and phantom reads without many of the concurrency bottlenecks created by Serializable isolation.

```
SET TRANSACTION ISOLATION LEVEL SNAPSHOT;
BEGIN TRANSACTION;
-- Example query
SELECT * FROM Orders WHERE CustomerID = 1;
-- Performing some operations
COMMIT;
```

Enabling Snapshot isolation requires configuring the database to support this level. This is done by allowing read-committed snapshot isolation (RCSI):

```
ALTER DATABASE [YourDatabaseName]
SET ALLOW_SNAPSHOT_ISOLATION ON;
ALTER DATABASE [YourDatabaseName]
SET READ_COMMITTED_SNAPSHOT ON;
```

When Snapshot isolation is enabled, SQL Server uses versioning to keep track of data modifications. The preferred version of the data is determined based on the transaction start time, ensuring a consistent view for all reads within the transaction.

Understanding and properly configuring transaction isolation levels is critical for managing data consistency and integrity in multi-user environments. Each isolation level offers different trade-offs between consistency and performance, allowing database administrators to optimize the system according to specific use cases and workloads.

9.7 Concurrency Control

Concurrency control is a critical aspect of database management systems (DBMS) to ensure the correctness of transactions when multiple users access the database simultaneously. The ultimate goal is to facilitate concurrent access while maintaining data integrity and consistency according to the ACID properties. Concurrency control typically revolves around preventing issues such as lost updates, temporary inconsistency, and uncommitted data from impacting the overall integrity of the database.

The two primary strategies for managing concurrency control in SQL Server are **pessimistic concurrency** and **optimistic concurrency**. Each approach has its strengths and weaknesses, which make them suitable for different types of applications and scenarios.

Pessimistic Concurrency Control: This strategy assumes that conflicts between transactions are likely to occur and hence uses locking mechanisms to prevent conflicts. Various types of locks (shared, exclusive, update) are used to ensure that other transactions cannot access data in a way that would lead to inconsistency. Consider the following SQL script that demonstrates how SQL Server implements pessimistic concurrency using locks:

```
BEGIN TRANSACTION

-- Select a record with a shared lock
SELECT * FROM Orders WITH (HOLDLOCK) WHERE OrderID = 1

-- Update the record
UPDATE Orders SET Quantity = Quantity + 1 WHERE OrderID = 1

COMMIT TRANSACTION
```

In this example, the HOLDLOCK hint ensures that the selected row is locked for the duration of the transaction, preventing other transactions from modifying it until the transaction is complete.

Optimistic Concurrency Control: This method assumes that conflicts are rare and allows transactions to proceed without locking resources. Before committing the transaction, the system checks whether any conflicts have occurred. If a conflict is detected, the transaction is rolled back. This strategy reduces the overhead associated with locks and can enhance performance in environments with low contention. The following example illustrates optimistic concurrency using a version column to detect conflicts:

```
BEGIN TRANSACTION

DECLARE @CurrentVersion INT

-- Retrieve the current version of the record
SELECT @CurrentVersion = Version FROM Orders WHERE OrderID = 1

-- Update the record only if the version number hasn't changed
UPDATE Orders
SET Quantity = Quantity + 1, Version = Version + 1
WHERE OrderID = 1 AND Version = @CurrentVersion

IF @@ROWCOUNT = 0
    -- Handle conflict scenario, as the version has changed
    ROLLBACK TRANSACTION
ELSE
    COMMIT TRANSACTION
```

Here, the UPDATE statement checks that the Version number of the record has not changed before applying the update. If the Version number has changed, it implies concurrent modification, and the transaction is rolled back.

Locking Mechanisms: SQL Server employs various types of locks to manage concurrent access. The primary locks include:

- **Shared Locks (S)**: Used for operations that do not change or update data (e.g., SELECT). Multiple transactions can hold shared locks on the same resource.
- **Exclusive Locks (X)**: Used for data-modifying operations (e.g., INSERT, UPDATE, DELETE). Only one transaction can hold an exclusive lock on a resource at a given time.
- **Update Locks (U)**: Initially held by transactions that are reading data with the intention to update it. They are later converted to exclusive locks during the update.

These locks are automatically managed by SQL Server based on the isolation level set for the transaction. The isolation level determines the degree of visibility one transaction has to changes made by other transactions and can be set using the SET TRANSACTION ISOLATION LEVEL statement, as shown below:

```
SET TRANSACTION ISOLATION LEVEL SERIALIZABLE

BEGIN TRANSACTION

-- Perform transactional operations
SELECT * FROM Products WHERE ProductID = 1

COMMIT TRANSACTION
```

The SERIALIZABLE isolation level ensures the highest level of isolation by holding locks until a transaction is complete, thereby preventing other transactions from inserting or updating rows that would conflict.

In addition to these standard locks, SQL Server also supports **intent locks**, which are a form of hierarchical locking mechanism ensuring that locks at one level of the hierarchy are understood appropriately at higher levels. For example, if a transaction holds an intention exclusive lock (IX) on a table, it can safely acquire an exclusive lock (X) on any row of the table.

Understanding these mechanisms allows for designing applications that effectively leverage SQL Server's concurrency control features to maintain data integrity and performance.

9.8 Handling Deadlocks

Deadlocks occur in a database system when two or more transactions are waiting indefinitely for each other to release locks, creating a cycle of dependencies. Consider two transactions, $T1$ and $T2$, where $T1$ holds lock A and needs lock B, and $T2$ holds lock B and needs lock A. Neither transaction can proceed, and the system reaches a deadlock state.

Understanding and handling deadlocks require recognizing their conditions, detecting their occurrence, and adopting strategies to resolve and prevent them.

Deadlock Detection and Resolution

SQL Server employs a deadlock monitor to detect deadlocks by periodically checking for cycles in the wait-for graph, which represents transactions waiting for resources locked by other transactions. When a deadlock is detected, SQL Server resolves it by choosing a victim transaction to terminate, thus breaking the cycle and allowing the remaining transactions to proceed.

SQL Server uses the following criteria to select a victim:

- The transaction with the lower cost, measured by the amount of resources it has consumed. This approach minimizes the impact on system performance.
- Transactions that are marked as DEADLOCK_PRIORITY LOW are more likely to be chosen as victims. Conversely, transactions marked as DEADLOCK_PRIORITY HIGH are less likely to be chosen.

The victim transaction is rolled back, and an error message 1205 is raised. Applications need to be designed to handle this error by retrying the transaction.

```
BEGIN TRANSACTION;
ALTER DATABASE SET DEADLOCK_PRIORITY LOW;
-- Transaction Statements Here
COMMIT TRANSACTION;
```

Deadlock Prevention Strategies

Preventing deadlocks proactively is preferable to merely detecting and resolving them. The following strategies can help reduce the frequency of deadlocks:

- **Consistent Lock Ordering:** Ensure that transactions acquire locks in a consistent order. By following the same sequence in accessing resources, the cycle of waiting can be avoided.
- **Short Transactions:** Keep transactions short and reduce the duration for which locks are held. This reduces the window of time during which deadlocks can occur.
- **Access Pattern Design:** Design access patterns to minimize overlapping locks. For example, acquiring table-level locks instead of row-level locks when large-scale operations are necessary.
- **Using the NOLOCK Hint:** In scenarios where dirty reads are acceptable, using the NOLOCK hint can prevent locks from being acquired, reducing the chances of deadlocks.

```
SELECT * FROM table\_name WITH (NOLOCK);
```

Handling Deadlock Scenarios

Here's an example of how to handle deadlocks in an application by employing retry logic. This approach retries a transaction a specified number of times before failing:

```
DECLARE @retry INT = 3;
DECLARE @success BIT = 0;

WHILE @retry > 0 AND @success = 0
BEGIN
    BEGIN TRY
        BEGIN TRANSACTION;
        -- Transaction Statements Here
        COMMIT TRANSACTION;
        SET @success = 1;
    END TRY
    BEGIN CATCH
        IF ERROR\_NUMBER() = 1205
        BEGIN
            -- Deadlock occurred, retry the transaction
            SET @retry = @retry - 1;
        END
        ELSE
        BEGIN
            -- Handle other errors
            ROLLBACK TRANSACTION;
            BREAK;
        END
    END CATCH
END

IF @success = 0
BEGIN
    -- Transaction failed after retries
```

```
    RAISERROR ('Transaction failed after multiple retries due to deadlocks.', 16, 1);
END
```

This implementation demonstrates retry logic with error handling for deadlocks, giving the transaction multiple opportunities to succeed.

Monitoring and Analyzing Deadlocks

SQL Server provides tools to monitor and analyze deadlocks. The deadlock graph can be captured using SQL Server Profiler or Extended Events (XE), providing detailed information on the transactions and resources involved in the deadlock.

Using Extended Events:

```
CREATE EVENT SESSION DeadlockGraph ON SERVER
ADD EVENT sqlserver.lock\_deadlock\_graph
ADD TARGET package0.event\_file (SET filename = 'C:\Temp\Deadlock.xel', max\
    _file\_size = 5);
ALTER EVENT SESSION DeadlockGraph ON SERVER STATE = START;
```

To analyze the resulting .xel file, use SQL Server Management Studio (SSMS) or other tools capable of parsing Extended Event files. The Event Viewer in SSMS provides a graphical representation of the deadlock, making it easier to identify the cause and take corrective action.

9.9 Using Savepoints

Savepoints provide a mechanism to roll back parts of a transaction without affecting the entire transaction. This functionality offers finer control over error handling within a transaction, allowing segments of the transaction to be undone while preserving the work done up to the savepoint. Implementing savepoints can help in complex transactional logic where partial transaction failure is an acceptable state, and recovery can be handled more gracefully.

A savepoint is set within a transaction using the SAVE_TRANSACTION statement. To utilize it effectively, follow these steps:

- Begin a transaction.
- Define a savepoint using SAVE_TRANSACTION.
- Execute transactional statements.
- If an error occurs and you need to roll back to the savepoint, use

the ROLLBACK_TRANSACTION statement with the savepoint name.

- Commit the transaction if all operations succeed.

Consider the following example to illustrate the use of savepoints:

```
BEGIN TRANSACTION;

-- First set of operations
INSERT INTO Accounts (AccountID, Balance) VALUES (1, 1000);
INSERT INTO Accounts (AccountID, Balance) VALUES (2, 2000);

-- Set a savepoint
SAVE TRANSACTION SavePoint1;

-- Second set of operations
UPDATE Accounts SET Balance = Balance - 500 WHERE AccountID = 1;
INSERT INTO Transactions (AccountID, Amount) VALUES (1, -500);

-- Simulate an error
IF (1 = 1) -- Error condition
BEGIN
    -- Roll back to savepoint
    ROLLBACK TRANSACTION SavePoint1;
END;

-- Commit transaction
COMMIT TRANSACTION;
```

In this script, a transaction is initiated to manage account balances and a set of operations is performed. A savepoint named SavePoint1 is created after the initial inserts. The subsequent operations within the transaction are executed, including an update and an insert. If an error condition arises (simulated by the condition IF (1 = 1)), the ROLLBACK_TRANSACTION statement reverts the database state to SavePoint1. The transaction can then proceed and is eventually committed if no other errors occur.

Savepoints allow multiple logical units of work to be defined within a single transaction. This capability is particularly useful in scenarios where complex validation and business rules need to be applied incrementally. Each logical unit can be enclosed between savepoints, and errors within any unit do not necessarily invalidate all preceding operations.

Key considerations when using savepoints include:

- Savepoints consume resources such as memory and logs. Excessive use in large transactions may impact performance.

- Nesting savepoints is allowed, but careful management is required to avoid unintentional rollbacks that could undo more work than intended.

- Rolling back to a savepoint does not release locks obtained since the savepoint was created. This means that the constraints around lock management must be carefully designed to prevent deadlocks.

- Ensure savepoint names are unique within a transaction context to avoid conflicts and unintentional overwrites.

A nested savepoint example, demonstrating the power of using multiple savepoints within a transaction, is illustrated below:

```
BEGIN TRANSACTION;

-- Initial operations
INSERT INTO Orders (OrderID, CustomerID, Amount) VALUES (1001, 2001, 300);

-- Set first savepoint
SAVE TRANSACTION SavePoint1;

-- More operations
INSERT INTO OrderDetails (OrderID, ProductID, Quantity) VALUES (1001, 101, 5);

-- Set second savepoint
SAVE TRANSACTION SavePoint2;

-- Further operations and a conditional error
UPDATE Inventory SET Quantity = Quantity - 5 WHERE ProductID = 101;
IF (Quantity < 0)
BEGIN
    -- Roll back to second savepoint
    ROLLBACK TRANSACTION SavePoint2;
END

-- Final operations
INSERT INTO Shipping (OrderID, Status) VALUES (1001, 'Shipped');
COMMIT TRANSACTION;
```

In this nested savepoint example, a transaction is managing an order and its details, as well as inventory updates and shipping status. Two savepoints, SavePoint1 and SavePoint2, are set at different stages. If an error occurs when updating the inventory, the transaction rolls back to SavePoint2 without affecting the preceding operations.

Savepoints offer a robust way to ensure transactional integrity at multiple granular levels. Used judiciously, they enable fine-tuned control over complex transactions and enhance error recovery mechanisms. Integrating savepoints with structured error handling leads to more resilient and maintainable transactional systems.

9.10 Optimistic vs. Pessimistic Concurrency

Optimistic and pessimistic concurrency control are two strategies used in database management systems to handle simultaneous access to data resources by multiple transactions while maintaining data integrity. Each approach has its unique mechanisms, advantages, and appropriate use cases, necessitating a comprehensive understanding to apply them effectively.

Optimistic concurrency control operates under the assumption that conflicts between transactions are rare. In this method, transactions execute without acquiring locks on the data. When a transaction is ready to commit, the system checks if any other transactions have modified the same data during its execution. If a conflict is detected, the committing transaction may be rolled back. This strategy relies on validation and versioning techniques to ensure data consistency.

Implementing optimistic concurrency often involves the use of version numbers or timestamps. Each data item is associated with a version number that increments with each modification. Before a transaction commits, it verifies that the data it has read has not changed since it was last read, as indicated by the version number.

Here is an example of optimistic concurrency control using SQL Server:

```
-- Enable Snapshot Isolation Level
ALTER DATABASE AdventureWorks
SET ALLOW_SNAPSHOT_ISOLATION ON;
GO

-- Transaction 1 starts
BEGIN TRANSACTION;
-- Transaction 1 reads a row
SELECT EmployeeID, FirstName, LastName
FROM Employees
WHERE EmployeeID = 1;

-- Transaction 2 starts (concurrently with Transaction 1)
BEGIN TRANSACTION;
-- Transaction 2 updates the same row
UPDATE Employees
SET LastName = 'Smith'
WHERE EmployeeID = 1;

-- Transaction 2 commits
COMMIT TRANSACTION;

-- Transaction 1 tries to update the row
UPDATE Employees
SET LastName = 'Doe'
WHERE EmployeeID = 1;
```

```
-- Since the data was changed by Transaction 2, Transaction 1 will fail
-- or be asked to retry by the system.
COMMIT TRANSACTION;
GO
```

In the example above, if Transaction 1 attempts to commit after Transaction 2 has already committed, the system detects the version change and prevents Transaction 1 from proceeding, possibly requiring it to retry.

Pessimistic concurrency control, on the other hand, is predicated on the assumption that conflicts between transactions are likely. This approach uses locks to prevent other transactions from accessing data that is being read or modified. Locks can be shared (allowing read access by multiple transactions but exclusive for writes) or exclusive (preventing any access by other transactions). The locking mechanism ensures that when one transaction is accessing data, others are blocked until the lock is released, hence avoiding conflicts but potentially causing delays.

Consider the following example of pessimistic concurrency control in SQL Server:

```
-- Transaction 1 starts
BEGIN TRANSACTION;
-- Transaction 1 acquires an exclusive lock to update a row
UPDATE Employees
SET LastName = 'Doe'
WHERE EmployeeID = 1;

-- Transaction 2 starts (concurrently with Transaction 1)
BEGIN TRANSACTION;
-- Transaction 2 tries to read the same row
SELECT EmployeeID, FirstName, LastName
FROM Employees
WHERE EmployeeID = 1;

-- Transaction 2 is blocked until Transaction 1 completes
-- Transaction 1 commits
COMMIT TRANSACTION;

-- Now Transaction 2 can proceed
COMMIT TRANSACTION;
GO
```

In the example, Transaction 1's exclusive lock on the data prevents Transaction 2 from reading it until Transaction 1 has completed and committed. This ensures that Transaction 2 reads a consistent and committed state of the data, thus avoiding read-write conflicts.

The choice between optimistic and pessimistic concurrency control depends on various factors, including the expected frequency of conflicts, performance requirements, and the nature of the application workload. Optimistic concurrency control is often preferable in environments with low contention, where conflicts are infrequent, and performance gains from reduced locking overhead are significant. Pessimistic concurrency control is more suitable for high-contention environments, where ensuring immediate consistency and avoiding significant data anomalies is a priority.

Ultimately, understanding the trade-offs and the operational implications of each concurrency control model is vital for database professionals tasked with maintaining data integrity and optimizing performance.

9.11 Best Practices for Transactions

In SQL Server and database management, ensuring the integrity and performance of your transactions is crucial. This section offers a comprehensive compilation of best practices that can greatly enhance your ability to manage transactions effectively. These practices encompass designing transactions to optimize performance, ensuring data integrity, and minimizing contention among concurrent transactions.

1. Keep Transactions Short and Efficient

Long-running transactions are a common culprit for blocking and deadlocks in databases. Therefore, it is advisable to keep the scope of your transactions as narrow as possible. This involves only including the queries that absolutely need to be grouped together to maintain atomicity, consistency, isolation, and durability (ACID) properties. Avoid including long-running operations, such as user inputs or extensive calculations, within a transaction.

2. Minimize Transaction Scope

Reducing the number of resources and objects accessed within a transaction minimizes the locking duration, thereby reducing contention. This can be achieved by structuring your SQL statements to accomplish the necessary operations in the shortest time possible. Additionally, you should always perform read operations before write operations to take advantage of shared locks.

3. Use Explicit Transactions Judiciously

While explicit transactions provide greater control, they should be used judiciously. Implicit transactions or auto-commit transactions are often sufficient for straightforward operations. For more complex operations that require multiple steps, explicit transactions are necessary to ensure all steps succeed or fail as a unit. Consider the following example of an explicit transaction for updating account balances:

```
BEGIN TRANSACTION;

UPDATE Accounts
SET Balance = Balance - 100
WHERE AccountId = 1;

UPDATE Accounts
SET Balance = Balance + 100
WHERE AccountId = 2;

IF @@ERROR <> 0
BEGIN
    ROLLBACK TRANSACTION;
    PRINT 'Transaction Rolled Back';
END
ELSE
BEGIN
    COMMIT TRANSACTION;
    PRINT 'Transaction Committed';
END
```

4. Avoid Unnecessary Locks

Using the appropriate isolation level for your transactions can help avoid unnecessary locks and improve concurrency. For read-heavy transactions where a high level of consistency is not critical, consider using the READ UNCOMMITTED isolation level to prevent shared locks. However, always ensure that the chosen isolation level aligns with your data integrity requirements.

5. Use Savepoints Tactically

Savepoints allow for partial rollbacks within transactions, which can be particularly useful in complex transactions that involve multiple steps. If an error occurs after a savepoint is set, you can roll back to that savepoint instead of rolling back the entire transaction. Here's an example of using savepoints:

```
BEGIN TRANSACTION;

-- Initial update
UPDATE Orders
SET Status = 'Processing'
WHERE OrderId = 10;

SAVE TRANSACTION SavePoint1;

-- Another update
UPDATE Inventory
```

```
SET Quantity = Quantity - 1
WHERE ProductId = 100;

IF @@ERROR <> 0
BEGIN
    ROLLBACK TRANSACTION SavePoint1;
    PRINT 'Rolled back to SavePoint1';
END

COMMIT TRANSACTION;
```

6. Evaluate Deadlock Risk

Look for patterns in your transaction design that might lead to deadlocks. Deadlocks occur when two or more transactions are waiting indefinitely for each other to release resources. Techniques to avoid deadlocks include:

- Accessing resources in a consistent order among transactions.
- Breaking down large transactions into smaller units.
- Using the right isolation level to minimize locking.
- Regularly monitoring and analyzing system logs to identify and rectify deadlock patterns.

7. Review and Optimize Query Plans

SQL Server provides tools such as execution plans and the Database Engine Tuning Advisor to analyze and optimize the performance of your queries. Regularly reviewing execution plans will help identify inefficient queries within your transactions. Efficient queries result in shorter transaction duration, thus reducing contention and enhancing concurrency.

8. Implement Proper Error Handling

Transactions should have robust error handling to ensure that resources are properly released, and data integrity is maintained. Utilize try-catch blocks in your SQL scripts to centralize and manage error handling efficiently. Here's an example:

```
BEGIN TRY
    BEGIN TRANSACTION;

    -- Your transactional code here

    COMMIT TRANSACTION;
END TRY
BEGIN CATCH
    ROLLBACK TRANSACTION;
```

```
    PRINT 'Error occurred: ' + ERROR_MESSAGE();
END CATCH;
```

9. Use Indexes Effectively

Indexes can significantly speed up the performance of queries within a transaction by reducing the amount of data scanned and improving seek times. However, excessive or improper indexing can lead to additional overhead during insert, update, and delete operations. Carefully design and optimize indexes to balance read and write performance.

10. Regularly Monitor Transaction Performance

Regular monitoring and auditing of transactions can provide insights into potential performance bottlenecks and areas for optimization. SQL Server's Dynamic Management Views (DMVs) can be used to gather detailed information about currently active transactions, locks, and resource usage. Regularly analyze these metrics to ensure optimal performance and to proactively address issues.

Adhering to these best practices will help you design efficient, reliable, and high-performing transactions, thus ensuring data integrity and consistency while optimizing system resources.

Chapter 10

Security and Permissions

This chapter covers the fundamentals of SQL Server security, including authentication modes and the creation and management of logins, database users, and roles. It explains schema-based permissions, row-level security, and data encryption techniques such as Transparent Data Encryption (TDE). The chapter also discusses using certificates and keys, auditing and monitoring security, and best practices for ensuring a secure SQL Server environment.

10.1 Overview of SQL Server Security

SQL Server security encompasses a wide range of features and mechanisms to protect data and control access. This section provides an in-depth examination of the core concepts and components involved in securing SQL Server installations. Ensuring strict security measures is essential for preserving data integrity, confidentiality, and availability.

The security framework of SQL Server revolves around several fundamental principles. These include authentication, authorization, encryption, and auditing. Each principle addresses different aspects of security within SQL Server, ensuring comprehensive protection against various threats.

SQL Server employs a layered security model, which provides multiple levels of security controls. This model enhances the system's resilience by ensuring that even if one layer is compromised, the subsequent layers continue to protect the data. The primary layers include network security, instance-level security, database-level security, and object-level security.

Network Security

Network security in SQL Server refers to measures that safeguard data as it travels over the network between clients and the server. It includes securing communication channels and using firewalls to control access. One common practice is the use of Secure Sockets Layer (SSL) or Transport Layer Security (TLS) to encrypt data during transmission. To configure SSL/TLS, administrators need to install a valid server certificate and configure SQL Server to use it.

```
-- Example: Configuring SQL Server to use SSL for encryption
EXEC sp_configure 'show advanced options', 1;
RECONFIGURE;
EXEC sp_configure 'force encryption', 1;
RECONFIGURE;
```

Another important aspect of network security is using firewalls to restrict access. SQL Server can be configured to allow connections only from specific IP addresses, thereby limiting potential attack vectors.

Instance-Level Security

Instance-level security focuses on controlling access to the SQL Server instance itself. This is achieved through authentication mechanisms that verify the identity of users and entities attempting to connect. SQL Server supports two primary authentication modes: Windows Authentication and Mixed Mode Authentication (which includes both Windows and SQL Server Authentication).

In Windows Authentication mode, SQL Server relies on the underlying Windows operating system to authenticate users. This mode leverages existing Windows accounts and groups, simplifying management and enhancing security by integrating with the broader network's security policies.

```
-- Example: Changing SQL Server Authentication Mode
EXEC xp_instance_regwrite N'HKEY_LOCAL_MACHINE',
    N'Software\Microsoft\MSSQLServer\MSSQLServer',
    N'LoginMode', REG_DWORD, 2;
-- 2 = Mixed Mode Authentication
```

Database-Level Security

At the database level, security revolves around users and roles. Users define individual entities that can access the database, while roles group users together to apply common permissions. Database roles can be predefined (fixed roles) or user-defined, allowing for flexible permission management. Each database user is associated with a login, which links the database user with a broader security context at the instance level.

```
-- Example: Creating a database user and assigning it to a role
USE [YourDatabaseName];
CREATE USER [YourUserName] FOR LOGIN [YourLoginName];
ALTER ROLE [db_datareader] ADD MEMBER [YourUserName];
```

Object-Level Security

Object-level security pertains to the permissions granted on individual database objects such as tables, views, procedures, and functions. These permissions determine who can access or modify specific data and objects. SQL Server uses schemas to group related objects, and permissions can be managed at both the schema and object levels.

```
-- Example: Granting SELECT permission on a table
GRANT SELECT ON [YourSchema].[YourTable] TO [YourUserName];
```

SQL Server supports various permission types including SELECT, INSERT, UPDATE, DELETE, EXECUTE, and more. These permissions can be granted, revoked, or denied to users and roles.

Encryption and Data Protection

Encryption plays a crucial role in SQL Server security by ensuring data confidentiality both at rest and in transit. SQL Server provides several mechanisms for encryption including Transparent Data Encryption (TDE), cell-level encryption, and backup encryption. TDE encrypts the entire database, using a database encryption key that is protected by a certificate stored in the master database.

```
-- Example: Enabling Transparent Data Encryption (TDE)
USE master;
CREATE MASTER KEY ENCRYPTION BY PASSWORD = 'YourStrongPassword';
CREATE CERTIFICATE YourCertificate WITH SUBJECT = 'YourCertSubject';
USE [YourDatabaseName];
CREATE DATABASE ENCRYPTION KEY WITH ALGORITHM = AES_256
    ENCRYPTION BY SERVER CERTIFICATE YourCertificate;
ALTER DATABASE [YourDatabaseName] SET ENCRYPTION ON;
```

For more granular encryption needs, SQL Server supports cell-level encryption, which allows individual columns within a table to be encrypted. This method provides the flexibility to encrypt sensitive data without affecting the entire database.

Auditing and Monitoring

Auditing and monitoring are essential components of SQL Server security, enabling administrators to track and review activities within the database. SQL Server Audit is a feature that provides comprehensive auditing capabilities. It allows the capture of detailed information about events including login attempts, object access, and data modifications.

```
-- Example: Creating a server audit and audit specification
CREATE SERVER AUDIT [YourServerAudit]
    TO FILE (FILEPATH = 'C:\AuditLogs\', MAXSIZE = 100 MB);
ALTER SERVER AUDIT [YourServerAudit] WITH (STATE = ON);
CREATE SERVER AUDIT SPECIFICATION [YourAuditSpec]
    FOR SERVER AUDIT [YourServerAudit]
    ADD (FAILED_LOGIN_GROUP);
ALTER SERVER AUDIT SPECIFICATION [YourAuditSpec] WITH (STATE = ON);
```

Additionally, SQL Server provides Dynamic Management Views (DMVs) and performance counters that can be used for real-time monitoring and troubleshooting. These tools help identify potential security issues and allow for prompt response to incidents.

Overall, a robust SQL Server security framework relies on the integration of various features and practices. Administrators must stay vigilant and continuously update their security measures to safeguard against evolving threats. The subsequent sections in this chapter will delve deeper into these topics, providing comprehensive guidance on how to implement and manage SQL Server security effectively.

10.2 Authentication Modes

SQL Server provides different authentication modes to validate the identity of users attempting to access the server. Understanding and properly configuring these authentication modes is crucial for ensuring secure access to your SQL Server instances. The two primary authentication modes supported by SQL Server are Windows Authentication mode and Mixed Authentication mode.

Windows Authentication mode exclusively relies on Windows credentials and is considered more secure because it utilizes Windows security features. In contrast, Mixed Authentication mode allows both Windows Authentication and SQL Server Authentication, the latter requiring SQL Server-specific credentials.

Windows Authentication Mode

When SQL Server is configured to use Windows Authentication mode, it leverages Active Directory (AD) to authenticate users. This process is more secure because it integrates with the Windows operating system, allowing the use of security features like Kerberos protocol. Windows Authentication provides several advantages:

- **Single Sign-On (SSO)**: Users authenticated by Windows do not need to re-enter credentials when accessing SQL Server.
- **Centralized Account Management**: User accounts and passwords are managed through Windows, facilitating easier and more consistent account management.
- **Enhanced Security**: Utilizes Windows security policies, such as account lockout, password complexity, and expiration policies.

Configuring SQL Server to use Windows Authentication can be done during installation. To change an existing installation to Windows Authentication, use the SQL Server Management Studio (SSMS) as follows:

```
-- Connect to the SQL Server instance using SSMS
-- Navigate to the server properties
-- Under the 'Security' tab, select 'Windows Authentication mode'
-- Restart the SQL Server instance for changes to take effect
```

Mixed Authentication Mode

Mixed Authentication mode permits both Windows and SQL Server logins. This flexibility is useful in environments where users may not have Windows accounts or in systems requiring SQL Server-specific authentication. While this mode offers greater versatility, it poses additional security risks and requires careful management.

SQL Server Authentication involves creating SQL Server logins with usernames and passwords stored within SQL Server. Unlike Windows Authentication, SQL logins do not utilize Windows security policies, making them potentially less secure.

- **User Accounts Management**: Separate from Windows, potentially increasing administrative efforts.
- **Password Policies**: Although SQL Server can enforce password policies, these are often less stringent compared to Windows policies.

- **Increased Exposure**: Passwords are more susceptible to brute-force attacks if not managed properly.

To enable Mixed Authentication mode, follow these steps:

```
-- Connect to the SQL Server instance using SSMS
-- Navigate to the server properties
-- Under the 'Security' tab, select 'SQL Server and Windows Authentication mode'
-- Restart the SQL Server instance for changes to take effect
```

Once Mixed Authentication mode is enabled, you can create SQL Server logins as follows:

```
-- Example: Creating an SQL Server login with SQL Authentication
CREATE LOGIN SqlUser WITH PASSWORD = 'ComplexPassword@123';
```

Below is an example of querying to check which authentication mode the server is currently using:

```
-- Query to check authentication mode
DECLARE @AuthenticationMode INT;
EXEC xp_instance_regread
    N'HKEY_LOCAL_MACHINE',
    N'Software\Microsoft\MSSQLServer\MSSQLServer',
    N'LoginMode',
    @AuthenticationMode OUTPUT;

SELECT CASE @AuthenticationMode
         WHEN 1 THEN 'Windows Authentication Mode'
         WHEN 2 THEN 'Mixed Mode'
         ELSE 'Unknown Mode'
       END AS Authentication_Mode;
```

Output from this query:

```
---------------------------
Authentication_Mode
---------------------------
Mixed Mode
---------------------------
```

Understanding and properly configuring your SQL Server authentication mode is the first step in securing your database environment. Careful consideration should be given to the scenario and requirements of your deployment environment when choosing between Windows Authentication and Mixed Authentication modes.

10.3 Creating and Managing Logins

In SQL Server, logins are crucial for authenticating users and managing access to the server. A login is associated with a specific SQL Server instance and provides a means for users to connect.

Creating a new login involves specifying an authentication method, which can be either Windows authentication or SQL Server authentication. Windows authentication relies on Active Directory accounts, while SQL Server authentication involves defining a SQL Server-specific username and password.

To create a new SQL Server login using SQL Server Management Studio (SSMS), follow these steps:

1. Open SSMS and connect to the desired SQL Server instance.
2. In the Object Explorer, expand the server instance.
3. Right-click on the Security directory, then select New Login... from the context menu.

In the Login - New dialog, there are several fields and options to configure. These include:

- **Login Name**: For Windows authentication, this should be in the format DOMAIN\username. For SQL Server authentication, choose a unique username that follows SQL Server's naming conventions.
- **Authentication Method**: Choose between Windows Authentication and SQL Server Authentication.
  - If SQL Server Authentication is selected, enter and confirm a password.
  - Enforce password policies by default, which includes complexity requirements, expiration, and must-change options.
- **Default Database**: Specify the database to be used by default upon login.
- **Default Language**: Specify the default language for the login.

```
CREATE LOGIN sql_user WITH PASSWORD = 'StrongPassword!123';
```

The example above demonstrates the creation of a new SQL Server login named sql_user with a specified password. This login employs SQL Server Authentication.

Windows authentication logins can also be created using T-SQL commands. For example:

```
CREATE LOGIN [DOMAIN\username] FROM WINDOWS;
```

This command creates a new login for a Windows user or group.

Managing Logins:

Management of logins involves several tasks, such as modifying login properties, renaming logins, resetting passwords, disabling or enabling logins, and dropping logins.

To modify an existing login, such as changing the default database or language:

```
ALTER LOGIN sql_user WITH DEFAULT_DATABASE = AdventureWorks2019;
```

Renaming a login requires the use of the sp_rename stored procedure, though it is generally not recommended due to potential security and access complications:

```
EXEC sp_rename 'sql_user', 'new_sql_user';
```

Resetting a password is common when users forget their credentials:

```
ALTER LOGIN sql_user WITH PASSWORD = 'NewStrongPassword!123';
```

A login can be disabled to temporarily prevent user access without dropping the login entirely:

```
ALTER LOGIN sql_user DISABLE;
```

Similarly, to enable a previously disabled login:

```
ALTER LOGIN sql_user ENABLE;
```

Dropping a login removes it from the SQL Server:

```
DROP LOGIN sql_user;
```

Care should be taken when dropping logins to ensure no adverse effects on user access or existing dependencies within the databases.

Logins represent the first step in securing SQL Server access. Integrating effectively with database users and roles, logins facilitate a robust security framework. Thus, understanding the creation and management of logins is fundamental for administering SQL Server environments securely.

10.4 Database Users and Roles

In SQL Server, the concepts of database users and roles are central to managing database security. Understanding these entities and how they interact is crucial for effectively controlling access to database resources.

A database user in SQL Server is an account within a database that is used to access database objects. A role is a collection of permissions that can be assigned to a database user or another role, effectively grouping several privileges together to simplify the management of access controls.

Creating Database Users

A database user is associated with a login, which is an account on the SQL Server instance level. This association allows the user to connect to the database using their SQL Server login credentials.

To create a new database user, the CREATE USER statement is employed. The following example creates a new user named *JohnDoe* for the login *john_login*:

```
CREATE USER JohnDoe FOR LOGIN john_login;
```

It is essential to note that the login *john_login* must already exist at the SQL Server instance level for this user creation to succeed.

Types of Users

- *SQL User*: A typical database user, which is associated with a SQL Server login.
- *Windows User*: A user based on a Windows account.
- *Windows Group*: A user that represents an entire Windows group, allowing all members of that group access.
- *Application Role*: A role used by applications to run with specific permissions.

The syntax for each type can vary slightly, for instance:

```
CREATE USER [Domain\User] FOR LOGIN [Domain\User];
CREATE USER GroupUsers FOR LOGIN [Domain\GroupName];
CREATE APPLICATION ROLE AppRole WITH PASSWORD = 'StrongPassword';
```

Managing Database Users

Modifying users is achieved using the ALTER USER statement. Below is an example of changing the default schema for the user *JohnDoe*:

```
ALTER USER JohnDoe WITH DEFAULT_SCHEMA = Sales;
```

Dropping a user is done using the DROP USER statement:

```
DROP USER JohnDoe;
```

Database Roles

Database roles simplify permission management by allowing a collection of permissions to be managed as a unit. Roles can be either fixed or user-defined.

Fixed Database Roles: These are predefined roles that come with SQL Server, each with a predefined set of permissions. Key fixed database roles include:

- **db_owner**: Full control over the database.
- **db_securityadmin**: Manages roles and permissions.
- **db_accessadmin**: Manages login access to the database.
- **db_backupoperator**: Permits the ability to backup the database.
- **db_datareader**: Can read all data from all user tables.
- **db_datawriter**: Can add, delete, or modify data in all user tables.

User-Defined Database Roles: These roles offer flexibility by allowing DBAs to define roles tailored to specific needs. To create a user-defined database role, the CREATE ROLE statement is utilized:

```
CREATE ROLE SalesRole;
```

Granting permissions to a role follows the GRANT statement:

```
GRANT SELECT, INSERT, UPDATE ON SCHEMA::Sales TO SalesRole;
```

Assigning users to roles can be done using the ALTER ROLE statement:

```
ALTER ROLE SalesRole ADD MEMBER JohnDoe;
```

To remove a user from a role:

```
ALTER ROLE SalesRole DROP MEMBER JohnDoe;
```

Dropping a role is performed with the DROP ROLE statement:

```
DROP ROLE SalesRole;
```

Role Membership Management

Reviewing role membership is a crucial aspect of managing security. The following SQL query retrieves all role memberships for a specific user:

```
SELECT dp1.name AS DatabaseRoleName,
       dp2.name AS DatabaseUserName
FROM sys.database_role_members AS drm
JOIN sys.database_principals AS dp1
       ON drm.role_principal_id = dp1.principal_id
JOIN sys.database_principals AS dp2
       ON drm.member_principal_id = dp2.principal_id
WHERE dp2.name = 'JohnDoe';
```

Permission Management

Permissions can be applied directly to users or roles. Here are key commands for managing permissions:

Granting Permissions:

```
GRANT SELECT ON OBJECT::Sales.Customers TO JohnDoe;
```

Revoking Permissions:

```
REVOKE SELECT ON OBJECT::Sales.Customers FROM JohnDoe;
```

Denying Permissions:

```
DENY SELECT ON OBJECT::Sales.Customers TO JohnDoe;
```

Utilizing roles and expertly managing users within SQL Server enhances security and operational efficiency, ensuring optimal performance and compliance with organizational policies.

10.5 Schema-Based Permissions

Schema-based permissions in SQL Server provide a robust and manageable way to handle access control for database objects. By grouping related objects into schemas, administrators can assign permissions at the schema level, thereby simplifying the management of object-level permissions and enhancing security.

At a basic level, a schema acts as a namespace within a database, allowing for the categorization of tables, views, stored procedures, and other database objects. This categorization not only aids in organizing the database but also plays a crucial role in permission management.

Creating Schemas

The creation of schemas in SQL Server is straightforward. One can use the CREATE SCHEMA statement to define a new schema. The following example demonstrates the creation of a schema named Sales:

```
CREATE SCHEMA Sales;
```

This command creates a schema that can house related database objects such as tables and stored procedures. To assign ownership of the schema to a specific user, include the AUTHORIZATION keyword in the CREATE SCHEMA statement:

```
CREATE SCHEMA Sales AUTHORIZATION [UserName];
```

Assigning Permissions to Schemas

Permissions can be granted, denied, or revoked at the schema level. By doing so, you ensure that the specified actions can apply to all objects within the schema, streamlining permission management. Consider granting the SELECT permission on the Sales schema to a user:

```
GRANT SELECT ON SCHEMA::Sales TO [UserName];
```

This command allows the specified user to perform SELECT operations on any object within the Sales schema. To deny a permission, the DENY keyword is used instead:

```
DENY SELECT ON SCHEMA::Sales TO [UserName];
```

Revoking permissions can be achieved with the REVOKE keyword:

```
REVOKE SELECT ON SCHEMA::Sales FROM [UserName];
```

Examples of Detailed Permission Management

The following examples illustrate various ways to manage permissions for schema-based objects effectively.

Example 1: Granting Multiple Permissions

To grant multiple permissions such as SELECT and INSERT on a schema to a role, use the following syntax:

```
GRANT SELECT, INSERT ON SCHEMA::Sales TO [RoleName];
```

Example 2: Denying Specific Permissions

To prevent a user from deleting any data within the Sales schema, employ the DENY keyword:

```
DENY DELETE ON SCHEMA::Sales TO [UserName];
```

Example 3: Reverting Permissions

If permissions need to be reverted to their initial state, REVOKE can be used to remove previously granted or denied permissions:

```
REVOKE DELETE ON SCHEMA::Sales FROM [UserName];
```

This command will remove the DELETE permission previously denied to the specified user.

Managing Permissions Across Multiple Schemas

In cases where multiple schemas are used, consistent permission management becomes vital. Permissions can be assigned to multiple schemas with a singular command by leveraging roles.

First, create a role and grant the necessary permissions to the role. Then, add users to this role. Below is an example of creating a role, granting permissions to it, and associating a user with the role:

```
CREATE ROLE SalesRole;
GRANT SELECT, INSERT, UPDATE ON SCHEMA::Sales TO SalesRole;
ALTER ROLE SalesRole ADD MEMBER [UserName];
```

This methodology ensures that permission changes are easily managed by altering the role rather than the individual user permissions.

Auditing Schema-Based Permissions

Monitoring and auditing schema-based permissions are essential for ensuring compliance and security integrity. SQL Server provides tools like SQL Server Audit and Database Audit Specifications to track permission changes and access attempts.

Create a server audit and a database audit specification to capture events related to schema permission changes:

```
-- Create a server audit
CREATE SERVER AUDIT SchemaAudit
TO FILE (FILEPATH = 'C:\Audit\');
ALTER SERVER AUDIT SchemaAudit WITH (STATE = ON);

-- Create a database audit specification
CREATE DATABASE AUDIT SPECIFICATION SchemaPermissionChanges
FOR SERVER AUDIT SchemaAudit
ADD (SCHEMA_OBJECT_ACCESS_GROUP);
```

```
ALTER DATABASE AUDIT SPECIFICATION SchemaPermissionChanges
WITH (STATE = ON);
```

To review audit logs, consult the relevant audit report generated by SQL Server or query the audit files directly using system views like sys.fn_get_audit_file.

Best Practices for Implementing Schema-Based Permissions

Adhering to best practices when implementing schema-based permissions ensures a secure and manageable environment:

- **Principle of Least Privilege:** Assign the minimum necessary permissions to users and roles to reduce the risk of unauthorized access.
- **Use of Roles:** Simplify permission management by using roles to group permissions and then adding users to these roles.
- **Regular Audits:** Perform regular audits to review permissions and ensure compliance with security policies.
- **Documentation:** Maintain thorough documentation of all permission assignments for accountability and ease of review.
- **Consistent Naming Conventions:** Implement consistent naming conventions for schemas and roles to improve clarity and maintainability.

Effective schema-based permission management is a cornerstone of maintaining a secure and efficient SQL Server environment. By organizing objects within schemas and assigning permissions accordingly, administrators can achieve a higher degree of control and oversight over database security.

10.6 Implementing Row-Level Security

Row-Level Security (RLS) in SQL Server allows for fine-grained control over which users can access specific rows in a table. This mechanism is crucial for ensuring that users can only view and manipulate data that they are authorized to handle, providing a highly granular layer of security.

RLS is implemented through a combination of security predicates—inline table-valued functions (TVFs) applied within security policies that filter rows during query execution. The principle is to create a predicate_function that defines the logic for row access and then bind this function to a table through a security policy. Let's delve into the details of this process.

We begin by creating an example setup where RLS will be implemented. Consider a database containing a table Sales.Orders, where each row represents an order and includes details such as the OrderID, CustomerID, and OrderAmount. The objective is to ensure that employees can only view and manage orders placed by customers assigned to them.

First, we'll create the necessary schema and table:

```
CREATE SCHEMA Sales;

CREATE TABLE Sales.Orders (
    OrderID int PRIMARY KEY,
    CustomerID int,
    OrderAmount decimal(10, 2),
    EmployeeID int
);
```

Next, populate the Sales.Orders table with some sample data:

```
INSERT INTO Sales.Orders (OrderID, CustomerID, OrderAmount, EmployeeID)
VALUES (1, 101, 250.00, 1),
       (2, 102, 450.00, 2),
       (3, 103, 300.00, 1),
       (4, 104, 150.00, 3);
```

Now, to implement RLS, we need a predicate function to enforce the row-level control. This function will restrict access to rows based on the EmployeeID column. Here's how to define it:

```
CREATE FUNCTION dbo.fn_securitypredicate(@EmployeeID int)
RETURNS TABLE
WITH SCHEMABINDING
AS
RETURN SELECT 1 AS fn_securitypredicate_result
    WHERE @EmployeeID = SESSION_CONTEXT(N'EmployeeID');
```

In the function dbo.fn_securitypredicate, we use SESSION_CONTEXT to fetch the employee ID of the currently logged-in user. The SESSION_CONTEXT is set at the start of a user session and ensures the predicate applies correctly per user.

The next step is to create a security policy that binds this function to the Sales.Orders table:

```
CREATE SECURITY POLICY Sales.OrdersSecurityPolicy
ADD FILTER PREDICATE
dbo.fn_securitypredicate(EmployeeID)
ON Sales.Orders
WITH (STATE = ON);
```

The FILTER_PREDICATE invokes dbo.fn_securitypredicate(EmployeeID), ensuring that only rows for the relevant EmployeeID are visible to the session.

Another important aspect of RLS implementation is setting the session context for each user session. Before any query operation, the application must set the appropriate session context value using the sp_set_session_context stored procedure:

```
EXEC sp_set_session_context @key = N'EmployeeID', @value = 1;
```

With the session context properly set, the user (employee) can then execute queries on the Sales.Orders table and only see rows applicable to them:

```
SELECT * FROM Sales.Orders;
```

Assuming the session context is set for EmployeeID = 1, the result would be:

```
OrderID  CustomerID  OrderAmount  EmployeeID
------------------------------------------------
1        101         250.00       1
3        103         300.00       1
```

For more complex scenarios requiring multiple predicates or different access rules, simply create additional predicate functions and extend the security policy to cater to diverse security requirements. This modular approach to RLS allows customization in data access, enhancing both security and flexibility.

Integrating RLS with other SQL Server security features such as auditing and encryption further strengthens data protection. Monitoring access patterns and fine-tuning security policies ensure optimal performance and compliance with organizational security standards.

10.7 Data Encryption

Data encryption is a critical aspect of SQL Server security, aiming to protect data at rest and in transit from unauthorized access. Encryption transforms readable data, or plaintext, into an unreadable format known as ciphertext. Only authorized entities with the appropriate keys can decrypt ciphertext and revert it to readable plaintext. This section delves into the fundamental concepts, types, and implementation strategies for data encryption in SQL Server.

Types of Data Encryption in SQL Server

SQL Server supports several types of encryption techniques that cater to different security requirements. The primary encryption methodologies are:

- **Column-Level Encryption**: Encrypts data within specific columns of a database table.
- **Transparent Data Encryption (TDE)**: Encrypts the entire database at rest, including the physical files.
- **Always Encrypted**: Encrypts sensitive data inside client applications and never reveals encryption keys to the SQL Server instance.
- **Backup Encryption**: Encrypts backup files to prevent unauthorized access to database backups.
- **Transport Layer Security (TLS)**: Encrypts data transmitted between SQL Server and a client to ensure confidentiality and integrity during transit.

Implementing Column-Level Encryption

Column-level encryption is used to protect highly sensitive data such as credit card numbers and social security numbers. It involves the use of symmetric keys and certificates to encrypt and decrypt data stored in specific columns. Below is a step-by-step example.

First, create a database master key, which is required to secure certificates and symmetric keys:

```
USE [master];
GO
CREATE MASTER KEY ENCRYPTION BY PASSWORD = 'StrongPassword123!';
GO
```

Next, create a certificate in the database:

```
USE [YourDatabase];
GO
```

```
CREATE CERTIFICATE YourCertName
WITH SUBJECT = 'Data encryption certificate';
GO
```

With the certificate in place, create a symmetric key. The symmetric key encrypts the data in the designated column:

```
CREATE SYMMETRIC KEY YourSymmetricKey
WITH ALGORITHM = AES_256
ENCRYPTION BY CERTIFICATE YourCertName;
GO
```

Encrypt data in a specific column using the symmetric key. Below is an example of encrypting data during the insert operation:

```
OPEN SYMMETRIC KEY YourSymmetricKey
DECRYPTION BY CERTIFICATE YourCertName;
GO

INSERT INTO YourTable(Column1, EncryptedColumn)
VALUES ('Data', ENCRYPTBYKEY(KEY_GUID('YourSymmetricKey'), '
      SensitiveData'));
GO

CLOSE SYMMETRIC KEY YourSymmetricKey;
GO
```

To decrypt the data, the symmetric key must be opened again:

```
OPEN SYMMETRIC KEY YourSymmetricKey
DECRYPTION BY CERTIFICATE YourCertName;
GO

SELECT Column1, CONVERT(VARCHAR, DECRYPTBYKEY(EncryptedColumn))
FROM YourTable;
GO

CLOSE SYMMETRIC KEY YourSymmetricKey;
GO
```

Transparent Data Encryption (TDE)

TDE encrypts the entire database, protecting data files and log files, thereby ensuring data is encrypted at rest. Implementing TDE involves the following steps:

Create a Database Encryption Key (DEK) that uses a certificate:

```
USE [YourDatabase];
GO
CREATE DATABASE ENCRYPTION KEY
WITH ALGORITHM = AES_256
ENCRYPTION BY SERVER CERTIFICATE YourTDEServerCert;
GO
```

Enable encryption for the database:

```
ALTER DATABASE YourDatabase
SET ENCRYPTION ON;
GO
```

To verify the encryption status, use the following query:

```
SELECT name, is_encrypted
FROM sys.databases;
GO
```

The output should indicate whether the database is encrypted:

```
name         is_encrypted
----------- ------------
YourDatabase 1
```

Backup Encryption

Backup encryption secures database backups, ensuring that data is protected even during disk or tape storage. Implementing backup encryption requires the use of certificates or asymmetric keys:

```
BACKUP DATABASE YourDatabase
TO DISK = 'YourDatabaseBackup.bak'
WITH COMPRESSION, ENCRYPTION
(
  ALGORITHM = AES_256,
  SERVER CERTIFICATE = YourBackupCert
);
GO
```

Always Encrypted

Always Encrypted provides client-side encryption, meaning that encryption keys remain entirely on the application side and are never exposed to SQL Server itself. This translates to a scenario where encrypted data remains confidential while in SQL Server. Configuration involves setting up column master keys and column encryption keys utilizing SQL Server Management Studio (SSMS) and necessary application configuration.

Transport Layer Security (TLS)

TLS ensures encrypted connections between SQL Server and clients, safeguarding data during transmission. TLS implementation typically involves configuring SQL Server to use certificates for encryption. Please ensure that certificates are properly issued and installed on the server. Below is a configuration outline:

Enable encryption on the server using SQL Server Configuration Manager:

```
1. Open SQL Server Configuration Manager.
2. Expand "SQL Server Network Configuration".
3. Right-click on "Protocols for <instance name>" and choose "Properties".
4. Under the "Flags" tab, set the "Force Encryption" option to "Yes".
5. Restart the SQL Server service.
```

This section has explored the various data encryption techniques available in SQL Server, providing the necessary SQL commands and configurations to implement each type effectively.

10.8 Implementing Transparent Data Encryption (TDE)

Transparent Data Encryption (TDE) is a method used to encrypt SQL Server databases to provide security at rest. TDE ensures that data stored in the database files and log files is encrypted, making it inaccessible to unauthorized persons who might directly access the disk storage. This encryption helps to protect against the threat of data theft by encrypting the data before it is written to disk and decrypting it when it is read into memory. By using TDE, we can achieve encryption without requiring changes to the existing applications.

To implement TDE, follow these detailed steps:

First, create a Master Key in the master database. The Master Key is a symmetric key that is used to secure the certificates and keys in the database. Use the following SQL command to create the Master Key:

```
USE master;
GO
CREATE MASTER KEY ENCRYPTION BY PASSWORD = 'StrongPassword!123';
GO
```

After creating the Master Key, create a certificate in the master database. This certificate is used to encrypt the Database Encryption Key (DEK). Execute the following SQL command:

```
USE master;
GO
CREATE CERTIFICATE \texttt{TDECert}
WITH SUBJECT = 'TDE Certificate';
GO
```

Now, within the user database that you wish to encrypt, create a Database Encryption Key. This key is protected by the certificate created in the previous step. First, switch to the user database:

```
USE [\texttt{YourDatabase}];
```

```
GO
CREATE DATABASE ENCRYPTION KEY
WITH ALGORITHM = AES\_256
ENCRYPTION BY SERVER CERTIFICATE \texttt{TDECert};
GO
```

Enable encryption for the database using the ALTER DATABASE statement:

```
ALTER DATABASE [\texttt{YourDatabase}]
SET ENCRYPTION ON;
GO
```

After enabling encryption, you can verify the encryption status of the database using the following query:

```
SELECT
    db.name,
    db.is\_encrypted,
    dm.encryption\_state,
    dm.encryptor\_type,
    dm.encryptor\_thumbprint
FROM
    sys.databases db
JOIN
    sys.dm\_database\_encryption\_keys dm
ON
    db.database\_id = dm.database\_id
WHERE
    db.name = '\texttt{YourDatabase}';
```

The possible values for encryption_state in the result are:

- 0 = No encryption
- 1 = Unencrypted
- 2 = Encryption in progress
- 3 = Encrypted
- 4 = Key change in progress
- 5 = Decryption in progress

Additionally, the state of the transaction log and the throughput implications of TDE should be considered. TDE has minimal impact on read-/write performance because the encryption and decryption processes are efficient. However, there may be an initial performance impact when the database is being encrypted for the first time.

In terms of administrative best practices, it is crucial to back up the certificate used for TDE. Without this certificate, you cannot restore or attach the encrypted database. To back up the TDE certificate, execute the following SQL commands, specifying a secure location and a strong password for the backup:

```
USE master;
GO
BACKUP CERTIFICATE \texttt{TDECert}
TO FILE = 'C:\Path\To\Backup\TDECert.cer'
WITH PRIVATE KEY (
    FILE = 'C:\Path\To\Backup\TDECert\_PrivateKey.pvk',
    ENCRYPTION BY PASSWORD = 'SecurePassword!123'
);
GO
```

Best practices also dictate routinely rotating the DEK for security purposes. This involves creating a new DEK, encrypting it with the existing certificate, and setting it as the active encryption key. To rotate the DEK, the following steps can be taken:

```
USE [\texttt{YourDatabase}];
GO
CREATE DATABASE ENCRYPTION KEY
WITH ALGORITHM = AES\_256
ENCRYPTION BY SERVER CERTIFICATE \texttt{TDECert};
GO
-- Optionally, drop the old encryption key if it is no longer needed
-- DROP DATABASE ENCRYPTION KEY <OldEncryptionKey>;
```

The impact of TDE on business continuity should not be underestimated. Encrypted backups need appropriate handling, and only authorized individuals with access to the certificate and key can restore encrypted databases. TDE also ensures compliance with various regulatory frameworks that mandate encryption to protect sensitive data.

By following these meticulous steps, TDE can be effectively implemented to safeguard your SQL Server databases.

10.9 Using Certificates and Keys

Certificates and keys are fundamental concepts in SQL Server security, providing essential mechanisms for ensuring data integrity and authenticity. Understanding how to effectively create, manage, and apply certificates and keys within SQL Server is crucial for database administrators aiming to maintain a secure environment. This section delves into the specifics of managing these security features.

Certificates in SQL Server are database-level entities that use public key cryptography to secure data. Certificates can be used for various purposes, such as securing communications using Secure Sockets Layer (SSL), signing code, or enabling database encryption. They consist of a public key, which is disseminated and used to encrypt data, and a private key, which is kept secret and used to decrypt data.

Keys are essential cryptographic entities. SQL Server supports several types of keys, including symmetric keys, asymmetric keys, and database encryption keys. Symmetric keys use the same key for both encryption and decryption, making them fast and efficient for large data sets. Asymmetric keys, employing a pair of public and private keys, are used for situations where higher security is needed, such as securing small amounts of critical data.

To manage certificates and keys in SQL Server, the following steps are commonly followed:

- **Creating a Certificate:** A certificate can be created using the Transact-SQL (T-SQL) command. The following example demonstrates how to create a self-signed certificate:

```
CREATE CERTIFICATE MyCertificate
WITH SUBJECT = 'MyDemoCertificate',
START_DATE = '2023-01-01',
EXPIRY_DATE = '2025-01-01';
```

  In this script, MyCertificate is the name of the certificate. The SUBJECT clause provides a description of the certificate, while START_DATE and EXPIRY_DATE specify the valid duration of the certificate.

- **Backing Up a Certificate:** It's vital to back up created certificates to avoid data loss. A certificate backup creates a file containing the certificate and its private key, which can be restored later if needed.

```
BACKUP CERTIFICATE MyCertificate
TO FILE = 'C:\Backup\MyCertificate.cer'
WITH PRIVATE KEY (FILE = 'C:\Backup\MyCertificate.pvk',
                  ENCRYPTION BY PASSWORD = 'StrongPassword123');
```

  Here, MyCertificate.cer and MyCertificate.pvk are the output files for the certificate and private key, respectively. The private key is encrypted with a password for added security.

- **Creating Symmetric Keys:** Symmetric keys are created and used similarly to certificates. The following command creates a symmetric key:

```
CREATE SYMMETRIC KEY MySymmetricKey
WITH ALGORITHM = AES_256
ENCRYPTION BY CERTIFICATE MyCertificate;
```

In this script, MySymmetricKey is created using the AES_256 algorithm and is encrypted by a previously created certificate, MyCertificate.

- **Using Symmetric Keys to Encrypt Data:** Once created, symmetric keys can be used to encrypt and decrypt data. Before using a key, it must be opened:

```
OPEN SYMMETRIC KEY MySymmetricKey
DECRYPTION BY CERTIFICATE MyCertificate;

DECLARE @EncryptText NVARCHAR(200) = 'Sensitive Information';
DECLARE @EncryptBinary VARBINARY(MAX);

SET @EncryptBinary = EncryptByKey(Key_GUID('MySymmetricKey'),
    @EncryptText);
PRINT 'Encrypted Data: ' + CAST(@EncryptBinary AS NVARCHAR(MAX));
```

This example opens the symmetric key using the associated certificate, encrypts a piece of text (Sensitive Information), and prints the encrypted data. EncryptByKey is the function used to perform the encryption.

- **Decrypting Data:** Decrypting previously encrypted data requires reopening the same symmetric key:

```
OPEN SYMMETRIC KEY MySymmetricKey
DECRYPTION BY CERTIFICATE MyCertificate;

DECLARE @DecryptText NVARCHAR(200);
SET @DecryptText = CONVERT(VARCHAR(200), DecryptByKey(
    @EncryptBinary));
PRINT 'Decrypted Data: ' + @DecryptText;
```

In this script, the encrypted binary data is decrypted using the DecryptByKey function and converted back into a readable string.

- **Creating Asymmetric Keys:** Asymmetric keys are created for scenarios demanding additional security. The following command creates an asymmetric key:

```
CREATE ASYMMETRIC KEY MyAsymmetricKey
WITH ALGORITHM = RSA_2048;
```

MyAsymmetricKey is created using the RSA_2048 algorithm, which provides a robust level of encryption suitable for most secure scenarios.

- **Using Asymmetric Keys:** Asymmetric keys are primarily used for encrypting smaller data sets like key material or small pieces of critical data, due to their computational complexity:

```
DECLARE @TextToEncrypt NVARCHAR(200) = 'Critical Info';
DECLARE @EncryptedText VARBINARY(MAX);

SET @EncryptedText = EncryptByAsymKey(AsymKey_ID('MyAsymmetricKey
    '), @TextToEncrypt);
PRINT 'Encrypted Data: ' + CAST(@EncryptedText AS NVARCHAR(MAX));

DECLARE @DecryptedText NVARCHAR(200);
SET @DecryptedText = DecryptByAsymKey(AsymKey_ID('MyAsymmetricKey
    '), @EncryptedText, N'MyAsymmetricKey');
PRINT 'Decrypted Data: ' + @DecryptedText;
```

  In this example, EncryptByAsymKey and DecryptByAsymKey functions are used to encrypt and decrypt text, respectively.

Maintaining the security of certificates and keys involves periodic rotation and auditing to ensure they remain secure and effective. Storing keys securely, employing strong passwords, and regularly backing up certificates and keys are critical practices. Applying sound key management policies and procedures helps mitigate security risks and ensures data remains protected against unauthorized access.

10.10 Auditing and Monitoring Security

Auditing and monitoring security in SQL Server is fundamental for ensuring that data access and modifications are appropriately tracked and reviewed. This process helps in detecting malicious activities, unauthorized access attempts, and understanding usage patterns, which is crucial for maintaining the integrity and privacy of data.

SQL Server provides a comprehensive suite of tools and techniques for auditing and monitoring, commonly classified into SQL Server Audit, Common Criteria Compliance, and using Extended Events and Profiler.

SQL Server Audit is a feature that enables tracking of events occurring on the system, primarily driven by audit specifications and logs. It is divided into server audits and database audits to cater to different levels of tracking.

To create a server audit specification, the following Transact-SQL (T-SQL) commands can be used:

```
CREATE SERVER AUDIT [AuditName]
```

```
TO FILE (FILEPATH = 'C:\AuditLogs\ServerAudit')
WITH (ON_FAILURE = CONTINUE);
GO

ALTER SERVER AUDIT [AuditName]
WITH (STATE = ON);
GO
```

The above code snippet initializes a server audit named AuditName directing its logs to a specified file path, and it ensures the audit is activated immediately.

Next, a server audit specification is created. An example targeting a login change group is shown below:

```
CREATE SERVER AUDIT SPECIFICATION [LoginChangeAudit]
FOR SERVER AUDIT [AuditName]
ADD (SERVER_PERMISSION_CHANGE_GROUP);
GO

ALTER SERVER AUDIT SPECIFICATION [LoginChangeAudit]
WITH (STATE = ON);
GO
```

Similarly, a database audit specification tracks events at the database level. An example snippet involving schema object changes is presented as:

```
CREATE DATABASE AUDIT SPECIFICATION [UserSchemaAudit]
FOR SERVER AUDIT [AuditName]
ADD (SCHEMA_OBJECT_CHANGE_GROUP)
WITH (STATE = ON);
GO
```

Server and database audits generate logs that can be analyzed to assess security events and compliance.

Common Criteria Compliance is another feature that enhances security monitoring by enforcing stricter measures for event logs, particularly useful in regulated environments. Enabling this compliance mode is straightforward:

```
EXEC sp_configure 'common criteria compliance enabled', 1;
RECONFIGURE WITH OVERRIDE;
GO
```

This command ensures a higher audit level, guaranteeing that even system-level events are captured rigorously.

Extended Events and SQL Server Profiler are advanced tools focusing on event management within SQL Server. Extended Events provide a lightweight performance monitoring system, capable of capturing detailed event data with minimal overhead. A quick example to set up an event session is:

```
CREATE EVENT SESSION [ExampleSession] ON SERVER
ADD EVENT sqlserver.error_reported
(
    ACTION (sqlserver.sql_text)
)
ADD TARGET package0.event_file
(SET filename=N'C:\AuditLogs\ExampleSessionFile.xel', max_file_size=(5))
WITH (MAX_MEMORY=4096 KB, EVENT_RETENTION_MODE=
      ALLOW_SINGLE_EVENT_LOSS, MAX_DISPATCH_LATENCY=30
      SECONDS, MAX_EVENT_SIZE=0 KB, MEMORY_PARTITION_MODE=
      NONE, TRACK_CAUSALITY=OFF, STARTUP_STATE=OFF)
GO

ALTER EVENT SESSION [ExampleSession] ON SERVER STATE = START;
GO
```

Such a session setup captures error reports along with the related SQL text and logs them into a file for detailed inspection.

SQL Server Profiler allows for the real-time capture and view of event data. However, it is generally recommended to leverage Extended Events due to performance efficiency.

Integral to auditing and monitoring is the ability to review, analyze, and understand the captured log data. SQL Server Management Studio (SSMS) provides a user interface for auditing configurations and log reviews. Logs can be read using T-SQL:

```
SELECT * FROM sys.fn_get_audit_file('C:\AuditLogs\*.sqlaudit', DEFAULT,
      DEFAULT);
GO
```

This function reads all audit files in the specified directory, and results can be cross-analyzed for any anomalies or security breaches.

Maintaining an efficient auditing system involves ensuring that logs are secured, managed correctly, and periodically reviewed. Using automated tools and scripts to analyze and report findings enhances the security posture significantly. Furthermore, combining audit logs with security information and event management (SIEM) systems can provide a holistic view of the entire security landscape, aiding quick responses to any incidents.

The practices discussed here are vital for a secure SQL Server setup, balancing rigorous monitoring while maintaining system performance. Implementing a robust auditing strategy is indispensable for adhering to regulatory standards and safeguarding critical data assets.

10.11 Best Practices for SQL Server Security

Ensuring the security of SQL Server databases is of paramount importance for maintaining data integrity, confidentiality, and availability. Adhering to industry-standard best practices helps mitigate risks associated with unauthorized access, data breaches, and other security threats. This section elaborates on key best practices that should be followed to secure SQL Server environments effectively.

1. **Utilize the Principle of Least Privilege (PoLP)**: The Principle of Least Privilege dictates that users and applications should be granted the minimum permissions necessary to perform their tasks. Over-privileged accounts can be exploited to carry out unauthorized activities. Implement PoLP by carefully defining roles and permissions and regularly reviewing and adjusting access rights.

2. **Enable Firewall Protection**: Ensure that the SQL Server instance is protected behind a firewall to restrict unwanted network traffic. Configure the firewall to allow connections only from trusted sources by defining specific IP address ranges or subnet masks. Use both hardware and software firewalls for layered security.

3. **Regularly Update and Patch SQL Server**: Keeping the SQL Server software up to date with the latest patches and updates is crucial to protect against known vulnerabilities. Enable automatic updates when possible, or establish a regular maintenance schedule to manually check and apply updates.

4. **Implement Strong Authentication Mechanisms**: Enforce strong password policies for SQL Server authentication, including complexity requirements, expiration periods, and account lockout thresholds. If possible, utilize Windows Authentication, which leverages Active Directory's secure authentication features. Implement Multi-Factor Authentication (MFA) for an added layer of security.

5. **Encrypt Sensitive Data**: Use encryption to protect sensitive data both at rest and in transit. Transparent Data Encryption (TDE) can be used to encrypt the entire database, while column-level encryption can be applied to specific sensitive fields. Ensure that SSL/TLS is used for encrypting data in transit between clients and the SQL Server.

6. **Perform Regular Security Audits and Monitoring**: Conduct regular security audits to identify and remediate potential vulnerabilities. Use SQL Server Audit and Extended Events to monitor and log access to sensitive data and configuration changes. Regularly review audit

logs to detect and respond to suspicious activities promptly.

7. Secure SQL Server Configuration: Configure SQL Server settings to enhance security. Disable unnecessary features and components to reduce the attack surface. For example, disable SQL Server Browser service, avoid enabling xp_cmdshell, and restrict the use of OPENROWSET and OPENDATASOURCE functions. Ensure that the SQL Server instance and SQL Server Agent services run under low-privilege accounts.

8. Backup and Disaster Recovery Planning: Implement a robust backup and disaster recovery strategy. Regularly back up SQL Server databases and test the restoration process to ensure that data can be recovered in the event of a failure or attack. Store backups securely, and consider using encryption for backups containing sensitive data.

9. Secure Physical Access: Ensure that physical access to the SQL Server hardware is restricted to authorized personnel only. Utilize access control mechanisms such as secure rooms, locked cabinets, and monitoring systems to prevent unauthorized physical access.

10. Educate and Train Personnel: Security is not solely reliant on technical measures; personnel must also be aware of security best practices and potential threats. Regularly educate and train staff on security policies, procedures, and emerging threats. Encourage a security-conscious culture within the organization.

11. Implement Regular Vulnerability Assessments: Regularly perform vulnerability assessments and penetration testing to identify security weaknesses. Use tools such as SQL Server vulnerability assessment features or third-party security assessment tools to scan for misconfigurations, vulnerabilities, and compliance issues.

12. Guard Against SQL Injection Attacks: SQL injection attacks remain a prevalent threat. Develop and implement input validation, parameterized queries, and stored procedures to mitigate the risk. Regularly review and test code to ensure it is resilient against SQL injection.

```
-- Using a parameterized query to prevent SQL injection
DECLARE @username NVARCHAR(50);
SET @username = 'john\_doe';

-- Correct way to execute a query with parameters
EXEC sp\_executesql N'SELECT * FROM Users WHERE Username = @username',
                  N'@username NVARCHAR(50)',
                  @username = @username;

-- Avoid executing dynamic SQL with concatenated input
-- Example of a vulnerable query (DO NOT USE)
-- EXEC('SELECT * FROM Users WHERE Username = ''' + @username + '''');
```

13. Limit Exposure of Metadata: Restrict access to metadata by limiting permissions on system databases such as master and msdb. Metadata can provide insights into the database structure and configuration, potentially aiding an attacker in crafting exploits.

14. Optimize Indexes and Queries for Performance: Although primarily a performance concern, poorly optimized indexes and queries can lead to increased load times and resource consumption, indirectly impacting security. Ensure that indexes are correctly configured and queries are optimized to maintain efficient and secure operations.

15. Secure the Supply Chain: Ensure that third-party components and dependencies used within your SQL Server environment are trustworthy and maintain updated versions. Evaluate the security posture of third-party vendors and software to avoid introducing vulnerabilities through the supply chain.

Regular adherence to these best practices forms the foundation of a secure SQL Server environment capable of withstanding evolving security threats. Each practice should be integrated into the organization's overall security strategy, with ongoing evaluation and adjustment as needed to address emerging risks and regulatory requirements.

Made in the USA
Monee, IL
13 September 2026

62976632R00167